MUSLIM SLAVE SYSTEM IN MEDIEVAL INDIA

By the same author

History of the Khaljis, 1950, 1967, 1980
Twilight of the Sultanate, 1963, 1980
Studies in Medieval Indian History, 1966
Studies in Asian History (edited), 1969
Growth of Muslim Population in Medieval India, 1973
Early Muslims in India, 1984
The Mughal Harem, 1988
Indian Muslims: Who are They, 1990, 1993
The Legacy of Muslim Rule in India, 1992

MUSLIM SLAVE SYSTEM IN MEDIEVAL INDIA

K.S. Lal

ADITYA PRAKASHAN
New Delhi

First published 1994
Second reprint 2020

ISBN 978-81-85689-67-8

Email: contact@adityaprakashan.com
Website: www.adityaprakashan.com

Published by Aditya Prakashan, 2/18, Ansari Road, New Delhi – 110 002.

Printed at EIH Ltd., Unit: Printing Press, IMT Manesar, Gurgaon.

CONTENTS

	Preface	vii
	Abbreviations	viii
I.	Introduction	1
II.	The Origins of Muslim Slave System	9
III.	Enslavement of Hindus by Arab and Turkish Invaders	17
IV.	The Slave Sultans of Hindustan	25
V.	Slave-taking during Muslim Rule	41
VI.	Enslavement and Proselytization	60
VII.	Struggle for Power among Slave Nobles	74
VIII.	Employment of Slaves	83
IX.	Ghilmans and Eunuchs	105
X.	Slave Trade	119
XI.	Rules regarding Manumission and Sale of Slaves	139
XII.	Sex Slavery	150
	Postscript	175
	Bibliography	178
	Index	189

PREFACE

In my book *The Legacy of Muslim Rule in India*, I had said that "It is not pertinent here to make a detailed study of the Muslim slave system which was an institution as peculiar as it was unique." A detailed study of the Muslim slave system in medieval India is being made here. In *The Legacy* I had also said that "the best way to understand the content and spirit of Muslim rule in India... is by going through Muslim scriptures (as) all medieval chroniclers were scholars of Muslim law." In their writings they often quote from their holy books to vindicate the actions of their conquerors and kings. Hence Muslim scriptural sources are referred to quite often in the present work which is a study both in the theory and practice of Islamic slavery

BA-57A Ashok Vihar
Delhi – 110 052

K.S.Lal
10 January 1994

ABBREVIATIONS USED IN REFERENCES TO TITLES OF WORKS

Afif.	*Tarikh-i-Firoz Shahi* by Shams Siraj Afif
Ain.	*Ain-i-Akbari* by Abul Fazl
Ashraful Hidayah.	Urdu trs. by *Hidayah* done at Deoband
Barani.	*Tarikh-i-Firoz Shahi* by Ziyauddin Barani
Badaoni.	*Muntakhab-ut-Tawarikh* by Abdul Qadir Badaoni
Bernier.	*Travels in the Mogul Empire* by Francois Bernier
C.H.I.	*Cambridge History of India*
E.D.	*History of India as told by its own Historians* by Henry M. Elliot and John Dowson
Farishtah.	*Tarikh-i-Farishtah* by Muhammad Qasim Hindu Shah Farishtah
Fatawa-i-Alamgiri.	Urdu trs. of Aurangzeb's *Fatawa-i-Alamgiri*, Deoband
Hamilton.	English trs. of the *Hedaya* by Charles Hamilton
Hodivala.	*Studies in Indo-Muslim History*
Ibn Battuta.	*The Rehla,* English trs. by Dr. Mehdi Husain
Isami.	*Futuh-us-Salatin* by Khwaja Abdullah Malik
Manucci.	*Storia do Mogor* by Niccolao Manucci
Minhaj.	*Tabqat-i-Nasiri* by Minhaj Siraj Jurjani
Pelsaert.	*Jahangir's India* by Francisco Pelsaert
Tuzuk.	*Tuzuk-i-Jahangiri* or Memoirs of Emperor Jahangir
Utbi.	*Tarikh-i-Yamini* by Abu Nasr Muhammad
Yahiya.	*Tarikh-i-Mubarak Shahi* by Yahiya bin Ahmad bin Abdullah

THE SLAVE TRADE IN AFRICA: A GANG ON THE MARCH

Chapter I
INTRODUCTION

Slavery is the system by which certain persons are kept as the property of others — a system of great antiquity and wide prevalence. Slavery originated during the age of savagery and continued into ancient civilizations. As Nieboer has said, "the taming of animals naturally leads to taming of men." It is supposed that the nomadic herdsman who domesticated animals also began to domesticate, to enslave, men. Slavery was there in Babylon and elsewhere in Mesopotamia; it was widely prevalent in ancient Egypt, Greece and Rome, centuries before the coming of Christ. Slaves were mainly prisoners of war, but destitutes, debtors and convicted criminals were also sometimes drafted into slavery and commandeered for specific assignments. The history of ancient civilizations in various countries is divided into dynasties, periods and kingdoms. We need not go into details of these; for our limited purpose we shall only attempt a general survey of the state of slavery in ancient Egypt, Greece, Rome etc. till the advent of Islam when slavery became inalienable with religion and culture and was accorded a permanent place in society.

In ancient Egypt, as elsewhere, slaves supplied the labour force and were used in any capacity and for any type of work. An almost fabulous number of slaves were employed for the building the Pyramids of Egypt dating from 3000 B.C. to 2300 B.C. "According to Herodotus, the Great Pyramid (of Cheops) took 100,000 men for ten years to make a causeway 3000 feet long in order to facilitate the transport of stone from the quarries, and the same number of men for twenty years more to complete the pyramid itself." Modern research considers these figures to be exaggerated as Herodotus inquired from people during his journeys and depended on hearsay. What is important in this regard is that the nine pyramids existing at present, are supposed to have been built by respective kings as tombs and memorials of themselves by a very substantial labour force. Slaves in Egypt were also employed on various other jobs.

Among the Greeks also slavery was a rooted institution. In two city states or *poleis* (singular *polis* means a city plus its environment) of Athens and Sparta slavery prevailed as also in other lesser known city states. Ancient Greek society was divided into three classes. The free-borncomprised the citizens. They enjoyed all kinds of privileges and took part in politics. The second class of *perioeci* consisted of foreigners. They possessed no political rights, but they were better off as compared to slaves because sometimes they handled economic affairs and enrolled in the infantry. The third category of *helots* comprised of slaves. In Greece the bulk of the peasants did not own their own land and had to supply a considerable portion of their crop to the landlords. They fell into debt and ultimately had no security to offer but their own persons. They were then sold into slavery. It is said about Athens that at one point of time there were 460,000 slaves and 2,100 citizens. Consequently, each master had a number of male and female slaves. The men worked in mines and on cultivation while women slaves worked as maids in homes. They were required to do all those works which provided leisure to the masters. Earlier among the Hebrews and later among the Greeks the slaves were treated with mildness, but not in every city state. At Athens the slaves were treated with mildness while in Sparta they are said to have been accorded very harsh treatment. By themselves the slaves were helpless, but the Constitution of Draco (621 B.C.) and laws of Solon ameliorated their condition.[1] They were the property of the state; they possessed certain elementary rights, and could not be put to death save by the authority of the state. However, the larger number of slaves in Greece left the privileged

[1] Stewart C. Easton, *The Heritage of the Past*, New York, 1957, 73.

classes enough time to give to politics and development of political philosophy for which ancient Greece has become famous.

In Rome also slavery was extensively prevalent. There the great landed estates were accumulated in a few hands and the cultivation of these lands was done mostly by swarms of slaves leaving war as the chief occupation of honour for the elitist citizens. Roman slaves were either captives or debtors who were unable to repay. There were purchased slaves also. In Rome the slaves had no rights at all; they could be put to death for the smallest misdemeanor. The slaves were so numerous that, in the time of Augustus, a single person is said to have left at his death over 4000 slaves. Besides cultivation the slaves were engaged in all the various professions, handicrafts and occupations. Supervision of the large number of slaves employed on cultivation was not easy. Consequently, they were chained with iron shackles. The iron rings on their wrists and ankles were not removed even when they went to sleep.

Hosts of slaves were employed in the sport of gladiatorial exhibitions. Gladiators were combatants who were obliged to fight wild animals or each other, often to the death, for the entertainment of the spectators. Some slaves were trained as regular gladiators. In the public exhibition, if a vanquished gladiator was not killed in the combat, his fate was decided by the spectators. If they wished his death for showing weakness or disinterestedness in the fighting, they held up their thumbs; the opposite motion was to save him. It was a cruel enjoyment at the cost of the helpless slaves.

There were sometimes slave revolts also. A revolt in Italy led by the gladiator Spartacus in 73 B.C. could be put down with considerable difficulty. Slaves, however, were sometimes set at liberty, and these freed-men were a well-known class at Rome. In the days of the Roman empire some great changes took place in the condition of the slaves. Augustus

Ceasar (63 B.C-14 C.E) granted the slaves a legal status and Antoninus Pius (86-161 C.E) took away from the masters the power of life and death. Emperor Constantine (C.E. 274-337) made it a rule that in case of the division of property of a master, the distribution of his slaves be so arranged that father and son, husband and wife and brothers and sisters should not be separated.

Galley slaves were also common in ancient Greece, Rome and especially France. They propelled ships or warships with oars. Small galleys carried as many as twenty oars on each side, each of them worked by one or more men; the large ones had 200 to 300 rowers on each side. In this work convicts or slaves were forced to labour. The slaves were sometimes chained to the deck and lashed with whip if found slack in work. The cruelties sometimes perpetrated by their masters have become proverbial in the annals of ancient European maritime activity.

As in most parts of the ancient world, slavery seems to have been a recognised institution of ancient Indian society also from the earliest times. In the Rigveda there are many references about slaves. Slaves were given as presents to relatives. Rulers gave female slaves as gifts. All these slaves served as domestic servants in the palaces of rulers as well as in the establishments of aristocrats and priests. Probably all those persons who could not repay their debts were reduced to slavery.

In ancient Indian society slaves were treated with consideration. Their condition was far better as compared to that of the slaves in ancient Egypt, Greece, and Rome. The Buddha enjoined on his lay followers to assign only as much work to their slaves as they could easily do. He also said that the master should attend to the needs of his slaves when the latter was ill. During the Maurya period (C. 300 B.C. to 100 B.C.), Kautilya laid down rules about how slaves should be treated by their masters. The master was not to punish a slave without reason. If a master ill-treated his slaves the state was to punish him. Emperor Ashoka says in his Rock Edict IX that all people should treat their slaves with sympathy and consideration. In ancient India slaves were so mildly treated that foreign visitors like Megasthenes, who were acquainted with their fate in other countries, failed to notice the existence of slavery in this country. He wrote, "All Indians are free. None of them is a slave.... They do not reduce even foreigners to slavery. There is thus no question of their reducing their own countrymen to slavery."[2] Megasthenes of course could not speak for the whole of India and for the entire ancient period. Slavery did exist in India, but it was tempered with humanism. There are philosophical and religious works in ancient India from the Rigveda onwards which do write about slaves. But none of them suggests that they were cruelly treated. In India slaves were not treated as commodities for earning profit through sale. Indian economy was not based on slavery. The number of slaves in ancient India was less than that in western countries and, aberrations apart, they were treated with kindness and as human beings.

An altogether new dimension — religious sanction — was added to the institution of slavery with the rise of Christianity to power in the Roman Empire. Hitherto, slavery had been a creation of the crude in human nature — the urge to dominate over others, to make use of others for private comfort and profit. Now it was ordained that the God of the Christians had bestowed the whole earth and all its wealth on the believers, that the infidels had no natural or human rights, and that the believers could do to the infidels whatever they chose — kill them, plunder them, reduce them to the status of slaves or non-citizens. In short, slavery became a divinely ordained institution.

Jesus Christ had seen nothing objectionable in slavery. St.

---

[2] *Indica* of Megasthenes, cited in Om Prakash, *Religion and Society in Ancient India*, Delhi, 1985, 140.

Paul thought that a slave who became Christian was better than an infidel freeman. The Church Fathers and the Popes sanctioned slavery on scriptural grounds, so that slavery and slave trade continued in Europe and other Christianised countries for more than fifteen centuries after the passing away of Roman Paganism. Christian monasteries in medieval Europe are known to have employed slaves on some scale for keeping their farms and gardens flourishing. Christian nations became major partners of the Muslim slave traders when slave trade reached its peak in the seventeenth and the eighteenth centuries. Many churches continued to come out openly in support of slavery right up to the Civil War (1861-65 C.E) in the USA.

Even so, it goes to the credit of Islam to create slave trade on a large scale, and run it for profit like any other business. Prophet Muhammad had accepted the prevailing Arab practice of making slaves and also set a precedent when he sold in Egypt some Jewish women and children of Medina in exchange for horses and arms. The Quran expressly permitted the Muslims to acquire slaves through conquest. Since every Muslim Arab was a partner in the revenues derived from war booty including slaves, coveting the goods and wives of the unbelievers by the Muslims was avowed, though not encouraged, by the Prophet. War was prescribed on religious grounds, and became an integral part of Islam. "War is ordained for you, even if it be irksome to you. Perchance ye may dislike that which is good for you and love that which is evil for you, but God knoweth, and ye know not."

The Prophet himself had made slaves in war and peace. Women and captives were sold as slaves in Najd. The Islamised Arabs started taking pride in keeping male and female slaves. The second Caliph, Umar, ordered that residents of Arabia were not to be enslaved since they had all become Muslims. This resulted in obtaining slaves from neighbouring countries. Prior to the Crusades, Muslims had kept black slaves imported from Africa. After that they began to obtain white slaves from Europe, not only through war but also by purchase —Rome and Mecca being the chief centres of this trade. The Muslims of the Barbary States (Morocco, Fez, Algeria, Tunis, and Tripoli in North Africa), also obtained white slaves by piracy in the Mediterranean.

The concept of *Jihad* against unbelievers, the share of every Muslim in the loot from war including slaves, and the profit obtained through the sale of slaves added new zest in Islam for practising and profiting from slavery. Slaves in Egypt, Greece and Rome used to be conscripted for constructing roads, working in mines, and on agricultural farms. They were treated cruelly, but there was no religious prejudice against them. In Islam, on the other hand, it was enjoined on the faithful to enslave non-Muslims for no other reason than that of their being non-Muslims. The outcome in due course was a large-scale slave trade and big slave markets all over the Islamic world. Muslim capitals such as Medina, Damascus, Kufa, Baghdad, Cairo, Cordova, Bukhara, Ghazni, Delhi and some other Muslim metropolises in India became crowded with slaves for sale as well as with slave traders out to maximise profits.

Alexander Gardner who later became the Colonel of Artillery in the service of Maharaja Ranjit Singh, had travelled extensively in Central Asia from 1819 to 1823 C.E. He saw a lot of slave-catching in Kafiristan, a province of Afghanistan, which was largely inhabited by infields at that time. He found that the area had been reduced to "the lowest state of poverty and wretchedness" as a result of raids by the Muslim king of Kunduz for securing slaves and supplying them to the slave markets in Balkh and Bukhara. He writes:

"All this misery was caused by the oppression of the Kunduz chief, who not content with plundering his wretched subjects, made an annual raid into the country south of Oxus, and by *chappaos* (night attacks) carried off all the inhabitants on whom his troops could lay their hands. These, after the best had been selected by the chief and his courtiers, were publicly sold in the bazaars of Turkestan. The principal providers of this species of merchandise were the Khan of Khiva, the king of Bokhara (the great hero of the Mohammedan faith), and the robber *beg* of Kunduz.

"In the regular slave markets, or in transactions between dealers, it is the custom to pay for slaves in money; the usual medium being either Bokharan gold *tillahs* (in value about 5 or 51/2 Company rupees each), or in gold bars or gold grain. In Yarkand, or on the Chinese frontier, the medium is the silver *khurup* with the Chinese stamp, the value of which varies from 150 to 200 rupees each. The price of a male slave varies according to circumstances from 5 to 500 rupees. The price of the females also necessarily varies much, 2 *tillahs* to 10,000 rupees. Even the double the latter sum has been known to have been given.

"However, a vast deal of business is also done by barter, of which we had proof at the holy shrine of Pir-i-Nimcha, where we exchanged two slaves for a few lambs' skins! Sanctity and slave dealing may be considered somewhat akin in the Turkestan region, and *the more holy the person the more extensive are generally his transactions in flesh and blood.*"[3]

Alexander Gardner subsequently found a Muslim fruit merchant at Multan "who was proved by his own ledger to have exchanged a female slave girl for three ponies and seven long-haired, red-eyed cats, all of which he disposed of, no doubt to advantage, to the English gentlemen at this station."[4] Small wonder that the Islamic system of slavery was revolting to the Hindu psyche because it was alien to Hindu Dharma and ideologically abhorrent to it.

---

[3] *Memoirs of Alexander Gardner,* edited by Major Hugh Pearce, first published in 1898, reprint published from Patiala in 1970, 103-04. Emphasis added. See also 32, 35-36, 92, 121-122, 124 and 148.

[4] Ibid., 104n.

CHAPTER II

THE ORIGINS OF MUSLIM SLAVE SYSTEM

From the day India became a target of Muslim invaders its people began to be enslaved in droves to be sold in foreign lands or employed in various capacities on menial and not-so-menial jobs within the country. To understand this phenomenon it is necessary to go into the origins and development of the Islamic system of slavery. For, wherever the Muslims went, mostly as conquerors but also as traders, there developed a system of slavery peculiar to the clime, terrain and populace of the place. For example, simultaneously with Muhammad bin Qasim's invasion of Sindh in early 8th century, the expansion of Arab Islam had gone apace as far as Egypt, North Africa and the Iberian Peninsula in the West, as well as in Syria, Asia Minor, Palestine, Iraq, Iran, Khurasan, Sistan and Transoxiana. In all these countries Muslim slave system grew and developed in its own way. There was constant contact between India and most of these countries in the medieval times. For example, as early as during the reigns of the slave sultans Iltutmish and Balban (1210-86), there arrived at their courts in Delhi a large number of princes with their followers from Iraq, Khurasan and Mawar-un-Nahr because of the Mongol upheaval.[1] Many localities in Delhi and its environs were settled by these elites and their slaves, soldiers and scholars. In Balban's royal procession 500 Sistani, Ghauri and Samarqandi slave-troops with drawn swords used to march by his side pointing to the fact that a large number of foreign slaves from these lands had come to India in 13th-14th centuries.[2] When the Mughals launched their conquest of India, there was the establishment of the Ottoman Empire in Turkey which at its height included

[1] Minhaj, 598-99; Farishtah, I, 73, 75.
[2] Barani, 57-58.

present-day Albania, Greece, Bulgaria, Serbia, Romania and several other contiguous countries. Then there was the Safavid empire in Iran. The Ottoman Empire traded with Europe and imported "there indispensable stock of slaves. (Slav, as the word indicates), supplied by merchants, sometimes Jewish, from Verdun, Venice or elsewhere in Italy. Other slaves were brought from black Africa, eastern Europe and Turkish Central Asia."[3] The Mughals of India had very close contacts with the Turkish Ottoman and Iranian Safavid empires. This contact certainly included exchange of slaves and ideas on slavery. But any attempt in this area of study, which is so vast and labyrinthine, is bound to deflect us from our main theme which is restricted to India. We shall therefore confine ourselves to the barest particulars of the beginnings of the institution outside India which will suffice for understanding the Muslim slave system in India in the medieval period.

Prophet Muhammad found slavery existing in Arabia, and recognised it in the Quran. The origins of Muslim slave system can thus be traced to Arabia, the original Muslim homeland, and the regions into which Islam spread. Quranic injunctions, Islamic conquests and Muslim administrative institutions gave it a continuity and legitimacy. According to T.P. Hughes, "Slavery is in complete harmony with the spirit of Islam.... That Muhammad ameliorated the condition of the slave, as it existed under the heathen law of Arabia, we cannot doubt; but it is equally certain that the Arabian legislator intended it to be a permanent institution."[4] D.S. Margoliouth elaborates on the theme adding that "On the whole... the Prophet did something to alleviate the existence of the captives... manumission was declared by him to be an act of

---

[3] *Cambridge History of Islam*, II, 524. The word slave, observes Ram Swarup, "is derived from *Slavs*, the Slavonic peoples of Central Europe. When they were captured and made bondsmen, they gave birth to the word 'slave' ", *The Word as Revelation: Names of Gods*, 23; also J.H. Kremers, *The Legacy of Islam*, 101.

[4] *Dictionary of Islam*, 596, 600.

piety... and murder or maiming of slaves was to be punished by retaliation."[5] In one of his last sermons, Muhammad exhorted his followers thus: "And your Slaves! See that ye feed them with such food as ye eat yourselves; and clothe them with the stuff ye wear. And if they commit a fault which ye are not inclined to forgive, then sell them, for they are the servants of the Lord, and are not to be tormented."[6] His first orthodox biographer, Ibn Ishaq, however mentions a transaction which set a precedent for Islamic slave trade at a later stage: "Then the apostle sent Sa'd b. Zayd Al-Ansari ...with some of the captive women of B Qurayza to Najd and he sold them for horses and weapons."[7] The women had been made captive after their menfolk had been slaughtered en masse in the market place at Medina.

Status of Slaves in Islam

The appeal of Muhammad contained some fundamental perceptions about the status of slaves in Islam. It recognised the slave as the property of the master. A slave could be sold but, being a Muslim or servant of the Lord, was not to be treated harshly. Here it needs to be observed that in the early days of Islam it was the scum of the society the flocked to the standard of Muhammad and became his fighting force. "Koran acknowledges so distinctly that the followers of the Prophet were the lowest of the people."[8] Arabian aristocracy "requested him to send away this scum before they would argue with him",[9] (as did the Turkish ruling classes treat the early Muslim converts in India). But the mission of Muhammad was to spread his creed and any non-humane regulations would have presented a very unfavourable picture of Islam to the captives. This would have discouraged

[5] Margoliouth, *Mohammed and the Rise of Islam*, 461-62.
[6] Cited in Muir, *The Life of Mahomet*, 473.
[7] *The Life of Muhammad:* A translation of Ibn Ishaq's *Sirat Rasul Allah* by A. Gillaume, OUP, Karachi (1955), Eighth Impression, 1987, 466.
[8] Margoliouth, 98 quoting Quran, 11:27.
[9] Ibid., 97

proselytization. On conversion also Muslim slaves could not be treated badly for that again would have been damaging to the reputation of the new creed and galling to the lives of the new converts. How these injunctions were later on followed or flouted by Muslim invaders and rulers in other countries is a different matter. In the original land of Islam, in Arabia, it was enjoined not to treat the slaves harshly; instead the masters were encouraged to utilize to the best the services of men slaves and enjoy the intimate company of women slaves.[10]

This tolerant treatment was not without conditions. A slave was the property of his master. His tenor of life was determined by the latter. For example, he could not marry without the master's permission. Although he was free to move from place to place, he could not hold pleasure parties nor pay visits to friends. A slave could not bestow alms or grant a loan or make a pilgrimage.[11] If he managed to accumulate any property, it was inherited not by his sons but by the master.[12] In theory a slave could purchase his freedom, but bond of freedom was granted to a slave in return for money paid, and until full money was paid there was no total redemption.[13] A slave should not seek his emancipation by running away, "The slave who fled from his master committed an act of infidelity", says Muhammad.[14]

The emancipation of slaves was not unknown in pre-Islamic Arabia. It was an old custom among the Arabs of more pious disposition to will that their slaves would be freed at their death. To Muhammad, the freeing of a slave was an act of charity on the part of the master, not a matter of justice, and only a believing slave deserved freedom.

---

[10] Ibid., 406-407; Quran, 4:3, 4:24, 4:25, 23:6; Muir, *Life of Mahomet*, 334-35, 365, 421.
[11] Hughes, *Dictionary of Islam*, 598.
[12] *Sahih Muslim*, Hadis, 3584, 3585, 3595.
[13] Quran, 24:33.
[14] Ram Swarup, *Understanding Islam through Hadis*, 76.

In short, slavery in Islam is a permanent and perennial institution. As Margoliouth points out, "the abolition of slavery was not a notion that ever entered the Prophet's mind."[15] "The fact remains," writes Ram Swarup "that Muhammad, by introducing the concept of religious war and by denying human rights to non-Muslims, sanctioned slavery on an unprecedented scale.... (and on) such massive proportions. Zubair, a close companion of the Prophet, owned one thousand slaves when he died. The Prophet himself possessed at least fifty-nine slaves at one stage or another, besides thirty-eight servants, both male and female. Mirkhond, the Prophet's fifteenth century biographer, names them all in his *Rauzat-us-Safa*. The fact is that slavery, tribute, and booty became the main props of the new Arab aristocracy....."[16] "The Slavery of Islam is interwoven with the Law of marriage, the Law of sale, and the Law of inheritance, of the system, and its abolition would strike at the very foundations of the code of Muhammadanism."[17]

Extension of Islamic Slavery

Islamic slave system spread and developed wherever Muslim rule was established. *Ghulam* or *quallar* ('slave') was the creation of the Safavid state. Mamluks were found in Egypt. In the Ottoman empire they were called kapi-kulus. "Kapi-kulu were recruited originally from the Sultan's share of prisoners of war, and subsequently from a periodical levy (*depshrime*) of Christian boys. Most of the youths entered the Janissary corps."[18] Christian slaves were drawn from the ranks of the Georgian, Armenian and Circassian prisoners or their descendants."[19] Black slaves, natives of East Africa, were called Zanj.[20] Majority of slaves who penetrated and flour-

[15] Margoliouth, *Mohammed and the Rise of Islam*,, 461.
[16] Ram Swarup, op.cit., 75.
[17] Hughes, *Dictionary of Islam*, 600.
[18] *Cambridge History of Islam*, I, 280 and n., 342.
[19] Ibid., 415, also 407.
[20] Ibid., 129-30, 179.

ished in India were Turks.

Immediately after its birth, Muhammadanism entered upon a career of aggressive and expansionist conquest. Its Caliphs conquered extensively and set up autocratic governments based on the tenets of Islam rather than democratic governments based on the will of the people. Conquests required large armies; despotic governments could not be run without a train of bureaucrats. From the ninth to the thirteenth century in particular it was a period of feverish activity in Muslim Asia; empires were established and pulled down; cities were founded and destroyed. In other words, the whole of Central Asia, Transoxiana and Turkistan was a very disturbed region in the medieval period. Armies and bureaucrats were needed in large numbers to administer the ever expanding dominions of Islam. The Turks came handy for such services.

Turkish Slaves

The Abbasids had built up a very large empire with capital at Baghdad,[21] and its provinces were administered by their Turkish slave officers and Turk mercenary troops. Caliph al-Mutasim (833-842 C.E.) introduced the Turkish element into the army, and he was the first Caliph to have Turkish slaves under his employment.[22] For it was soon discovered that the young slaves acquired from Turkistan and Mawar-un-Nahr formed an excellent material for such a corps.

Turks is a generic term comprehending peoples of sundry denominations and tribes. The Turkistan of the medieval historians was an extensive country. It was bounded on the east by China, on the west by Rum or Turkey, on the north by the walls of Yajuj and Majuj (Gog and Magog) and on the south by the mountains of Hindustan.[23] The Turks as a

---

[21] Ruben Levy, *The Baghdad Chronicle*, Cambridge, 1929, 13.
[22] Hamdullah Mustaufi, *Tarikh-i-Guzidah*, ed. E.G. Browne, London, 1910, 318.
[23] Fakr-i-Mudabbir, *Tarikh-i-Fakhruddin Mubarak Shah*, 38.

people were both civilised town-dwellers and the migratory tribes trekking across the desert or wilderness. With the extension of the Muslim frontier to the north and west of Persia one tribe after another, like Turks, Tartars, Turkomen and even Mongols and Afghans came under subjection. They attracted the attention of their conquerors by their bravery and spirit of adventure. They were acquired in groups and droves as slaves. The Caliphs of Islam also purchased Turkish slaves to manage their far-flung empire. The Turkish slaves helped the cause of Islam through their fighting spirit.

But as their numbers grew, they became unmanageable. For example, Caliph al-Mutasim's own guard was of 4000 Turks; the number later rose to 70,000 slave mercenaries.[24] With time the tyranny, lawlessness and power of the Turks went on increasing.[25] The unscrupulous policy of religious persecution followed by the Caliph Mutawakkil was responsible for the alienation of the subject races. His own son entered into a conspiracy with the Turks, which ended in the Caliph's murder in 861. The Caliph Mutadid (892-902) was unable to suppress the power of the Turks. The final decline of the Caliphate set in just after the murder of Muqtadir in 932 C.E. "The Turkish soldiers made and murdered Caliphs at their pleasure."[26] As the Caliphal empire disintegrated, in the third century of Islam, its provincial governors became independent.[27]

But technically these Turkish governors were only slaves and their tenure of power rested on military force and chance-victory and not on any moral foundations. On the other hand, the Caliphs were objects of respect. The first four Caliphs were directly related to Muhammad. Muawiyah, the founder of the Ummayad Caliphate, was a cousin of Abbas, an uncle of the Prophet. Abbas himself was founder of the

---

[24] *Cambridge History of Islam*, I, 125.
[25] Ibn Asir, *Kamil-ut-Tawarikh*, Urdu trs. Hyderabad, 1933, VI, 319.
[26] Sykes, P.M., *History of Persia*, 2 vols., London, 1915, II, 83.
[27] Ruben Levy, *The Social Structure of Islam*, Cambridge, 1962, 282.

Abbasid Caliphate. The Turkish slaves, therefore, considered it politic to keep a sort of special relationship with the Caliph: they went on paying him tribute and seeking from him recognition of their 'sovereignty'. That is how, in course of time, their political power was firmly established.

CHAPTER III
ENSLAVEMENT OF HINDUS BY ARAB AND TURKISH INVADERS

Turks were not the first Muslims to invade India. Prior to the coming of Turks the Arab general Muhammad bin Qasim invaded Sindh in the early years of the eighth century. In conformity with the Muslim tradition, the Arabs captured and enslaved Indians in large numbers. Indeed from the days of Muhammad bin Qasim in the eighth century to those of Ahmad Shah Abdali in the eighteenth, enslavement, distribution, and sale of Hindu prisoners was systematically practised by Muslim invaders and rulers of India. It is but natural that the exertion of a thousand years of slave-taking can only be briefly recounted with a few salient features of the system highlighted.

Enslavement by the Arabs

During the Arab invasion of Sindh (712 C.E.), Muhammad bin Qasim first attacked Debal, a word derived from Deval meaning temple. It was situated on the sea-coast not far from modern Karachi. It was garrisoned by 4000 Kshatriya soldiers and served by 3000 Brahmans. All males of the age of seventeen and upwards were put to the sword and their women and children were enslaved.[1] "700 beautiful females, who were under the protection of Budh (that is, had taken shelter in the temple), were all captured with their valuable ornaments, and clothes adorned with jewels."[2] Muhammad despatched one-fifth of the legal spoil to Hajjaj which included seventy-five damsels, the rest four-fifths were distributed among the soldiers.[3] Thereafter whichever places he attacked like Rawar, Sehwan, Dhalila, Brahmanabad and Multan,

[1] C.H.I., III, 3.
[2] Al Kufi, *Chachnama*, Kalichbeg, 84.

Hindu soldiers and men with arms were slain, the common people fled, or, if flight was not possible, accepted Islam, or paid the poll tax, or died with their religion. Many women of the higher class immolated themselves in Jauhar, most others became prize of the victors. These women and children were enslaved and converted, and batches of them were despatched to the Caliph in regular instalments. For example, after Rawar was taken Muhammad Qasim "halted there for three days during which he massacred 6000 (men). Their followers and dependents, as well as their women and children were taken prisoner." Later on "the slaves were counted, and their number came to 60, 000 (of both sexes?). Out of these, 30 were young ladies of the royal blood.... Muhammad Qasim sent all these to Hajjaj" who forwarded them to Walid the Khalifa. "He sold some of these female slaves of royal birth, and some he presented to others."[4] Selling of slaves was a common practice. "From the seventh century onwards and with a peak during Muhammad al-Qasim's campaigns in 712-13", writes Andre Wink, "a considerable number of Jats was captured as prisoners of war and deported to Iraq and elsewhere as slaves."[5] Jats here is obviously used as a general word for all Hindus. In Brahmanabad, "it is said that about six thousand fighting men were slain, but according to others sixteen thousand were killed", and their families enslaved.[6] The garrison in the fort-city of Multan was put to the sword, and families of the chiefs and warriors of Multan, numbering about six thousand, were enslaved.

In Sindh female slaves captured after every campaign of the marching army, were converted and married to Arab

---

[3] C.H.I., III, 3.

[4] *Chachnama*, Kalichbeg, 154. Raja Dahir's daughters also were counted among slave girls, 196. E.D., I, 172-73 gives the number of captives as 30,000.

[5] Andre Wink, *Al Hind*, 161.

[6] Mohammad Habib, "The Arab conquest of Sind." in *Politics and Society During the Early Medieval Period*, being Collected Works, of Habib, ed. K.A. Nizami, II, 1-35. Al Biladuri, 122, has 8000 to 26000.

soldiers who settled down in colonies established in places like Mansura, Kuzdar, Mahfuza and Multan. The standing instructions of Hajjaj to Muhammad bin Qasim were to "give no quarter to infidels, but to cut their throats", and take the women and children as captives.[7] In the final stages of the conquest of Sindh, "when the plunder and the prisoners of war were brought before Qasim... one-fifth of all the prisoners were chosen and set aside; they were counted as amounting to twenty thousand in number... (they belonged to high families) and veils were put on their faces, and the rest were given to the soldiers".[8] Obviously a few lakh women were enslaved in the course of Arab invasion of Sindh.

Ghaznavid capture of Hindu slaves

If such were the gains of the 'mild' Muhammad bin Qasim in enslaving *kaniz wa ghulam* in Sindh, the slaves captured by Mahmud of Ghazni, "that ferocious and insatiable conqueror", of the century beginning with the year 1000 C.E. have of course to be counted in hundreds of thousands. Henry Elliot and John Dowson have sifted the available evidence from contemporary and later sources—from Utbi's *Tarikh-i-Yamini*, Nizamuddin Ahmad's *Tabqat-i-Akbari*, the *Tarikh-i-Alai* and the *Khulasat-ut-Tawarikh* to the researches of early European scholars. Mohammad Habib, Muhammad Nazim, Wolseley Haig and I myself have also studied these invasions in detail.[9] All evidence points to the fact that during his seventeen invasions, Mahmud Ghaznavi enslaved a very large number of people in India. Although figures of captives for each and every campaign have not been provided by contemporary chroniclers, yet some known numbers and data about the slaves taken by

[7] *Chachnama*, Kalichbeg, 155; E.D.I, 173, 211.
[8] Ibid., 163; E.D., I, 181.
[9] Appendix D, 'Mahmud's invasions of India,' in E.D., II, 434-478.
Habib, *Sultan Mahmud of Ghaznin*, 23-59.
M. Nazim, *The Life and Times of Mahmud of Ghazni*, 42-122.
Lal, *Growth of Muslim Population*, 102-04, 211-16.

Mahmud speak for themselves.

When Mahmud Ghaznavi attacked Waihind in 1001-02, he took 500,000 persons of both sexes as captive. This figure of Abu Nasr Muhammad Utbi, the secretary and chronicler of Mahmud, is so mind-boggling that Elliot reduces it to 5000.[10] The point to note is that taking of slaves was a matter of routine in every expedition. Only when the numbers were exceptionally large did they receive the notice of the chroniclers. So that in Mahmud's attack on Ninduna in the Punjab (1014), Utbi says that "slaves were so plentiful that they became very cheap; and men of respectability in their native land (India) were degraded by becoming slaves of common shop-keepers (in Ghazni)".[11] His statement finds confirmation in later chronicles including Nizamuddin Ahmad's *Tabqat-i-Akbari* which states that Mahmud "obtained great spoils and a large number of slaves". Next year from Thanesar, according to Farishtah, "the Muhammadan army brought to Ghaznin 200,000 captives so that the capital appeared like an Indian city, for every soldier of the army had several slaves and slave girls".[12] Thereafter slaves were taken in Baran, Mahaban, Mathura, Kanauj, Asni etc. When Mahmud returned to Ghazni in 1019, the booty was found to consist of (besides huge wealth) 53,000 captives. Utbi says that "the number of prisoners may be conceived from the fact that, each was sold for from two to ten *dirhams*. These were afterwards taken to Ghazna, and the merchants came from different cities to purchase them, so that the countries of Mawarau-un-Nahr, Iraq and Khurasan were filled with them". The *Tarikh-i-Alfi* adds that the fifth share due to the Saiyyads was 150,000 slaves, therefore the total number of captives comes to 750,000.[13]

---

[10] *Tarikh-i-Yamini*, E.D., II, 26; Elliot's Appendix, 438; Farishtah, I, 24.
[11] Utbi, E.D., II, 39.
[12] Farishtah, I, 28.
[13] Lal, *Growth of Muslim Population in Medieval India*, 211-13; also Utbi, E.D., II, 50 and n. 1.

Before proceeding further, let us try to answer two questions which arise out of the above study. First, how was it that people could be enslaved in such large numbers? Was there no resistance on their part? And second, what did the victors do with these crowds of captives?

During war it was not easy for the Muslim army to capture enemy *troops*. They were able-bodied men, strong and sometimes 'demon like'. It appears that capturing such male captives was a very specialised job. Special efforts were made by 'experts' to surround individuals or groups, hurl lasso or ropes around them, pin them down, and make them helpless by binding them with cords of hide, ropes of hessian and chains and shackles of iron. Non-combatant males, women and children of course could be taken comparatively easily after active soldiers had been killed in battle. The captives were made terror-stricken. It was a common practice to raise towers of skulls of the killed by piling up their heads in mounds. All captives were bound hand and foot and kept under strict surveillance of armed guards until their spirit was completely broken and they could be made slaves, converted, sold or made to serve on sundry duties.

In a letter Hajjaj instructed Muhammad bin Qasim on how to deal with the adversary. "The way of granting pardon prescribed by law is that when you encounter the unbelievers, strike off their heads.... make a great slaughter among them... (Those that survive) bind them in bonds... grant pardon to no one of the enemy and spare none of them" etc., etc.[14] The lives of some prisoners could be spared, but they could not be released. That is how the Arab invaders of Sindh could enslave thousands of men and women at Debal, Rawar and Brahmanabad. At Brahmanabad, after many people were killed, "all prisoners of or under the age of 30 years were put in chains... All the other people capable of bearing arms were beheaded and their followers and depen-

[14] *Chachnama*, Kalichbeg, 155 and n.

dents were made prisoners."[15]

That is also how Mahmud of Ghazni could enslave 500,000 "beautiful men and women" in Waihind after he had killed 15,000 fighting men in a "splendid action" in November 1001 C.E. Utbi informs us that Jaipal, the Hindu Shahiya king of Kabul, "his children and grandchildren, his nephews, and the chief men of his tribe, and his relatives, were taken prisoners, and being strongly bound with ropes, were carried before the Sultan (Mahmud) like common evil-doers... Some had their arms forcibly tied behind their backs, some were seized by the cheek, some were driven by blows on their neck."[16] In every campaign of Mahmud large-scale massacres preceded enslavement.

The sight of horrendous killing completely unnerved the captives. Not only were the captives physically tortured, they were also morally shattered. They were systematically humiliated and exposed to public ridicule. When prisoners from Sindh were sent to the Khalifa, "the slaves, who were chiefly daughters of princes and Ranas, were made to stand in a line along with the menials (literally shoe-bearers)".[17] Hodivala gives details of the humiliation of Jaipal at the hands of Mahmud. He writes that Jaipal "was publicly exposed at one of the *slave-auctions in some market in Khurasan,* just like the thousands of other Hindu captives.... (He) was paraded about so that his sons and chieftains might see him in that condition of shame, bonds and disgrace.... inflicting upon him the public indignity of 'commingling him in one common servitude".[18] No wonder that in the end Jaipal immolated himself, for such humiliation was inflicted deliberately to smash the morale of the captives. In short, once reduced to such straits, the prisoners, young or old,

[15] Ibid., 83-86, 154, 159, 161 ff.

[16] Utbi, E.D., II, 26. Minhaj, 607, n., 5. Al Utbi and other chroniclers refer to Jaipal on many occasions. H.G. Raverty suggests that "Jaipal appears to be the title, not the actual name, of two or more persons", Minhaj, 81n.

[17] *Chachnama*, Kalichbeg, 152.

[18] Hodivala, 192-93.

ugly or handsome, princes or commoners could be flogged, converted, sold for a tuppence or made to work as menials.

It may be argued that Mahmud of Ghazni could enslave people in hundreds of thousands because his raids were of a lightning nature when defence preparedness was not satisfactory. But even when the Muslim position was not that strong, say, during Mahmud's son Ibrahim's campaign in Hindustan when "a fierce struggle ensued, but Ibrahim at length gained victory, and slew many of them. Those who escaped fled into the jungles. Nearly 100,000 of their women and children were taken prisoners..."[19] In this statement lies the answer to our first problem. There was resistance and determined resistance so that all the people of a family or village or town resisted the invaders in unison. If they succeeded, they drove away the attackers. If not, they tried to escape into nearby forests.[20] If they could not escape at all they were made captives but then all together. They did not separate from one another even in the darkest hour. Indeed adversity automatically bound them together. So they determined to swim or sink together.

Besides, right from the days of prophet Muhammad, and according to his instructions, writes Margoliouth, "parting of a captive mother from her child was forbidden... The parting of brothers when sold was similarly forbidden. On the other hand captive wife might at once become the concubine of the conqueror."[21] This precept of not separating the captives but keeping them together was motivated by no humanitarian consideration but it surely swelled their numbers to the advantage of the victors. Hence large numbers of people were enslaved.

And now our second question — what did the victors do with slaves captured in large crowds? In the days of the early invaders like Muhammad bin Qasim and Mahmud Ghaznavi, they were mostly sold in the Slave Markets that had come up

---

[19] Maulana Ahmad and others, *Tarikh-i-Alfi*, E.D., V, 163; Farishtah, I, 49.
[20] Lal, *Legacy*, 263-68.
[21] Margoliouth, *Muhammad*, 461; also Gibbon, II, 693.

throughout the Muslim dominated towns and cities. Lot of profit was made by selling slaves in foreign lands. Isami gives the correct position. Muhammad Nazim in an article has translated relevant lines of Isami's metrical composition.[22] "He (Mahmud) scattered the army of the Hindus in one attack and took Rai Jaipal prisoner. He carried him to the distant part of his kingdom of Ghazni and delivered him to an agent of the *Slave Market* (*dalal-i-bazar*). I heard that at the command of the king (Mahmud), *the Brokers of the Market,* (*maqiman-i-bazar* in the original) sold Jaipal as a slave for 80 *Dinars* and deposited the money realised by the sale in the Treasury."[23]

When Muslim rule was established in India, the sale of captives became restricted. Large numbers of them were drafted for manning the establishments of kings and nobles, working as labourers in the construction of buildings, cutting jungles and making roads, and on so many other jobs. Still they were there, enough and to spare. Those who could be spared were sold in and outside the country, where slave markets, slave merchants and slave brokers did a flourishing business, and the rulers made profit out of their sale.

Mahmud of Ghazni had marched into Hindustan again and again to wage Jihad and spread the Muhammadan religion, to lay hold of its wealth, to destroy its temples, to enslave its people, sell them abroad and thereby earn profit, and to add to Muslim numbers by converting the captives. He even desired to establish his rule in India.[24] His activities were so multi-faceted that it is difficult to determine his priorities. But the large number of captives carried away by him indicates that taking of slaves surely occupied an anteriority in his scheme of things. He could obtain wealth by their sale and increase the Muslim population by their conversion.

---

[22] In his article 'Hindu Shahiya kingdom of Ohind', in J.R.A.S., 1927.
[23] Cited in Hodivala, 192-93.
[24] C.E. Bosworth, *The Ghaznavids*, 235.

CHAPTER IV
SLAVE SULTANS OF HINDUSTAN

Slavery was wide-spread in Islam. The early Turkish invaders and rulers of India were slaves or scions of slaves. Mahmud of Ghazni was the son of a purchased slave, Subuktigin. Subuktigin in his turn had been bought by one Alptigin who himself was a purchased slave. Alptigin was the first Turkish slave-warrior-ruler who carried his arms into Hindustan. His career and resourcefulness are symbolic of the Turkish slaves as a whole.

Alptigin was purchased by Ahmad bin Ismail, the Samanid king of Khurasan and Bukhara. The Samanid rulers had adopted the Abbasid custom of enrolling slaves. They used to purchase small Turkish children and impart to them training in arms and religious education. In course of time these slaves were appointed to various offices but primarily as bodyguards to Amirs and sentinels of frontiers. Such an one was Alptigin. He began his career as a Sarjandar (Life Guard) and soon became the head of Sarjandars. He proved to be a man of great ability and courage and at the age of thirty-five was placed in charge of the Iqta of Khurasan by the Samanid governor, Abdul Malik (954-961 C.E.). As the Muqta of Khurasan he had 500 villages and about 2,000 slaves of his own. Deprived of his office at the death of his patron, he betook himself to Ghazni where his father had been governor under the Samanids. At Ghazni he acted more or less as an independent chief.[1] After his death a number of his slaves like Baltagin, Pirai and Subuktigin ruled over Ghazni, but of them the last one alone proved to be successful.

Alptigin had purchased Subuktigin at Nishapur[2] from a certain merchant, Nasir Haji, who had brought him from Turkistan to Bukhara. Subuktigin was born in 942 C.E. (331

[1] M. Ufi, *Jami-ul-Hikayat*, E.D., II, 179.
[2] Minhaj, 70, 71.

H.) He was captured by some Turk marauders when he was about 12.[3] Alptigin brought him up and gradually raised him in posts of honour. He married his daughter to Subuktigin and, in course of time, conferred upon him the title of Amir-ul-Umara in recognition of his talents and because of the psychological awe which self-asserting slaves instilled in the masters' minds, to which Juwayni refers. Subuktigin "made frequent raids into Hind, in the prosecution of holy wars."[4] After his master's death he was raised to the throne by his nobles. He turned out to be an ambitious ruler. With the help of his Turk and Afghan retainers and troops he mounted attacks upon the Samanid power at Bukhara and after years of continued fighting succeeded in securing the province for his son Mahmud in 994 C.E. Mahmud took the title of sultan and was so recognized by the Caliph. We meet Mahmud of Ghazni again and again during his campaigns in India.

About two centuries later, the Ghauris wrested Ghazni from the Ghaznavids. One of its great sultans was Sultan Shihabuddin (also known as Muizzuddin bin Sam and Muhammad Ghauri). Just as Mustasim was the first caliph to have collected a large force of Turkish slaves under his employment, Sultan Muizzuddin bin Sam Ghauri also "took considerable delight in purchasing Turkish slaves and educating them."[5] The Sultan did not have a son who could succeed him, but this fact did not cause him any worry because of his liking for and faith in his slaves. Minhaj Siraj writes that on one occasion when a favourite courtier spoke to the Sultan about the default of male heirs, he replied with absolute confidence: "Other monarchs may have one or two sons: I have so many thousand sons, namely, my Turkish slaves, who will be the heirs of my dominions, and who, after me, will take care to preserve my name in the *Khutbah*

[3] Isami, I, 119. Also Majumdar, *Struggle for the Empire*, V, 2.
[4] Utbi, *Tarikh-i-Yamini*, E.D., II, 18-19, 22-23.
[5] Khondmir, *Khulasat-ul-Akhbar*, E.D., IV, 145 besides others.

throughout those territories."[6] And so it happened. With the help of his Turkish slaves Sultan Muizzuddin built up a large empire in India. He sent them there first as invaders and later as governors and viceroys in various parts for its governance.

As said earlier, Sultan Muizzuddin possessed thousands of slaves many of whom he purchased. Others must have been captured in campaigns because financial constraints would not have permitted buying of all of them. The life story of every Turkish slave who rose to any position of prominence was full of adventure and hazard, "accidents and vicissitude of the world". Some of these have been recorded by contemporary and later chroniclers. It is not possible here to study about them all in detail. However, the careers of two, Aibak the ugly and Iltutmish the handsome, may receive our particular attention as being samples for most of them.

Qutbuddin Aibak, who rose to be the first slave-sultan of Hindustan, was purchased, early in life, by Fakhruddin, the chief Qazi of Nishapur who appears to have been a great slave trader. Through his favours and along with his sons, Aibak received training in reciting the Quran and practising archery and horsemanship. Expenditure on such instructions used to be regarded as an investment by slave merchants: a trained slave fetched a better price in the market. After the Qazi's death his sons sold Aibak to a merchant who took him to Ghazni and sold him to Sultan Muizzuddin. Though ugly in external appearance, Aibak's training had endowed him with "laudable qualities and admirable impressions". He cultivated his compatriots by being most liberal with the "Turkish guards, the slaves of the household."[7] Thereby he won their affection and support. Merit raised him to the position of Amir Akhur (Master of the Horse Stables). He was deputed to campaign in India extensively, a task he accomplished with determination and success. In course of time, loyalty

---

[6] Minhaj, 497.

[7] Minhaj 513, 514 and n.

and signal services to Sultan Muizzuddin secured him the post of vice-regent in Hindustan. In accordance with Muizzuddin's desire, Tajuddin Yaldoz, another slave of the Sultan, married his daughter to Aibak.[8] Aibak extended Muslim dominions in India by undertaking expeditions on behalf of his master. The Sultan seems to have desired that Aibak should succeed him in Hindustan, and after the death of the Sultan, he ascended the throne of Hindustan at Lahore in 1206 and ruled up to 1210.

The career of Shamsuddin Iltutmish, who reigned as Sultan from 1210 to 1236, was more romantic and more eventful. He was a purchased slave of Aibak and thus he became "the slave of a slave". He originally belonged to "the territory of Turkistan and the families of the Ilbari (tribe)". His father, Ilam Khan, happened to have numerous kindred, relations, dependents and followers. Iltutmish, from his earliest years, "was endowed with comeliness, intelligence, and goodness of disposition to a great degree, so much so that his brothers began to grow envious of these endowments". They took him away from his parents on some pretext and sold him to a slave merchant by the name of Bukhara Haji. The merchant sold him to the Sadr Jahan or the chief ecclesiastic of the place. He remained in "that family of eminence and sanctity... and the family used to nourish him like his own children in infancy." Subsequently, another merchant by the name of Jamaluddin Muhammad bought him and brought him to the city of Ghazni, where he was mentioned in terms of commendation to Sultan Muizzuddin. After a long stay at Ghazni, where the merchant wanted a high price for Iltutmish but could not get it, he brought him to Delhi. Iltutmish had received good training as a soldier and had also learnt the art of reading and writing. After many vicissitudes, he was at last purchased by Qutbuddin Aibak for a high price. Sultan Muizzuddin is believed to have said to Qutbuddin: "Treat

[8] Hasan Nizami, *Tajul Maasir*, E.D., II, 221.

Iltutmish well, for he will distinguish himself."

Iltutmish was first made Sarjandar to Qutbuddin. He was later promoted to the offices of Amir-i-Shikar (Master of Hunt), governor of Gwalior and governor of Badaon in succession. Qutbuddin Aibak had three daughters, of whom two, one after the death of the other, were married to Nasiruddin Qubacha, and the third was married to Iltutmish.[9] Such close relationships ensured continuance of the governance of Hindustan to the people of one tribe, that of the Turki slaves. But relationships did not restrain their ambition. After Aibak's sudden death, the Amirs and Maliks placed on the throne his son, Aram Shah, and Qubacha marched to Uchch and Multan and seized those places. The nobles then invited Iltutmish from Badaon to assume charge of the empire. Aram's small army was overpowered. He was probably done to death and Iltutmish ascended the throne of Delhi. He waded through blood to the throne by doing away with most of the Muizzi and Qutbi Amirs. According to the standards of behaviour then prevailing among Turkish slaves, he could not be accused of disloyalty to Aibak's salt for doing away with his son, nor for that matter shedding the blood of his rival compatriots.

Similar fluctuations of fortune attended the careers of other Sultans. Tajuddin Yaldoz was purchased by Sultan Muhammad Ghauri when he was young. In course of time he was appointed head of a group of Turkish slaves. His ability and courage won him the confidence of the Sultan who conferred upon him the office of the Wali of Kirman. Minhaj writers, "He was a great monarch (of Kirman) of excellent faith, mild, beneficent, of good disposition and very handsome." After Muizzuddin's death he became ruler of Ghazni with the consent of Maliks and Amirs. He was a great warrior but was expelled by Qubacha who made himself master of the country. Yaldoz hit back and occupied Qubacha's Sindh

[9] Minhaj, 529-30.

and established himself in the Punjab. But Iltutmish defeated him in 1215. Yaldoz was taken prisoner, sent to the fortress of Badaon and there done to death. Qubacha made his submission to Iltutmish in 1217 and was finally eliminated in 1227.

Qubacha was the son-in-law of both Aibak and Yaldoz. By the command of Sultan Muizzuddin a daughter of Yaldoz was married to Aibak and another to Qubacha.[10] It may be remembered that as per the Islamic law, slaves could not enter into matrimony except with the consent and permission of the master. Through Muizzuddin's favour, Qubacha had acquired considerable experience of civil and military affairs in passing from humble to high posts. He was made governor of Uchch. In a short time he made himself master of Multan, Siwistan and the whole country of Sindh. But his ambition came in clash with that of Yaldoz and Iltutmish and he lost in the game of power politics. Similarly, the scions of Iltutmish lost to Balban, another ambitious Turkish slave.

Balban was a Turk of the Ilbari tribe from which Iltutmish himself had descended. His father was a Khan of 10,000 families. In his youth, he was captured by the Mongols who took him to Baghdad. Khwaja Jamaluddin of Basrah purchased him from the Mongols, brought him up like his own son and along with other slaves brought him to the capital city of Delhi in the year 1232.[11] Shortly after, Balban entered the service of Iltutmish. This is the version of the official chronicler Minhaj Siraj. According to Isami, however, some Chinese merchants brought forty Turkish slaves along with other goods and displayed them before Sultan Iltutmish. The Sultan rejected Balban, short statured as he was. But the Wazir Kamaluddin Muhammad Junaidi, *noticing marks of promise in Balban*, purchased him. Ibn Battuta's version is like this: Sultan Iltutmish purchased in bulk a hundred slaves leaving out only Balban. When the latter asked the Sultan for

---

[10] Minhaj, 500.
[11] Ibid., 777-78.

whom he had purchased the other slaves, Iltutmish replied, "for myself". Balban pleaded that he may purchase him for "God's sake". Touched by the appeal Iltutmish bought him too. In short, Balban entered the service of Iltutmish and was appointed his Khasabardar (Personal Attendant) and then enrolled in the famous corps of Forty Slaves. Raziyah promoted him to the rank of Amir-i-Shikar. When some nobles rose against Raziyah, Balban joined their faction and assisted in her deposition. He helped in the accession of the new king, Bahram, who rewarded him with the fief of Rewari to which later on Hansi also was added. His shrewdness and cunning played an important role in raising Nasiruddin Mahmud to the throne. In 1246, he became the principal adviser to the king.[12] A few years later he further strengthened his position by marrying his daughter to the Sultan, whereupon he was given the title of Ulugh Khan (the Great Khan), and appointed Naib Mumlikat (Deputy Sultan). He was all powerful in the politics of the Sultanate until he himself became king in 1265, some say after poisoning Sultan Nasiruddin.[13]

Slave Kings

The success of slaves such as these has made many scholars praise the medieval Muslim slave system as being marvellous, asserting that it provided unlimited scope for rise so much so that a slave could even become a king. This is not a correct assessment. Slaves were not captured to be made kings; they were not purchased to be made kings. They were abducted, captured, or purchased to serve as domestics, guards, troopers etc. They were sold to make money. 'Slave' and 'king' are contradictory terms. If a few slaves could become kings, it was not because the system provided them with such opportunities but mainly because of their ability to indulge in unscupulous manipulations,

[12] Nigam, *Nobility under the Sultans*, 38.
[13] Lal, *Early Muslims*, 64-65.

muster armed band of followers, and strike for the throne at an appropriate moment. Isami puts the idea in suitable words in the mouth of the slave Sultan Shamsuddin Iltutmish who declared: "You cannot take the world through inheritance and boasting, you can take it only by wielding the sword in battle."[14] Kingship was won through the sword, not by mere loyalty or service. Slave adventurists openly supplanted the forces of the reigning monarch to seize authority. The killings and blindings of Caliph Umar (644 C.E.), scions of Alauddin Khalji (1316), Mubarak Khalji (1320), Farrukhsiyar (1719) and Shah Alam (1788) by slave nobles clearly shows that treachery stalked every step of the reigning monarch, so that courtesy and conspiracy by slaves went hand in hand throughout the medieval period. In such an atmosphere, loyalty was a luxury only a few could indulge in. One thing is certain. In these 'favourable openings' for rise to the highest office no moral principles were involved. All this is seen in the careers of the Turkish slave rulers of India, who, just because they were successful, are called remarkable men by some modern historians. In all their cases applies the dictum: "Nothing succeeds like success." For if some slaves rose to become kings, myriads of others, equally ambitious and efficient, got nowhere.

Such an one was Ikhtiyaruddin Bakhtiyar Khalji. He had a hard time getting recognition. He belonged to the Khalji tribe of Ghaur in the province of Garmsir. He came to the court of Sultan Muizzuddin at Ghazni and applied for enrolment in the Diwan-i-Arz (Military Department), but he was rejected. Consequently, from Ghazni he proceeded towards Hindustan, but was again rejected by the Diwan-i-Arz at Delhi. He went to Badaon and later on to Avadh. The ruler of Avadh Malik Hisamuddin Aghilbek (Aghilbek is a Turkish word meaning Lord of the flock), gave him two fiefs for subsistence. He soon acquired all the requisites of power like

[14] Isami, II, 221.

arms, men and horses, and began to raid the territory of Bihar and Munghir. The fame of his bravery and news of his plundering raids spread abroad, attracting to his standard a body of Khalji warriors then found hanging about all over Hindustan. His exploits were reported to Qutbuddin Aibak, who sent him a robe of honour and appointed him to invade Bihar as the Sultan's general in 1202 C.E.[15] Ikhtiyaruddin Bakhtiyar Khalji conquered extensively in Bihar and Bengal but then died unhonoured and unsung.

In short, as Yahiya concluded in the fifteenth century, "each and every noble wanted to become sultan",[16] but of course only a few succeeded. Slave nobles who attained fame, position and crown, were feared, befriended and flattered; others were not given much attention. About the first set a few encomiums by Minhaj Siraj are worth reproducing. Qutbuddin Aibak was ugly and deformed, but because he ascended the throne, he was, according to our author, "endowed with all laudable qualities and admirable impressions... the beneficent Qutbuddin Aibak, the second Hatim, was a high spirited and open handed monarch. The Almighty God had endowed him with intrepidity and beneficence the like of which, in his day, no sovereign of the world, either in the east or west, possessed..."[17] Nasiruddin Qubacha "was endowed with very great intellect, sagacity, discretion, skill, wisdom and experience...,"[18] while Bahauddin Tughril, the governor of Thangir or Bayana, "was a Malik of excellent disposition, scrupulously impartial, just, kind to the poor and strangers, and adorned with humility."[19] Sultan Iltutmish was "just and munificent Sultan, upright, beneficent, zealous and steadfast warrior against infidels, the patronizer of the learned, the dispenser of justice...through his sovereignty...

[15] Lal, *Early Muslims*, 65-66.
[16] Yahiya, *Tarikh-i-Mubarak Shahi*, 140.
[17] Minhaj, 512, 513.
[18] Ibid., 531.
[19] Ibid., 544.

(and) valour the Ahmadi faith acquired pre-eminence. In intrepidity he turned out to be another impetuous Ali, and, in liberality, a second Hatim-i-Tai..."[20] Even the belatedly recognized Ikhtiyaruddin Bakhtiyar Khalji was "a man impetuous, enterprising, intrepid, bold, sagacious, and expert."[21] But when he lay dying of age and exhaustion after the Tibetan debacle, our author could say nothing more than that "Ali Mardan in some way went unto him, drew the sheet from his face, and with a dagger assassinated him", and add nothing more than that "these events and calamities happened in the year 602 H (1205-06 C.E.)."[22]

Exaggerated praise was normal with the panegyrists for those slaves who succeeded in wresting the throne. In all cases the length of the sword and the strength of the supporters was more important than any claims on the basis of inheritance or even an investiture from the Caliph. The first four Caliphs were directly related to the Prophet. There was therefore very great respect for the Caliphs in the world of Islam. Conscious of the moral benefits accruing from Caliphal support, there developed a tradition with medieval Muslim rulers to request for and receive recognition of their sovereignty from the Caliph. But even this recognition was of no avail before the power of arms. As Prince Masud, son of Mahmud Ghaznavi, once declared, when his claims were being superseded by his brother Muhammad, "the sword is a truer authority than any writing"[23] (or investiture from the Caliph).

In such a situation there was no sanctity of any letter of manumission either. Manumission was of great importance in law, polity and society of Islam. It is even asserted that "no slave could ascend the throne unless he had obtained a letter of manumission (*khatt-i-azadi*) from his master. ...because a slave is no longer slave when he is manumitted by his mas-

[20] Ibid., 597-98.
[21] Ibid., 548.
[22] Ibid., 572-73.
[23] Ibid., 91-92.

ter."[24] Sure enough, many of the slaves tried to obtain such letters; it provided legitimacy to their office. But many slaves whose star was in ascendance lived almost like kings without receiving or caring to receive any manumission letter. For example, as mentioned earlier, Alptigin in Khurasan had 500 villages of his own and an assemblage of 2000 slave troopers. As such as governor of Khurasan his position was not inferior to that of any sultan, although he had not been manumitted. But since the sword was the ultimate arbiter, even this moral prop was not that important. Most of the slave Maliks of Muizzuddin requested for letters of manumission from the Sultan's successor, Mahmud, and did receive them. Tajuddin Yaldoz and Nasiruddin Qubacha received their letters of manumission on request,[25] but Qutbuddin Aibak received his letter of manumission more than one year after he had ascended the throne of Delhi.[26] It is not clear when Balban received his letter of freedom. At one place the contemporary chronicler, Ziyauddin Barani, says that Balban used to maintain the paraphernalia of royalty even when he was a khan,[27] at another that he ascended the throne after becoming free,[28] and yet at another that all the Forty Amirs (Chahlgani) had obtained freedom (*buzurgi*) at one and the same time so that no one considered himself inferior to any other.

Slave Nobles

These Turkish slaves formed the ruling class of Muslim kings and nobles in Hindustan. A few became kings while most others remained nobles. The nobles were called Khans, Maliks and Amirs. The official status of a noble was deter-

---

[24] M.A. Ahmad *Political History and Institutions of the Early Turkish Empire of Delhi*, 1.

[25] Minhaj, 398-99.

[26] Aibak ascended the throne at Lahore on 24 June 1206 (17 Zilqada 602) more than three months after Muizzuddin's death. His formal manumission, sent by Sultan Mahmud, the nephew and successor of the deceased Sultan, was not obtained till 603 H/1208. Habibullah, *The Foundation of Muslim Rule in India*, 88-89, notes 7-11.

[27] Barani, p. 26.

[28] Ibid., 25.

mined by his *shughl* (office), *khitab* (title), *iqta* (land assignment) and *maratib* (status and position at the court). Each nobleman of any importance commanded his own army and held his own miniature court. Sometimes he gathered so much strength that the Sultan began to live in fear of him. Alauddin Ata Malik Juwaini in his *Tarikh-i-Jahan Gusha* writes that often the ruler of a Muslim country "talks with fear with his own purchased slave, if the latter possesses ten horses in his stable...If an army is placed under his command, and he attains to position of authority, he simply cannot be commanded. And often it happens that the officer himself rises in revolt (against the king)."[29] This was precisely the situation during the period of the early sultans. When Sultan Muizzuddin was killed, the inheritance of his dominions was contested between his relatives and Amirs in the homeland and the Turkish slaves operating in India. "These slave Maliks and Amirs, deprived the Maliks and Amirs of Ghaur, by force, of the bier of the late Sultan, together with precious treasures, and took possession of them" while they sent his body to Ghazni.[30] This conveys the idea of the clout of the Turkish slaves appointed in Hindustan. Aibak, Iltutmish, Yaldoz, Qubacha and Balban were all purchased slaves. They fought amongst themselves and faced opposition from their slave nobles. The nobles flouted the wishes and dictates of the rulers to make a show of strength. They formed pressure groups and rejected the king's nominee to the throne. Qutbuddin Aibak wanted his slave Iltutmish to succeed him, but the nobles raised Aram Shah to the throne of Delhi. Sultan Iltutmish made Raziyah his successor, but the Maliks raised Ruknuddin Firoz to the throne. Balban designated Kai Khusrau as his heir apparent, but the nobles placed Kaiqubad on the throne. As if this was not bad enough, in

---

[29] Juwaini, *Tarikh-i-Jahan Gusha* (Tehran), 19-21 and summarized in Muhammad Aziz Ahmad, *Political History and Institutions in the Early Turkish Empire of Delhi*, Lahore 1949, Delhi reprint 1972, 40-41.

[30] Minhaj, 492.

the thirteenth century, during the Slave Dynasty's rule in Hindustan, out of ten rulers they killed six — Aram Shah, Ruknuddin Firoz, Raziyah, Bahram, Alauddin Masaud and Nasiruddin Mahmud. As we shall see later on, these slave nobles extended Muslim dominions in India, collected huge treasures through loot, and made their constructive and destructive contribution in the various spheres of life. But they always posed a challenge to the king about how to control them.

No king could rule by himself; he had to govern through the nobles or Umara. They used to be appointed as Walis, Muqtis or Iqtadars to administer their assignments. W.H. Moreland enumerates the services rendered by some slave nobles like Tughan Khan, Saifuddin Aibak, Tughril Khan and Ulugh Khan Balban.[31] But they had to be kept under control and there were many levers in the administrative machinery through which the Sultan kept a control over them. The lives of nobles, their titles and grants, were all dependent on the pleasure and mercy of the monarch. The absolute powers of the king regarding appointment and dismissal made the nobles completely dependent on him. The Sultan took extreme care in selecting them, and appointed to this cadre either his relatives or the most trusted persons. As a further safeguard some sort of a spoil system was resorted to. On accession a new monarch removed all nobles of his predecessor and appointed his own loyal slave supporters to important offices. Hence the Muizzi, Qutbi, Shamsi and Balbani slave Amirs (*Ghulams*) or nobles of Muizzudin bin Sam, Qutbuddin Aibak, Shamsuddin Iltutmish and Ghiyasuddin Balban.

Turkish nobles suffered from an inborn arrogance. Devoid of humanitarian learning and proud of military prowess, every one of them felt and said to the other: "What art thou

[31] Moreland, *The Agrarian System of Moslem India*, 216-220.

and what shalt thou be, that I shalt not be?"[32] Their continuous conflict born out of jealousy and intrigue, was a constant danger to the stability of the Muslim state and the monarch's position. To show them their place the Sultan used to inflict humiliating and barbarous punishments on those found guilty of some crime. Malik Baqbaq, the Governor of Badaon and holder of a Jagir of 4000 horse, got a servant beaten to death. Sultan Balban ordered Malik Baqbaq to be publicly flogged. Balban also publicly executed the spies who had failed to report the misconduct of Malik Baqbaq. Another great noble, Haibat Khan, was the Governor of Avadh. In a state of drunkenness, he got a man killed. Balban ordered Haibat Khan to be flogged with five hundred stripes. He was also made to pay a compensation of 20,000 *tankahs* to the widow of the victim. Haibat Khan felt so ashamed that after this incident he never came out of his house till the day of his death. Amin Khan, the Governor of Avadh, was hanged at the gate of the city of Ayodhya because he had failed to defeat in battle the rebel Tughril Beg of Bengal. Balban is said to have poisoned even his cousin, Sher Khan, the Governor of Bhatinda. A well-established espionage system helped in keeping the nobles terrorized. While terror tactics made individual nobles squirm, junior Turks were promoted to important positions and placed on par with the important. That is how the slave rulers tried to keep individual slave nobles under control.

Under the Khaljis and Tughlaqs (fourteenth century) the nobles lived under constant fear of the Sultan. "Nor did they do anything nor utter a single word which could subject them to reproof or punishment.[33]" The Afghan nobles, who were considered to be difficult of control and therefore fairly independent, were no better. Whenever a *farman* was sent

---

[32] *"tu kesti ki man na am va tu ki bashi ki man na basham"*, Barani, 28. For the struggle of Iltutmish with his compatriots see Minhaj, 610, 774 and n. Also Tripathi, *Some Aspects of Muslim Administration*, 26.

[33] Barani, 284; also *Fatawa-i-Jahandari*, 30.

to a district officer by Sultan Sikandar Lodi (fifteenth century), the former received it with the utmost respect. Sikandar reduced the highest nobles to the position of slaves so that he could boast that "if I order one of my slaves to be seated in a palanquin, the entire body of nobility would carry him on their shoulders at my bidding."[34] Badaoni gives an eye-witness account of the situation under Islam Shah Sur (sixteenth century). "In the year 955H (1548 A.D.), when he was of tender age (the chronicler Badaoni) went to the country of Bajwara, one of the dependencies of Baiana ... and witnessed the customs and rules in practice" — that the high nobles holding ranks of 500 to 20000 *sawars* were ordered to set up a lofty tent every Friday; a chair was placed in its centre on which were kept the shoes of Islam Shah (how could the shoes of the Sultan be procured ? Were they sent along with the *farman* ?). The nobles sat at their proper places with bowed heads in front of them to show their respect. Thereafter, the *amin* read out the *farman* containing new regulations and reforms to be carried out by the nobles. If any one disobeyed the royal orders, the officer concerned informed the Sultan and "the disobedient Amir would forthwith be visited with punishment together with his family and relations." The Sultan also took away the elephants and even *patars* (dancing girls) of the nobles at will.[35]

Under the Mughals the nobles enjoyed a fair amount of respect but in principle their status was not changed. In fact, all nobles took pride in calling themselves *ghulams* of their superiors or the king. This indeed became a part of Muslim etiquette and culture. This explains how sometimes poets, physicians, musicians and scholars have all been bracketed together as slaves. In fact, they all were. It is true that some of them were not captured in war or pur-

---

[34] *Tarikh-i-Daudi*, 40; *Waqiat-i-Mushtaqui*, 13(b). For more references, Lal, *Twilight*, 189.

[35] Badaoni, I, 496-97.

chased in slave markets. But there were certain conditions of slavery which were applicable to them as to the meanest of slaves. They were prohibited from visiting one another or holding get-together parties without the permission or at least the knowledge of the king. Further, they were prohibited from contracting any matrimonial alliances without permission of the king or the master. The king was heir to the noble; on his death his property went to the king and not to his children, and the sons of the noble became slaves of the king in their turn. Most of the kings kept a strict watch on the activities of their greatest nobles. Hence there should be no misgivings about the status of nobles and slaves. They were all slaves, whether high or low. As pointed out by Pelsaert, their ranks, assignments, "wealth, position, confidence, everything hangs by a thread". The king could take away everything at any time. "A trifling mistake may bring a man to the depth of misery or to the scaffold."[36] The position of the highest noble was as uncertain as that of any slave.

[36] Pelsaert, 56 for the Mughal period; Barani, 282 ff for the Sultanate.

Chapter V
SLAVE-TAKING DURING MUSLIM RULE

Slavery forms an integral part of the history of Islam. The Turks practised it on a large scale before they entered India as invaders. Slaves were abducted or captured by marauders (Subuktigin, Balban), they were sold by jealous or needy relatives (Iltutmish), and they were purchased by slave-traders to be sold for profit (Aibak). These methods were known to Muslim rulers in India. All these and many other methods were employed by them and their nobles in making slaves in India. The phenomenon and its application was shocking to the Hindu mind; the Muslims, however, thought otherwise. According to Ibn Khaldun, the captives were "brought from the House of War to the House of Islam under the rule of slavery, which hides in itself a divine providence; cured by slavery, they enter the Muslim religion with the firm resolve of true believers..."[1] Muslims took pride in enslaving people; the feelings of Hindu victims were just the opposite.

Qutbuddin Aibak entered upon a series of conquests. He despatched Ikhtiyaruddin Bakhtiyar Khalji to the East and himself concentrated in Hindustan proper. He captured Kol (modern Aligarh) in 1194. There "those of the garrison who were wise and cute were converted to Islam, but those who stood by their ancient faith were slain with the sword."[2] Surely, those who embraced Islam during or immediately after the battle were 'cute' and wise, because by this initiative on their part they were counted as free-born Muslims as against those who fought, were captured in battle, and then enslaved. T.P. Hughes gives the legal position: "If a captive embraced Islam on the field of battle he was a free man; but if he were made captive, and afterwards embraced Islam, the

---

[1] Ibn Khaldun; *Ibar*, trs. by Bernard Lewis in *Islam*, 98.

[2] Hasan Nizami, *Taj-ul-Maasir*, E.D., II, 222.

change of creed did not emancipate him." Women captives were invariably taken prisoner. "Atiyat-ul-Qurazi relates that, after the battle with the Banu Quraizah, the Prophet ordered all those who were able to fight to be killed, and the women and children to be enslaved."[3]

Both these traditions were followed in India. In 1195 when Raja Bhim was attacked by Aibak 20,000 slaves were captured, and 50,000 at Kalinjar in 1202. "The temples were converted into mosques," writes Hasan Nizami, "and the voices of the summoners to prayer ascended to the highest heavens, and the very name of idolatry was annihilated."[4] Call to prayer five times a day with a loud voice carried an invitation and a message — join us, or else. People "could refuse this invitation or call at their own peril, spiritual and physical. As His followers became more powerful, the peril became increasingly more physical."[5] This process helped in the conversion of captives. Murry Titus pertinently remarks that "we may be sure that all those who were made slaves were compelled to embrace the religion of the masters to whom they were allotted."[6] Farishtah specifically mentions that during the capture of Kalinjar "fifty thousand *kaniz va ghulam*, having suffered slavery, were rewarded with the honour of Islam." Thus enslavement resulted in conversion and conversion in accelerated growth of Muslim population.

Minhaj Siraj assigns twenty (lunar) years to Qutbuddin's career in Hindustan from 'the first taking of Delhi' up to his death, both as a commander of Sultan Muizzuddin and as an independent ruler.[7] During this period Aibak captured Hansi, Meerut, Delhi, Ranthambhor and Kol.[8] When Sultan Muizzuddin personally mounted another campaign against

---

[3] *Dictionary of Islam*, 597.
[4] Hasan Nizami, *Taj-u-Maasir*, E.D., II, 231. Farishtah, I, 62.
[5] Ram Swarup, Introduction to the Reprint of William Muir's *The Life of Mahomet*, New Delhi, 1992, 9.
[6] Titus, *Islam in India and Pakistan*, 31.
[7] Minhaj, 523 n. Also Farishtah, I, 63.
[8] Ibid., 528.

Hindustan, Aibak proceeded as far as Peshawar to meet him, and the two together attacked the Khokhar stronghold in the Koh-i-Jud or the Salt Range. The Hindus (Khokhars) fled to the highest in the mountains. They were pursued. Those that escaped the sword fled to the dense depth of the Jungle; others were massacred or taken captive. Great plunder was obtained and many slaves.[9] According to Farishtah three to four hundred thousand Khokhars were converted to Islam by Muizzuddin;[10] but this figure is inflated. More than a hundred years later, Amir Khusrau refers to Khokhars as a non-Muslim tribe, and the way they were constantly attacked and killed by Sultans Iltutmish and Balban confirms Khusrau's contention.[11] Minhaj also says that "the Khokhars were not annihilated in this affair (Muizzuddin-Aibak attack) by any means, and gave great trouble in after years."[12]

Under Aibak most of Hindustan from Delhi to Gujarat, and Lakhnauti to Lahore, was brought under the sway of the Turks. In his time a large number of places were attacked and many more prisoners were captured than for which actual figures are available. Figures of slaves made during campaigns of Kanauj, Banaras (where the Muslims occupied "a thousand" temples),[13] Ajmer (attacked thrice), Gujarat, Bayana and Gwalior are not available. Similar is the case with regard to Bihar and Bengal. About the end of the twelfth or the beginning of the thirteenth century, Ikhtiyaruddin Bakhtiyar Khalji marched into Bihar and attacked the University centres at Nalanda, Vikramshila and Uddandpur.[14] The Buddhist monks and Brahmans mistaken for monks were massacred and the common people, deprived of their priests

[9] Minhaj 483-84.
[10] Farishtah, I, 59-60.
[11] Amir Khusrau, *Tughlaq Nama*, Aurangabad text, 128.
[12] Minhaj, 484n.
[13] Farishtah, I, 58.
[14] Opinions differ on the date of this raid. Ishwari Prasad, *Medieval India*, 138, places it probably in 1197; Wolseley Haig, C.H.I, III, 45-46, a little earlier than this, and Habibullah, 70 and 84, in 1202-03.

and teachers, became an easy prey to capture and enslavement. But no figures of such captives are known. Ibn Asir only says that Qutbuddin Aibak made "war against the provinces of Hind.... He killed many, and returned with prisoners and booty."[15] In Banaras, according to the same author, "the slaughter of the Hindus was immense, none was spared except women and children,"[16] who would have been enslaved as per practice. Habibullah writes that Muslim sway extended from Banaras through the strip of Shahabad, Patna, Monghyr and Bhagalpur districts,[17] and repeated references to the presence of Muslims in this tract from the early times indicates that taking of slaves and conversion was common in the region. Fakhr-i-Mudabbir informs us that as a result of the Turkish achievements under Muizzuddin and Aibak, "even poor (Muslim) householder became owner of numerous slaves."[18]

The narratives of contemporary and later chroniclers should not lead us to the conclusion that taking of Hindus as slaves was a child's play. There was stiff resistance to Muslim conquest and Muslim rule. Besides, the Sultans of Delhi had always to deal with a number of problems simultaneously. Most of the time of Sultan Iltutmish (1210-1236) was spent in suppressing his Turkish opponents, Qutbi and Muizzi Amirs in Delhi and rivals Yaldoz and Qubacha in Punjab and Sindh. He also faced the threat of invasion from the Mongol conqueror Chingiz Khan and the Khwarizmi Prince Jalaluddin Mangbarni fleeing before Chingiz. Therefore it was only sixteen years after his accession that he could march against Ranthambhor in 1226. During this period many Hindu kingdoms subdued by Aibak were becoming independent. Mandor near Jodhpur was attacked a little later. Here "much booty fell into the hands" of the victors, which obviously

---

[15] Ibn Asir, *Kamil-ut-Tawarikh*, E.D., II, 250.
[16] Ibid., 251.
[17] Habibullah, op.cit., 147.
[18] *Tarikh-i-Fakhruddin Mubarak Shah*, 20.

included slaves also.[19] The year 1231 witnessed his invasion of Gwalior where he "captured a large number of slaves". In 1234-35 he attacked Ujjain, broke its temple of Mahakal, and as usual made captives "women and children of the recalcitrants."[20] But most of his compatriot Muslims were not satisfied with the Sultan's achievements in the sphere of slave-taking and converting the land into Dar-ul-Islam all at once.

It is true that foreign Muslims — freemen and slaves — were flocking into Hindustan and this development was of great significance for the Sultanate. Adventurers and job seekers were flocking into Hindustan, the new heaven of Islam. More importantly, because of the Mongol upheaval, as many as twenty-five Muslim refugee princes with their retinues arrived at the court of Iltutmish from Khurasan and Mawaraun Nahr.[21] During the reign of Balban fifteen more refugee rulers and their nobles and slaves arrived from Turkistan, Khurasan, Iraq, Azarbaijan, Persia, Rum (Turkey) and Sham (Syria).[22] Their followers comprised masters of pen and of sword, scholars and Mashaikh, historians and poets. The pressure of these groups on the Sultan for Islamization of Hindustan would have been great. In 1228 C.E. Iltutmish received a patent of investiture from Al-Mustansir Billah, the Khalifa of Baghdad, in recognition of his enormously augmenting the prestige of the Muhammadan government in India. This was a booster as well as a further pressure. No wonder, the capital city of Delhi looked like Dar-ul-Islam and its ruler the leader of the eastern world of Islam.[23] But since the whole country was not conquered and converted, it did not amuse the Ulama and the Mashaikh.

---

[19] Minhaj, 611.
[20] Farishtah, I, 66.
[21] Farishtah, I, 73; Minhaj, 598-99.
[22] Farishtah, I, 75. Also Habibullah, 272.
[23] Barani, 57-58; Farishtah, I, 75; Habibullah, 294-95.

Slave-taking a matter of policy

Some Ulama therefore approached the 'pious' Sultan Iltutmish to rule according to the Shariat and confront the Hindus with choice between Islam and death. Muslims had set up their rule and so the country had become Dar-ul-Islam. Any opposition to it was an act of rebellion. The Hindus who naturally resisted Muslim occupation were considered to be rebels. Besides they were idolaters (*mushrik*) and could not be accorded the status of Kafirs, of the People of the Book — Christians and Jews. For them the law provided only Islam or death. Islamic jurisprudence had crystallized over the last five centuries. Besides the evolvement of the four schools of Islamic jurisprudence, Shaikh Burhauddin Ali's *Hidayah* (530-596 H./1135-1199 C.E.), the Compendium of Sunni Law, based on the Quran and the Hadis, was also readily available in the time of Iltutmish. Muslim scriptures and treatises advocated Jihad against idolaters for whom the law advocated only Islam or death.

In such a situation the answer of the Sultan to the Ulama was: "But at the moment in India... the Muslims are so few that they are like salt (in a large dish)... However, after a few years when in the capital and the regions and all the small towns, when the Muslims are well established and the troops are larger... it would be possible to give Hindus, the choice of death or Islam."[24] Such an apologetic plea was not necessary to put forward. The fact was that the Muslim regime was giving a choice between Islam and death only. Those who were killed in battle were dead and gone; but their dependents were made slaves. They ceased to be Hindus; they were made Musalmans in course of time if not immediately after captivity.

There was thus no let up in the policy of slave-taking. Minhaj Siraj writes that Ulugh Khan Balban's "taking of cap-

[24] Ziyauddin Barani, *Sana-i-Muhammadi*, trs. in Medieval India Quarterly, (Aligarh), I, Part III, 100-105.

tives, and his capture of the dependents of the great Ranas cannot be recounted". Talking of his war in Avadh against Trailokyavarman of the Chandela dynasty (Dalaki va Malaki of Minhaj), the chronicler says that "All the infidels' wives, sons and dependents... and children... fell into the hands of the victors." In 1253, in his campaign against Ranthambhor also, Balban enslaved many people. In 1259, in an attack on Haryana, many women and children were enslaved.[25] Twice Balban led expeditions against Kampil, Patiali, and Bhojpur, and in the process enslaved a large number of women and children. In Katehar he ordered a general massacre of the male population of over eight years of age and carried away women and children.[26] In 658 H. (1260 C.E.) Ulugh Khan Balban marched with a large force on a campaign in the region of Ranthambhor, Mewat and Siwalik. He made a proclamation that a soldier who brought a live captive would be rewarded with two silver *tankahs* and one who brought the head of a dead one would get one silver *tankah*. Soon three to four hundred living and dead were brought to his presence.[27] Like Balban other slave commanders of Iltutmish, or the "Shamsia Maliks of Hind" were marching up and down the Hindustan, raiding towns and villages and enslaving people. This was the situation prevailing from Lakhnauti to Lahore and from Ajmer to Ujjain. The Hindus used to reclaim their lands after the Muslim invaders had passed through them with fire and sword, and Turkish armies used to repeat their attacks to regain control of the cities so lost. But the captives once taken became slaves and then Musalmans for ever. The exact figures of such slaves have not been mentioned and therefore cannot be computed. All that is known is that they were captured in droves. Only one instance should suffice to convey an idea of their numbers. Even in the reign of a weak Sultan like Nasiruddin, son of Iltutmish,

---

[25] Minhaj 680, 683, 391, 828; E.D., II, 348, 367, 371, 380-81, Farishtah, I, 73.
[27] Farishtah, I. 73.

the ingress of captives was so large that once he presented *forty heads of slaves* to our chronicler Minhaj Siraj to send to his "dear sister" in Khurasan.[28]

Enslavement under the Khaljis

The process of enslavement during war gained momentum under the Khaljis and the Tughlaqs. In two or three generations after Iltutmish the Muslims were digging their heels firmly into the country. Their territories were expanding and their armies were becoming larger. All the time, the desire to convert or liquidate the idolaters remained ever restless. Achievements in this regard of course depended on the strength, resources and determination of individual Muslim rulers. For example, although Jalaluddin Khalji was an old and vacillating king, even he did not just remain content with expressing rage at the fact of not being able to deal with the Hindus according to the law.[29] During six years of his reign (June 1290 — July 1296), he mounted expeditions and captured prisoners. While suppressing the revolt of Malik Chhajju, a scion of the dynasty he had ousted, he marched towards Bhojpur in Farrukhabad district and ruthlessly attacked Hindus in the region of Katehar (later Rohilkhand). During his campaign in Ranthambhor he broke temples, sacked the neighbouring Jhain and took booty and captives, making "a hell of paradise".[30] Later on Malwa was attacked and large quantity of loot, naturally including slaves, was brought to Delhi.[31] His last expedition was directed against Gwalior.[32]

Jalaluddin's nephew and successor Alauddin Khalji (1296-1316) turned out to be a very strong king. He marched against Devagiri in 1296. On his way through Gondwana and

---

28 Minhaj, 686; 675 n.5, 719-868.
29 Barani, 216-17.
30 Khusrau, *Miftah-ul-Fatuh,* Aligarh text, 1954, 35-36; Barani, 213.
31 Khusrau, *Miftah-ul-Fatuh*, 38-39; Farishtah, I, 94.
32 Barani, 222-23; Farishtah, I, 95-97.

Khandesh he took prisoners a large number of Mahajans and cultivators and ransomed them for wealth.[33] At Devagiri he enslaved a number of the Raja's relatives, and Brahmans and Mahajans. He put them in shackles and chains and paraded them in front of the fort to pressure the besieged king. After victory, he released many of the captives because of compulsions of the situation. He was only a prince who had marched to the Deccan without the Sultan's permission. But his taking of slaves in large numbers was in consonance with the policy of Muslim sultans and gave a foretaste of what was to follow during the course of his reign.

After ascending the throne, Alauddin Khalji embarked upon a series of conquests. He turned out to be the greatest king of the Sultanate period (cir. 1200-1500), and his success as regards capture of slaves was stupendous. He started by seizing the families and slaves of his brothers and brother-in-law.[34] In 1299 he despatched a large army for the invasion of Gujarat. There all the major towns and cities like Naharwala, Asaval, Vanmanthali, Surat, Cambay, Somnath etc. were sacked. There the temples were broken, wealth looted and large numbers of captives of both sexes captured, including the famous Malik Kafur[35] and the Vaghela king's consort Kamala Devi.[36] In the words of Wassaf, the Muslim army in the sack of Somnath "took captive a great number of handsome and elegant maidens, amounting to 20,000, and children of both sexes.... the Muhammadan army brought the country to utter ruin, and destroyed the lives of inhabitants, and plundered the cities and captured their offspring...."[37] In 1301 Ranthambhor was attacked and in 1303 Chittor. In the invasion of Chittor, 30,000 people were massacred in cold blood and obviously females and minors of their families were captured.[38]

---

[33] Farishtah, I, 95-96.
[34] Barani, 249; Farishtah, I, 102: Badaoni, Ranking, I, 248.
[35] Isami, 243; Barani, 251-52.
[36] For detailed references see Lal, *Khaljis*, 69-71.
[37] Wassaf, Bk. IV, 448. Also trs. in E.D. III, 43.
[38] *Khazain*, Habib trs., 49; Lal, *Khaljis*, 101.

Slaves were also taken in large numbers in the expeditions to Malwa, Sevana and Jalor (1305-1311); these will be referred to again in the course of this study. Maybe the number of captives obtained from Rajasthan was not that large knowing the bravery and chivalry of the Rajputs and their prevailing customs of Jauhar and Sati. But the highly successful Deccan campaigns of Malik Kafur must have supplied a large corps of captives. Besides, Alauddin did not confine to obtaining Hindu slaves. During the invasion of the Mongol Saldi (1299), the commanders of the Sultan captured 1,700 of his officers, men and women and sent them as slaves to Delhi.[39] During the raid of Ali Beg, Tartaq and Targhi (1305), 8,000 Mongol prisoners were executed and their heads displayed in the towers of the Siri Fort which were then under construction.[40] The women and children accompanying the Mongol raiders Kubak and Iqbalmand were sold in Delhi and the rest of Hindustan. "The Mongol invaders were certainly infidels," says Mahdi Husain. This enslavement was as beneficial to Islam as that of the Hindus. Muslims were not enslaved because they were already Muslim.[41]

Sultan Alauddin's collection of slaves was a matter of successful routine. Under him the Sultanate had grown so strong that, according to Shams Siraj Afif, in his days "no one dared to make an outcry."[42] Similar is the testimony of the Alim and Sufi Amir Khusrau. In *Nuh Sipehr* he writes that "the Turks, whenever they please, can seize, buy or sell any Hindu."[43] No wonder, under him the process of enslavement went on with great vigour. As an example, he had 50,000 slave boys in his

[39] Barani, 253-54; Farishtah, I, 103: Futuh, 241.

[40] Farishtah, I, 114-15; Barani, 320; *Khazain*, Habib, 28; Wassaf, IV, 526-27. The walls of the towers popularly known as Chor Minar in modern Hauz Khas Enclave are pierced with 225 holes. In medieval India apertures on the walls of towers were used by Muslims not only as windows but also to display heads of captured and executed prisoners. The custom was to cut off their heads and stick them into those holes, to be seen by everybody. During wars, only the heads of chiefs were displayed; those of common soldiers were simply piled into pyramids.

[41] For references Lal, *Khaljis*, 146-48.

[42] Afif, 37-38.

[43] Trs, in E.D., III, 561. Also in his *Ashiqa*, ibid., 545-46.

personal service[44] and 70,000 slaves worked continuously on his buildings.[45] We must feel obliged to Muslim chroniclers for providing such bits of information on the basis of which we can safely generalize. For instance, it is Barani alone who writes about the number of slaves working on buildings and Afif alone who speaks about the personal 'boys' of Sultan Alauddin who looked after his pigeons. Ziyauddin Barani's detailed description of the Slave Markets in Delhi and elsewhere during the reign of Alauddin Khalji, shows that fresh batches of captives were constantly arriving there.[46]

Enslavement under the Tughlaqs

All sultans were keen on making slaves, but Muhammad Tughlaq became notorious for enslaving people. He appears to have outstripped even Alauddin Khalji and his reputation in this regard spread far and wide. Shihabuddin Ahmad Abbas writes about him thus: "The Sultan never ceases to show the greatest zeal in making war upon infidels... Everyday thousands of slaves are sold at a very low price, so great is the number of prisoners".[47] Muhammad Tughlaq did not only enslave people during campaigns, he was also very fond of purchasing and collecting foreign and Indian slaves. According to Ibn Battuta one of the reasons of estrangement between Muhammad Tughlaq and his father Ghiyasuddin Tughlaq, when Muhammad was still a prince, was his extravagance in purchasing slaves.[48] Even as Sultan, he made extensive conquests. He subjugated the country as far as Dwarsamudra, Malabar, Kampil, Warangal, Lakhnauti, Satgaon, Sonargaon, Nagarkot and Sambhal to give only few prominent place-names.[49] There were sixteen major rebel-

---

[44] Afif, 272.

[45] Barani, 341.

[46] Barani, 318; Lal, *Khaljis*, 214-15.

[47] *Masalik-ul-Absar*, E.D., III, 580.

[48] Ishwari Prasad, *Qaraunh Turks*, 39-40 citing Battutah, Def. and Sang., II, 212-14.

[49] *Qaraunah Turks*, 96, 126, 129-30, 173.

lions in his reign which were ruthlessly suppressed.[50] In all these conquests and rebellions, slaves were taken with great gusto. For example, in the year 1342 Halajun rose in rebellion in Lahore. He was aided by the Khokhar chief Kulchand. They were defeated. "About three hundred women of the rebels were taken captive, and sent to the fort of Gwalior where they were seen by Ibn Battutah."[51] Such was their influx that Ibn Battutah writes: "At (one) time there arrived in Delhi some female infidel captives, ten of whom the Vazir sent to me. I gave one of them to the man who had brought them to me, but he was not satisfied. My companion took three young girls, and I do not know what happened to the rest."[52] Iltutmish, Muhammad Tughlaq and Firoz Tughlaq sent gifts of slaves to Khalifas outside India. To the Chinese emperor Muhammad Tughlaq sent, besides other presents, "100 Hindu slaves, 100 slave girls, accomplished in song and dance... and another 15 young slaves."[53]

Ibn Battutah's eye-witness account of the Sultan's gifting captured slave girls to nobles or arranging their marriages with Muslims on a large scale on the occasion of the two Ids, corroborates the statement of Abbas. Ibn Battutah writes that during the celebrations in connection with the two Ids in the court of Muhammad bin Tughlaq, daughters of Hindu Rajas and those of commoners, captured during the course of the year were distributed among nobles, officers and important foreign slaves. "On the fourth day men slaves are married and on the fifth slave-girls. On the sixth day men and women slaves are married off."[54] This was all in accordance with the Islamic law. According to it, slaves cannot marry on their own without the consent of their proprietor.[55] The marriage

---

[50] Mahdi Husain *Tughlaq Dynasty*, 195-257.
[51] *Qaraunah Turks*, 148 citing Battutah, Def. and Sang, III, 332.
[52] Battutah, 123.
[53] *Qaraunah Turks*, 138-39.
[54] Battutah, 63; Hindi trs. by S.A.A. Rizvi in *Tughlaq Kalin Bharat*, part I, Aligarh 1956, 189.
[55] Hamilton, *Hedaya*. I, 161.

of an infidel couple is not dissolved by their jointly embracing the faith.[56] In the present case the slaves were probably already converted and their marriages performed with the initiative and permission the Sultan himself were valid. Thousands of non-Muslim women[57] were captured by the Muslims in the yearly campaigns of Firoz Tughlaq, and under him the Id celebrations were held on lines similar to those of his predecessor.[58] In short, under the Tughlaqs the inflow of women captives never ceased.

Similar was the case with males, especially of tender and young age. Firoz Tughlaq acquired them by all kinds of methods and means, so that he collected 180,000 of them.[59] Shams Siraj Afif, the contemporary historian, writes that under Firoz, "slaves became too numerous" and adds that "the institution took root in every centre of the land". So that even after the Sultanate broke up into a number of kingdoms, slave-hunting continued in every "(Muslim) centre of the land."[60]

Sufferings of the enslaved

This is the version of the slave-capturing victors. The humiliation and suffering of the victims finds no mention in Muslim chronicles. Sustained experience of grief and pain and loss of dignity and self-respect used to turn them into dumb driven animals. The practice and pattern of breaking the spirit of the captives under Aibak, Iltutmish and Balban, indeed throughout the medieval period, was the same as during the days of the Khaljis and the Tughlaqs. Only one case may be cited as an instance. Balban, when he was Ulugh Khan Khan-i-Azam, once brought to Delhi (in about 1260) two hundred fifty "Hindu leading men and men of

---

[56] Ibid., 174.
[57] Afif, 265. also 119-120.
[58] Ibid., 180.
[59] Ibid., 267-73.
[60] Ibid., 270-71.

position" from Mewat and Siwalik, bound and shackled and chained. During the expedition he had proclaimed that a royal soldier would be rewarded with two silver *tankahs* if he captured a person alive and one *tankah* if he brought the head of a dead one. They brought to his presence 300 to 400 living and dead everyday. The reigning Sultan Nasiruddin ordered the death of the leading men. The others accompanying them were shaken to the bones and completely tamed. Depiction of their suffering is found in an Indian work — *Kanhadade Prabandha*. Written in 'old Rajasthani or old Gujarati', it was composed in mid-fifteenth century and records the exploits of King Kanhardeva of Jalor against Alauddin's General Ulugh Khan who had attacked Gujarat in 1299 and taken a number of prisoners. In the Sorath (Saurashtra) region "they made people captive — Brahmanas and children, and women, in fact, people of all (description)... huddled them and tied them by straps of raw hide. The number of prisoners made by them was beyond counting. The prisoners' quarters (*bandikhana*) were entrusted to the care of the Turks." The prisoners suffered greatly and wept aloud. "During the day they bore the heat of the scorching sun, without shade or shelter as they were [in the sandy desert region of Rajasthan], and the shivering cold during the night under the open sky. Children, torn away from their mother's breasts and homes, were crying. Each one of the captives seemed as miserable as the other. Already writhing in agony due to thirst, the pangs of hunger... added to their distress. Some of the captives were sick, some unable to sit up. Some had no shoes to put on and no clothes to wear. ...Some had iron shackles on their feet. Separated from each other, they were huddled together and tied with straps of hide. Children were separated from their parents, the wives from their husbands, thrown apart by this cruel raid. Young and old were seen writhing in agony, as loud wailings arose from that part of the camp where they were all huddled up....

Weeping and wailing, they were hoping that some miracle might save them even now."[61] The miracle did happen and Kanhardeva was successful in rescuing them after a tough fight.

But the description provides the scenario in which the brave and the strong, the elite and the plebeian, were made captives and their spirit broken. That is how Timur was enabled to massacre in one day about 100,000 of captives he had taken prisoner on his march to Delhi. They had been distributed among his officers and kept tied and shackled. That is how Maulana Nasiruddin Umar, a man of learning in Timur's camp, "slew with his own sword fifteen idolatrous Hindus, who were his captives". If the prisoners could 'break their bonds', such a carnage could not have been possible. Prisoners were often brought to Timur's presence with hands bound to their necks.[62] Jahangir (1605-27) also writes that "prisoners were conducted to my presence yoked together."[63] Most of them were kept yoked together even when they were sent out to be sold in foreign lands or markets in India.

The captives, on their part, clung together and did not separate from one another even in their darkest hour. Nor were they permitted an opportunity to do so under Islamic law which the victors always observed with typical Muslim zeal. The *Hidayah* lays down that "if the Mussulmans subdue an infidel territory before any capitation tax be established, the inhabitants, together with their wives and children, are all plunder, and the property of the state, as it is lawful to reduce to slavery all *infidels*, whether they be *Kitabees*, *Majoosees* or *idolters*."[64] The *Hidayah* also lays down that "whoever slays an infidel is entitled to his private property,"[65] which invariably included his women and children. That is

[61] Padmanabh, *Kanhadade Prabandh*, trs. Bhatnagar, 11, 16, 18.
[62] Yazdi, *Zafar Nama*, II, 92-95; *Mulfuzat-i-Timuri*, trs. E.D., III, 436, 451.
[63] *Tarikh-i-Salim Shahi*, 165. This was the fate of the captives throughout the medieval period and therefore there is no need to cite any more instances.
[64] *Hedaya*, Hamilton, II, 213.
[65] Ibid., 181.

how a large number of people were involved, whether it was a matter of taking captives, making converts, or ordering massacres. About women and children of a single family of a slain infidel, or of droves of slaves captured in an attack on a region or territory Fakhre Mudabbir furnishes information on both counts during the campaigns of Muhammad Ghauri and Qutbuddin Aibak. He informs us that during their expeditions *ghulams* of all descriptions (*har jins*) were captured in groups and droves (*jauq jauq*) so that even a poor householder (or soldier) who did not possess a single slave (earlier) became the owner of numerous slaves..."[66]

In short, the captives swam or sank together so that if they were captured they were taken in large numbers. A manifest example of this phenomenon is that during a rebellion-suppressing expedition of Muhammad bin Tughlaq in the Deccan (1327), all the eleven sons of the Raja of Kampil (situated on the River Tungbhadra, Bellary District), were captured together, and made Muslims.[67] Generally, able bodied men and soldiers were massacred, and their helpless women and children were made prisoners in large numbers or groups.[68] Even in peace times people of one or more villages or groups acted in unison. When Firoz Shah Tughlaq proclaimed that those who accepted Islam would be exempted from payment of Jizyah, "great number of Hindus presented themselves.... Thus they came forward day by day from every quarter..."[69] Similarly, from the time of entering Hindustan, up to the time of reaching the environs of Delhi, Amir Timur had "taken more than 100,000 infidels and Hindus prisoners..."[70] Timur massacred them all, but the fact that people could be made slaves in such unbelievably large

[66] *Tarikh-i-Fakhruddin Mubarak Shah*, ed. Denison Ross, 20.

[67] Battutah, 95. For details see Ishwari Prasad, *Qarunah Turks*, 65-66; Mahdi Husain, *Tughlaq Dynasty*, 207-208.

[68] Barani, 56; Afif, 119-120; Lal, *Growth of Muslim Population*, 106, 113-16, 211-217 for copious references from Muslim chronicles.

[69] *Fatuhat-i-Firoz Shahi*, E.D., III, 386.

[70] *Mulfuzat-i-Timuri*, E.D., III, 435-36; Z.N. Yazdi II, 192, *Rauzat-us-safa*, VI, 109.

numbers was due to their keeping together through thick and thin, howsoever desperate the situation. Nobody knew the reality better than Ibn Battuta who travelled in India extensively. During his sojourn he found villages after villages deserted.[71] Nature's ravages or man's atrocities might have made them flee, or more probably they would have been enslaved and converted, or just carried away. But the fact of habitations being completely deserted shows that large groups suffered together and did not forsake one another in times of trial and tribulation. This factor swelled the number of slaves.

Special Slaves of Firoz Shah Tughlaq

By the time of Firoz Shah Tughlaq, the institution of slavery had taken root in every region of Muslim domination. The Sultanate of Delhi was now two hundred years old and well entrenched. The need of slaves for all kinds of errands was great. So that slaves were ever needed in hundreds, and slave-taking did not remain confined to their capture during wars. Firoz Tughlaq resorted to some other methods of acquiring slaves. One of these was akin to the famous Dewshrime widely practised in the Ottoman Empire.

The practice of Dewshrime (Greek for 'collecting boys'), "is the name applied to the forcible pressing of Christian children to recruit the Janissary regiments.... of the Turkish Empire.... mainly in the European parts with a Christian population (Greece, Macedonia, Albania, Serbia, Bosnia and Herzegovina, and Bulgaria)."[72] These Christians, Jews and Gypsies turned Muslims were trained to fight against their own erstwhile brethren. "Instituted by Urkhan in 1330, it formed for centuries the mainstay of the despotic power of the Turkish sultans, and was kept alive by a regular contribution exacted every four years (or so), when the officers of the

[71] Battuta, 10, 20, 155-56.
[72] *Encyclopaedia of Islam*, First ed., 1913-38, II, 952.

Sultan visited the districts over and made a selection from among the children about the age of seven. The Muhammadan legists attempted to apologise for this inhuman tribute by representing these children as the fifth of the spoil which the Quran assigns to the sovereign."[73]

Sultan Firoz commanded his great fief-holders and officers to capture slaves whenever they were at war, and to pick out and send the best for the service of the court. The fifth part of slaves captured in war in India were always despatched to the ruler (or Caliph) ever since the days of Muhammad bin Qasim. Firoz Tughlaq desired slaves to be collected in the Dewshrime fashion. Great numbers of slaves were thus collected, and when they were found to be in excess, the Sultan sent them to Multan, Dipalpur, Hissar Firozah, Samana, Gujarat, and all the other feudal dependencies."[74]

The policy of Delhi Sultanate of leaving the bare minimum to the peasant helped in Firoz's 'Dewshrime'. Under Muslim rule, a substantial portion of the agricultural produce was taken away by the government as taxes and the people were left with the bare minimum for subsistence in order to impoverish them because it was thought that "wealth" was the source of "rebellion and disaffection."[75] This policy was in practice throughout the medieval period, both under the Sultans and the Mughals. Conditions became intolerable by the time of Shahjahan as attested to by Manucci and Manrique. Peasants were compelled to sell their women and children to meet the revenue demand. Manrique writes that "the peasants were carried off.... to various markets and fairs (to be sold), with their poor unhappy wives behind them carrying their small children all crying and lamenting, to meet

[73] Arnold, *The Preaching of Islam*, 150; Quran, 8:42. Bernard Lewis, *Islam*, 226-27 also traces its origin to the fourteenth century.

[74] Afif, 267-73.

[75] Barani, *Tarikh* 2, 16-17, 287, 291, 430, and *Fatawa-i-Jahandari*, 46-48; Afif, E.D., III, 289-90.

the revenue demand." Bernier too affirms that "the unfortunate peasants who were incapable of discharging the demand of their rapacious lords, were bereft of their children who were carried away as slaves."[76] As in the Ottoman Empire, Christians and Jews turned Muslim were trained to fight their erstwhile brethren, so also in India in the medieval period Hindus captured and converted were made to fight their erstwhile brethren in Muslim wars of conquest. Trained or accustomed to fighting their own people, these converts to Islam are posing various kinds of problems in the present-day India and Eastern Europe.

---

[76] Manucci, II. 451; Manrique, II, 272; Bernier, 205. For details see Lal, *Legacy*, 249-55.

CHAPTER VI
ENSLAVEMENT AND PROSELYTIZATION

Wherever the Muslims conquered — in West Asia, Eastern Europe, Africa and India — there they made people slaves and converted them to Islam. In this mission they were most successful in Africa and the least in India.

At the advent of Islam, part of Arabia was under Abyssinian rule. When Arabia was Islamized, the tide turned and the Abyssinians came under the Arabs and they made slaves of Abyssinians and Ethiopians without much opposition. Muslims have been quite satisfied with their achievements in slave-making in Africa. Many Western scholars also have romanticised and even defended black slavery in the Islamic world. Bernard Lewis quotes many European historians to say that "slavery is a divine boon to mankind, by means of which pagan and barbarous people are brought to Islam and civilization... Slavery in the East has an elevating influence over thousands of human beings, and but for it hundreds of thousands of souls must pass their existence in this world as wild savages, little better than animals; it, at least, makes *men* of them, *useful men* too...".[1] T.W. Arnold also writes that "devout minds have even recognised in enslavement God's guidance to the true faith, as the Negroes from the Upper Nile countries... In those Africans there is no resentment that they have been made slaves... even though cruel men-stealers rent them from their parentage... freedom is in many instances the reward of conversion.... The patrons who paid their price have adopted them in their households, the males are circumcised and... God has visited them in their mishap; they can say '*it was His grace*', since they are thereby entered into the saving religion."[2] Lewis, however

---

[1] David Brion Davis, in review article on Bernard Lewis's *Race and Slavery in the Middle East* in *The New York Review of Books*, 11 October 1990.

[2] Arnold, *The Preaching of Islam*, 416-17.

admits "that there are evils in Arab slavery" and that even emancipated blacks are "rarely able to rise above the lowest level."[3] Slavery is a degrading condition, and many people do lose their dignity when they are kept in this condition for a long time. It has been universally acknowledged that the later Western managed slave trade in which Muslim Arabs were often the intermediaries, has had a devastating consequence for African countries. There is no reason to assume that the consequences of the earlier Islamic slavery in Africa had more benign results for the Africans.

The Muslims kept black slaves as well as white ones. While West Asia by and large became Muslim, bondage was a condition from which no one was exempt including Greeks, Turks and Scandinavians, comprising even scholars and poets. As late as the fourteenth and fifteenth centuries, continuing shipments of white slaves, some of them Christians, flowed from the booming slave markets on the northern Black Sea coast into Italy, Spain, Egypt and the Mediterranean islands.... But as "Africa became almost synonymous with slavery the world forgot the eagerness with which the Tatars and other Black Sea peoples had sold millions of Ukrainians, Georgians, Circassians, Armenians, Bulgarians, Slavs and Turks."[4]

Hindu Resistance to enslavement

In India, however, the resistance by Hindus to enslavement by Muslims was persistent and perennial. We have made a detailed study of Hindu resistance against enslavement and concomitant cruelties of the Muslim rulers elsewhere.[5] Here only a few facts may be restated not to leave any lacunae in the narrative.

The peasants scared by the prospect of enslavement, and

---

[3] D.B. Davis, op. cit.

[4] Davis, ibid.; Elst, *Indigenous Indians*, 377.

[5] Lal, *Growth of Muslim Population in Medieval India, Indian Muslims: Who are they* and *The Legacy of Muslims Rule in India*.

finding the treatment by the government unbearable, sometimes left the fields and fled into the jungles. Often vanquished Rajas and aggrieved Zamindars also retired into the forests and organized resistance from there. In this confrontation Zamindars played the role of leaders and the peasants joined under their banner. Medieval Indian society was to some extent an armed society. In cities and towns the elite carried swords like walking sticks. In villages few men were without at least a spear or bow and arrows. Armed peasants provided contingents to Baheliya, Bhadauriya, Bachgoti, Mandahar and Tomar Rajputs in the earlier period, to Jats, Marathas and Sikhs in the later.

In the early period some angry rulers like Balban and Muhammad bin Tughlaq hunted down these escapists in the jungles like wild beasts. Muhammad Tughlaq was very keen on enslaving people and converting them to Islam. The flight of peasants sent him into paroxyms of rage. Many other rulers captured and clamped them in jails, but by and large the peasants did succeed in fighting the enslavement policy of the Muslim regime and did survive in the process.[6] Nature, climate and determination were on their side. Amir Khusrau, Ziyauddin Barani and Vidyapati and many chroniclers of the fifteenth century described how "the Muslims dominated the infidels" through powerful armies.[7] "But the latter fortify themselves in mountains... (and uneven and rugged places) as well in bamboo groves which serve them as ramparts," writes Ibn Battutah.[8] Two hundred years later Babur also noted that "in many parts of the plains thorny jungles grow, behind the good defence of which the people... become stubbornly rebellious..." Timur, when he invaded India, describes the defences provided by forests. The defence of the people, writes he, "consists of woods and forests and trees,

[6] Afif. 98-99.
[7] Barani, 268; Khusrau, *Dewl Rani*, 50; Vidyapati *Kirtilata*, 42-44, 70-72.
[8] Battutah, 124. Also Khusrau, *Nuh Sipehr*, E.D., III, 558.

which interweaving with stem and branch, render it very difficult to penetrate the country... (where) landlords and princes... who inhabit fastnesses in those forests... live there like wild beasts."[9] This was in response to the policy of enslavement and proselytization practised by the sultans and their governors in all the centuries of Muslim rule. Even a weak Sultan like Khizr Khan, and indeed all Saiyyad rulers (1414-51) put the countryside of the Doab-Katehar region to indiscriminate plunder while the Rajas and Zamindars retaliated with scorched earth policy. Like Ikhtiyaruddin Bakhtiyar Khalji before him, Bahlul Lodi also turned a freebooter in his exertions to attain to power and with his gains from plunder built up a strong force. This policy of totally destroying villages and towns continued even when he became the Sultan. According to Abdullah, the Sultan plundered Nimsar Misrik in Hardoi district and "depopulated it of all riff-raff and undesirable elements."[10] In the fifteenth century important Afghan governors like those of Bihar, Ghazipur, Avadh and Lakhnau had thirty to forty thousand retainers each. What havoc they must have created can only be imagined.

To flee and settle down in forests was a very successful survival strategy of the Indian people and this is vouched by many observers including Babur. He says that when he arrived in Agra, "neither grain for ourselves nor corn for our horses was to be had. The villagers, out of hostility, and hatred to us had taken to thieving and highway-robbery; there was no moving on the roads... All the inhabitants (*khalaiq*) had run away in terror."[11] And naturally they had sought refuge elsewhere. For at another place he writes that "In Hindustan... villages and towns are depopulated and set up in a moment... If they (the people) fix their eyes on a place in

[9] *Mulfuzat-i-Timuri*, E.D., III, 395.
[10] Abdullah, *Tarikh-i-Daudi*, 25; Ahmad Yadgar, *Tarikh-i-Salatin-i-Afghana*, 23-27, 68; *Babur-Nama*, trs. A. Beveridge, 487; Nizamuddin Ahmad, *Tabqat-i-Akbari*, I, 342-43; *Tarikh-i-Daudi*,107; *Mankhzan-i-Afghani*, 74(a).
[11] *Babur-Nama*, 524.

which to settle,... they make a tank or dig a well... *Khas*-grass abounds, wood is unlimited, huts are made and straightaway there is a village or a town." There was no dearth of forests and no dearth of water therein.[12] The countryside was studded with little forts, many in inaccessible forests, some surrounded with nothing more than mud walls, but which nevertheless provided centres of the general tradition of opposition and unrest. For, the more the repression the more the resistance. Even emperor Jahangir in the seventeenth century confessed that "the number of the turbulent and the disaffected never seems to diminish; for what with the examples made during the reign of my father, and subsequently of my own, ...there is scarcely a province in the empire in which, in one quarter or the other, some accursed miscreant will not spring up to unfurl the standard of rebellion; so that in Hindustan never has there existed a period of complete repose."[13] In short, in such a society, "the millions of armed men," observes Dirk H. Kolf, "cultivators or otherwise, were its (government's) rivals rather than its subjects."[14] The one attacked from the open, the other often warded off the attack from jungle hide-outs. Those who took to the forest, stayed there, eating wild fruits, tree-roots, and coarse grain if and when available,[15] but surely all the time guarding their freedom.

To be brief, many Zamindars and peasants escaped into the forests because of fear of defeat and enslavement, but in course of time they were reduced to the position of Scheduled Castes, Scheduled Tribes and Backward Classes. For example, many Parihars and Parmars, once upon a time belonging to the proud Rajput castes, are now included in lower castes. So are the 'Rajputs' counted as Backward Classes in South India. Take the case of the Thaaru women in the Tarai region as described by Hugh and Colleen Gantzer.

---

[12] *Ibid.*, 487-88; Lal, *Legacy*, 270.
[13] *Tarikh-i-Salim Shahi*, trs. Price, 225-26.
[14] Kolf, *Naukar, Rajput and Sepoy*, 7.
[15] Badaoni, Ranking, I, 377.

"Once upon a time... a group of beautiful Sisodia Rajput princesses were spirited out of their kingdom by their loving father. Though the old man was prepared to die in the battlefield, with all honour, he could not bear the thought of all his beautiful daughters dying in the fiery self-immolation pit of *Jauhar*. He therefore summoned some of his bravest old retainers, charged them with the task of guarding the princesses, gave them a posse of Bhil warriors, and sent them to the safety of a remote Himalayan kingdom with which he had ties of blood. Sadly, on their arduous journey the old retainers succumbed to malaria and the other debilitating diseases that the Tarai produces. Eventually when the last old Rajput male had died, the princesses realised that they could go no further: neither they nor their posse of Bhils knew the way and delirium had struck the old retainers too swiftly to permit them to speak coherently.... They were young women, full of life. They didn't want to die. So they made an agreement with their Bhils that they would settle down there, in a clearing in the fertile Tarai, marry them but on one condition. From that day on their female descendants would always be superior to their males. They would cook their food. Yes, for that is the tradition, and they would have to cook food for themselves any way. So they would cook their food but they would not serve them. And that is the way it still is. Thaaru women cook their men's food. But then they place the *thali* on the floor and kick it towards their men.... They had a trace of the high cheek bones and almond eyes... But the most striking thing about the women were the extraordinary bright, embroidered skirts and backless *cholis* they wear. Also the columns of metal bangles they carried on their arms and ankles [which points to their Rajput ancestry]... These women were not the docile, subservient (type) we had often encountered in northern Indian villages: they were proud (and) independent..."[16]

[16] Sunday Magazine, *Indian Express*, 19 January 1992.

One has to travel through the country like Hugh and Colleen Gantzer to meet such types, almost everywhere. Today the SC/ST and OBC (Other Backward Classes) all count to fifty percent or thereabout of the population of India. This staggeringly high figure has been reached because of historical forces operating in the medieval times primarily. Muslim rule spread all over the country. Resistance to it by the Hindus also remained widespread. Jungles abounded throughout the vast land from Gujarat to Bengal and Kashmir to Kanyakumari, and flight into them was the safest safeguard. That is how SC/ST people are found in every state in large numbers. During the medieval period, in the years and centuries of oppression, they lived almost like wild beasts in improvised huts in forest villages, segregated and isolated, suffering and struggling. But by settling in the forests, these freedom fighters of medieval India were enabled to preserve their religion and their culture. Their martial arts, preserved in their *Akharas*, are even now practised in different forms in many states.

The forest-village dwellers, whether escapees or resisters, suffered untold privations. Still they had the satisfaction of being able to preserve their freedom. But all victims of aggression were not so lucky. Many groups and individuals could not escape from the clutches of the Muslim invaders and tyranny of their rulers; they used to be captured and enslaved. So that from the days of Muhammad bin Qasim in the eighth century to those of Ahmad Shah Abdali in the eighteenth, enslavement and distribution and sale of captives was systematically carried on by Muslim conquerors and rulers.[17] A Sufi of the stature of Amir Khusrau wrote in the *Ashiqa*: "Had not the law granted exemption from death by the payment of poll-tax, the very name of Hindu, root and branch, would have been extinguished." A few years later he asserted that "the Turks, whenever they please, can seize, buy, or sell any Hindu."[18] If this was

[17] For details see Lal, *Legacy*, 271-287.
[18] Amir Khusrau, *Ashiqa*, E.D., III, 546; *Nuh Sipehr*, 561.

the mind-set of the ruling elite as expositioned by the famous Sufi, the vulnerability of the Hindu to enslavement was truly great.

Attack on Hindu learning

The task of enslavement and proselytization could be made easy if the intellectual elite, the leaders of Hindu society, could be first dealt with and un-Islamic education suppressed. That is why in the early years of Muslim rule priests and monks, Brahman and Buddhist teachers, were generally slaughtered and their colleges and universities sacked.

For example, in the early years of Muslim rule, Ikhtiyauddin Bakhtiyar Khalji sacked the Buddhist University centres in Bihar (1197-1202). There, according to the contemporary chronicler Minhaj Siraj, "the greater number of the inhabitants of the place were Brahmans, and the whole of those Brahmans had their heads shaven (probably Buddhist monks mistaken for Brahmans) and they were all slain. There were a great number of books there; and the Musalmans... summoned a number of Hindus that they might give them information respecting the import of these books; but the whole of the Hindus had been killed." All that the invader could learn was that "the whole of the fortress was a college and in the Hindi tongue, they call a college (*madrasa*) Bihar."[19] During this period there were a large number of centres of learning spread all over India.[20] So thorough was

---

[19] Minhaj, I, 552.

[20] B.P. Mazumdar has listed some of these centres in the eleventh and twelfth centuries as existing in Northern India. In Bihar they were Nalanda, Vikramsila, Odantapuri and Phullahari monasteries near Monghyr. In North and Eastern Bengal they were Jagaddala, Somapura and Devikota in North Bengal, Vikrampuri in Dacca, Pattikeraka in Comilla, and Panditavihara in Chittagong. Minor *Viharas* were in existence at Gaya and Valabhi and in Bundelkhand.

Hieun Tsang, in the seventh century, noted that monasteries existed at the following places; although "we have no means to find out (how many) continued to flourish in the eleventh-twelfth centuries". But many surely did. Hieun Tsang's list included "Nagarkot, Udyana, Jalandhar, Sthanesvara, Srughna Matipura, Brahmapura, Govisana, Ahichchatra, Samkasya, Kanauj, Navadevakula, Ayodhya, Hayamuka, Prayag, Visoka, Kapilvastu, Banaras, Ramagrama, Ghazipur, Tilosika, Gunamati, Silabhadra near Gaya, Kajangala, Pundravardhana, Kamarupa, Samatata, Orissa, Berar, Malwa, Valabhi, Anandapura, Surat, Ujjayini and Chitor" (Mazumdar, *Socio-Economic History of Northern India*, 153-56).

the massacre by the Khalji warrior in Bihar and later on by others in other places that those who could read ancient inscriptions became rare if not extinct. So that when Sultan Firoz Shah Tughlaq (fourteenth century) shifted two Ashokan pillars from Khizarabad and Meerut to Delhi and installed them there, he called some learned Brahmans to read the inscriptions engraved in Ashokan Brahmi/Pali on the pillars; they failed to read the script. Some of them tried to please the Sultan with cock and bull stories by saying that it was recorded in the inscriptions that no one would be able to remove the monoliths until the advent of Firoz.[21]

It would appear that after the major and minor massacres of the type of Ikhtiyaruddin's, there were no pandits or monks left to read the Ashokan Brahmi script for centuries; suppression of Hindu learning by "demolition of schools and temples of the infidels," continued with most Muslim rulers right up to the time of Aurangzeb. Ashokan Edicts were lying scattered throughout the country but these could not be read as the experience of Firoz Tughlaq shows. It was left to the archaeologist and Mint Master James Prinsep to decipher the script in the nineteenth century and reveal to the world the glorious deeds of the great emperor Ashoka. Muslim rulers in general and Firoz Tughalq and Sikandar Lodi in particular considered the Brahmans as "the very keys of the chamber of idolatry in whom the Hindus reposed their trust."[22] Therefore they treated them with great severity. Brahmans, as leaders of Hindu society, were the real obstacles in the Islamization of India. If they could be suppressed, the task of proselytization would become easy.

---

[21] Afif, 302-315; Carr Stephen, *Archaeology of Delhi*, 292-293. Thomas, *Chronicles*, 292-93.

[22] Afif, 379-82. *Zunnardaran kalid-i-hujra-i-kufr und wa kafiran bar eshan muatqid und*; Dorn, *Makhzan*, I, 65. Farishtah, I, 182; Saqi Mustaad Khan, *Maasir-i-Alamgiri*, 51-52.

Slave-taking most successful missionary activity

It needs no reiteration that every slave captured in war or purchased in the market or sent in lieu of revenue or tribute was invariably converted to Islam, so that slave-taking in medieval India was the most flourishing and successful missionary endeavour. As K.M. Ashraf notes, "the slaves added to the growing Muslim population of India."[23] Every sultan, as champion of Islam, considered it a political necessity to plant or raise Muslim population all over India for the Islamization of the country and countering native resistance.[24] This slave-taking in war for spreading Islam was not new or special to India; the system prevailed wherever Muslim rule obtained. Throughout the medieval period Islam's conquests and aggressive wars were common and captured slaves helped in raising Muslim numbers. As at one time or the other, most Muslims invaders and conquerors were themselves slaves, and these slave-catching kings and nobles experienced happiness at the possession of a dependent species of property; this slave-property contributed to alleviate the hardships of the noble's own servitude. In their numerous families, particularly in their county estates, they encouraged the marriage of their slaves and let the Muslim numbers grow. On the other hand, once the captives were reconciled to Islam and obedience (about which, in any case, there was hardly any choice), their careers were opened to any new opportunities. In the flowery language of Edward Gibbon, "by the repetition of a sentence and the loss of a foreskin, the subject or the slave, the captive or the criminal, arose in a moment the free or equal companion of the victorious Moslems."[25] Although this freedom and equality did not come at once, their servile origins were allowed to be obliterated in the third or fourth generation. This was the reward of conversion. There

[23] Ashraf, 151. Also Arnold, *Preaching of Islam*, 365.
[24] Qureshi, *Administration*, 69, fn 1; Ishwari Prasad, *Qaraunah Turks*, 173.
[25] Gibbon, II, 782, also 720.

also developed a feeling of freedom even in slavery and a vanity in belonging to the 'ruling class'. After a few generations the Indian Muslim forgot the circumstances of his ancestors' enslavement and conversion; he began to take pride in his new faith because it opened up for him new avenues of rise and gave him a share in the rulers' or masters' wealth and loot. And so enslavement and proselytization went on hand in hand.[26]

Of the various channels of slave-catching, mounting a campaign or fighting a war was the most rewarding. Muslim rulers had come to realise that in the occasional or minor campaigns the harvest of slaves collected was as good, if not better, as in major expeditions. There was no harm if the operations were carried on in a low key. Thereby, because of the sustained pressure, "the infidel captives might abandon their false religion and accept Islam."[27] This was written by Muhammad Bihmad Khani, himself originally a slave (as the name Khani indicates), in the context of the wars that broke out in Hindustan after the death of Sultan Firoz Tughlaq. The exertions of the Saiyyad rulers in establishing their authority (1414-1451) also resulted in campaigns in Katehar, Khor Kampil, Saket, Badaon, Rapri, Jalesar, Chandwar, Etawah etc.[28] In all these places, especially in the Katehar-Doab region, the Muslim army contented itself "with the ignoble but customary satisfaction of plundering the people" and putting the country to indiscriminate devastation and enslavement.[29] Meanwhile foreigners like Shaikh Ali, the Mongol Governor of Kabul, also marched into the Punjab, "slew a large number of people and took prisoner many others."[30] During these continual campaigns Muslim captives were sometimes re-

[26] Barani, *Fatawa*, 98. Titus, *Islam in India and Pakistan*, 177.

[27] Muhammad Bihamad Khani, *Tarikh-i-Muhammadi*, English tr. by Muhammad Zaki, Aligarh Muslim University, 1972, 57-58. Also Afif, 180; Yahiya, 184-88; Badaoni, Ranking, I, 377; T.A., I, 266.

[28] For identification of places see Lal, *Twilight*, 74-75.

[29] Haig, C.H.I., III, 207; Farishtah, I, 162.

[30] Yahiya, 218; Farishtah, I, 167; Bihamad Khani, 95.

leased, but not the infidels who were enslaved and converted.[31]

The Lodis who gradually reestablished the authority of the Sultanate (1451-1526) continued with the traditional business of slave-taking. Bahlul, the founder of the dynasty, "turned a free-booter and with his gains from plunder built up a strong force."[32] If as a ruler Bahlul led his army into Nimsar (in Hardoi district), and plundered the place and depopulated it by killing and enslaving its people,[33] his successor Sikandar did the same in the Rewa and Gwalior regions.[34]

During the fifteenth century exertions for proselytization through enslavement were going on in the Muslim ruled regions which had broken away from the Delhi Sultanate and established independent kingdoms like Gujarat, Malwa, Jaunpur, Khandesh, Bengal and the Deccan. Detailed accounts of these are found in my two books,[35] and one who wants to delve deep into the subject has to go through them. For obvious reasons, major portions of the books cannot be reproduced here though they are very relevant in the present context. However, a page or two from one of them may be repeated here for two reasons: (1) not to leave a gaping vacuum in the present narrative and (2) to give an idea of slave-making in South India because we have, by and large, concentrated only on the North in the preceding pages. "The first Bhamani King, Alauddin Bahman Shah (1347-1358) despatched an expedition against the northern Canatic Hindu chieftains, and his booty included '1000 singing and dancing girls, *Murlis*, from Hindu temples'.[36] In 1406 Sultan Tajuddin Firoz (1397-1422) fought a war with

[31] For detailed references Lal, *Twilight*, 103-104.
[32] Ibid., 118.
[33] Abdullah, *Tarikh-i-Daudi* 25; Yadgar, *Tarikh-i-Salatin-i-Afghana*, 23-27.
[34] Lal, *Twilight*, 170-72, 176-78.
[35] *Growth of Muslim Polpulation in Medieval India*, New Delhi, 1973 and *Indian Muslims: Who are They*, New Delhi, 1990.
[36] C.H.I., III, 391.

Vijayanagar and captured 60,000 youths and children from its territories. When peace was made Bukka gave, besides other things, 2,000 boys and girls skilled in dancing and music[37]... His successor Ahmad Vali (1422-36) marched through Vijayanagar kingdom, 'slaughtering men and enslaving women and children.'[38] The captives were made Musalmans.[39] Sultan Alauddin (1436-58) collected a thousand women in his harem. When it is noted that intermittent warfare between the Bahmani and Vijayanagar kingdoms continued for more than a century and half, the story of enslavement and conversions need not be carried on. Even ordinary soldiers used to get many slaves and, at the end of the Battle of Talikot (1565), 'large number of captives consigned to slavery, enriched the whole of the Muslim armies, for the troops were permitted to retain the whole of the plunder.'[40] ..."[41]

The Mughal emperor Akbar, disapproved of the custom of enslaving women and children in times of war.[42] He also prohibited enslavement and sale of women and children of the peasants who had defaulted in the payment of revenue. He knew, as Abul Fazl says, that many evil hearted and vicious men used to proceed to villages and *mahals* and sack them.[43] According to W.H. Moreland, "It became a fashion to raid a village or group of villages without any obvious justification, and carry off the inhabitants as slaves."[44] It is appropriate to suffix this statement with the cryptic remark of Koenraad Elst that "A left-over from this period is the North-Indian custom of celebrating weddings at midnight: this was

---

[37] Sewell, *A Forgotten Empire* (Vijayanagar), 57-58.
[38] C.H.I., III, 397.
[39] *ibid*, 398.
[40] C.H.I., 449. Also Sewell, 198.
[41] *Indian Muslims: Who are they*, 53-54.
[42] *Akbar Nama*, II, 246. Du Jarric, *Akbar and the Jesuits*, 152-59. Also 28, 30, 70, 92.
[43] *Akbar Nama*, II, 451.
[44] Moreland, *India at the Death of Akbar*, 92; Sarkar, *Aurangzeb*, III, 331-32; *Maasir-ul-Umara*, III, 442.

a safety measure against the Islamic sport of bride catching."[45] Jahangir had ordered that "a government collector or *jagirdar* should not without permission intermarry with the people of the *pargana* in which he might be"[46], for abductions and forced marriages were common enough. But there was never an abjuration of the policy of enslavement as mainly it was not the Mughal emperors but the Mughal nobility who must have taken the lion's share of enslavement, deportation and sale by the state. It was not only Jahangir, a comparatively kind hearted emperor, who used to capture poor people during his hunting expeditions and send them to Kabul in exchange for dogs and horses; all Muslim rulers and governors collected slaves and exploited them in the manner they pleased. Under Shahjahan, as seen earlier, peasants were compelled to sell their women and children to meet the revenue demand.

In any case, warfare went on as usual even under Akbar and Jahangir and Mughal Generals went on with their usual ways in spite of the failings of Emperors whose writ was not very effective. Abdulla Khan Uzbeg's force of 12,000 horse and 20,000 foot destroyed, in the Kalpi-Kanauj area alone, all towns, took all their goods, their wives and children as slaves and beheaded and 'immortered' (fixed heads with mortar in walls and pillars) the chiefest of their men.[47] No wonder he once declared that "I made prisoners of five lacs of men and women and sold them. They all became Muhammadans. From their progeny there will be crores by the day of judgement."[48]

[45] Elst, *Negationism in India*, 28.
[46] *Tuzuk*, I, 9.
[47] For action in this region in the reign of Akbar see Abul Fazl, *Akbar Nama*, II, 195-96.
[48] Shah Nawaz Khan, *Maasir-ul-Umara*, I, 105.

Chapter VII
STRUGGLE FOR POWER AMONG SLAVE NOBLES

Abdulla Khan's words were prophetic. The population of Indian Muslims grew rapidly through enslavement. This rapid growth gave rise to new problems. One was a tussle for power between foreign slave-Amirs and Indian slaves some of whom also attained to the position of nobles. As among the Turkish Amirs themselves, a bitter struggle for clout also raged between foreign Turks and Indian Muslims. The Hindus resisted enslavement and conversion. But once made Musalmans, they asserted their claim to equality with foreign Muslims. Distinction between the two has always been there and it is reflected in the writings of medieval chroniclers like Minhaj and Barani and the observations of Europeans like Bernier and Robert Orme.[1] The Turks asserted that they belonged to the blue blood and were founders of Muslim rule in India. The India Muslims knew that the Turks were good fighters, but for administrative work indigenous Muslims were better suited. To keep them under control the sultans resorted to the time honoured policy of playing the one against the other. On one occasion Sultan Iltutmish dismissed thirty-three persons from service on account of their low birth, or their Indian ancestry.[2] On the other hand Sultan Nasiruddin raised Indian-born Imad-ud-din Rayhan to the position of Vakil-i-Dar (Custodian of the keys of Palace Gates) after dismissing the all powerful foreign Turk Ghiyasuddin Balban. Minhaj Siraj's description of the situation shows how high the feelings ran between the foreign Turkish and Indian 'Julaha' nobles. "The Maliks and servants

---

[1] Minhaj, 827-28; Barani, *Tarikh*, 38-39, *Fatawa-i-Jahandari*, 97, 98, also 47; Bernier, 209. Orme, 'Of the Moors of Indostan' in *A General Idea of the Government of Indostan.*

[2] Barani, 38-39.

of the Sultan's Court were all Turks of pure lineage" (*Turkan-i-pak*) writes he, and Taziks of noble birth (*Tazikan-i-guzida was*). "Imad-ud-Din Rayhan (who) was castrated and mutilated, and of the tribe of Hind, was ruling over the heads of lords of high descent, and the whole of them were loathing that state, and were unable to suffer any longer that degradation."[3] The Turkish nobles rose in arms and the Sultan was persuaded to order the dismissal of Rayhan and recall of Ulugh Khan-i-Azam Balban (February, 1254). The language of Ziyauddin Barani is not less vituperative. He was a staunch believer in the racial superiority of the Turks and the baseness of Indian Muslims. He recommended that "Teachers of every kind are to be sternly ordered not to thrust precious stones down the throats of dogs... that is, to the mean, the ignoble, the worthless... To the low-born they are to teach nothing more than the rules about prayer, fasting, religious charity and the Hajj pilgrimage along with some chapters of the Quran and some doctrines of the faith... They (Indian Muslims) are not to be taught reading and writing for plenty of disorders arise owing to the skill of the low-born in knowledge... the low-born are capable only of vices... so they are called low-born, worthless, plebeian, shameless and of dirty birth."

In this strife, the foreign slave-nobles had an edge over their Indian counterparts. They were closer to the Sultan and had influence with him. For most of them Indian-born Muslims were originally all slaves, "scum captives taken in thousands by chance of war or purchased at a vile price". But like Turks they intrigued and maneuvred to rise to power. Malik Kafur and Nasiruddin Khusrau even staked their claims to the throne. In any case it took a few generations' time for them to reach the stature of foreign nobles.[4] Muslim society tended

[3] Minhaj, 829.

[4] Bernier, 209; Titus, *Islam in India and Pakistan,* 117.

Here are a few examples. Bahadur Nahar was a converted Rajput from Mewat. So also were Rai Daud of Jalandhar and Rai Kamaluddin Main of Ludhiana. Similarly three brothers, Sarang Khan, Mallu Khan and Khandu converted to Islam and rose to be nobles. Mallu Khan later became Mallu Iqbal Khan and Khandu was entitled

to be divided into ruling and other classes.

Strife among nobles

The attitude of 'what art thou that I am not' prevailed not only among some individual nobles but among all nobles, foreigner and Indian, and at all times. Besides the Turks, who were in majority but belonged to many clans, there were Abyssinians, Afghans (of many clans and groups), Tajiks, Persians and Mongols.[5] All these sections had vested interests as individuals and groups. All sections had among them seasoned veterans, hardened by life's tough experience. As their names indicate, Malik Qabul Ulugh Khani, the Superintendent of the Grain Market (*Shahna-i-Mandi*) under Alauddin Khalji, Muhammad Bihamad Khami, the historian, Jahangir Quli Khan, the nobleman of Jahangir, and Murshid Quli Khan, the Subedar of Bengal were all slave-nobles. No wonder, intrigue and manoeuvring went on throughout, and tooth and claw, sword and poison, were freely used to destroy rivals.[6]

In the beginning the number of the Turkish slaves was the largest. Besides the Turks, slaves from many other tribes, ethnic groups and countries also went on arriving in good numbers. Whether they were captured, purchased or lured into the country because of the bright prospects here, whether they were adventurers or were invited because they possessed talent as administrators, musicians or poets, in

---

Adil Khan. Soon enough Mallu was dropped and he became just Iqbal Khan, a pure Muslim, like of foreign lineage. Iqbal Khan's sons were Saifuddin and Khudadad. By now the family had become *pucca* Muslim having dropped all Hindu appellations. Therefore it was not harmed by Sultan Mahmud when settling the affairs of Delhi after the upheaval of Timur. Mahmud sent the family of Iqbal Khan to Kol (Aligarh) just as Sher Shah returned the consort of Humayun to the Mughal because in both cases families of Muslims were involved. Such examples of claiming pure Muslim. (or foreign) lineage after a few generations of conversion abound in medieval Indian history.

Yahiya, *Tarikh-i-Mubarak Shahi*, 175; Nizamuddin, *Tabqat-i-Akbari*, I, 260. Also Yazdi, *Zafar Namaii*, II, 116; Farishtah, I, 158; Lal, *Twilight*, 21-22 and notes 52-53.

[5] Many more are mentioned by Fakhre Mudabbir in his *Tarikh-i-Fakhruddin of Mubarak shah*.

[6] Barani 47-48.

whatever capacity or through whatever channel they arrived, officially and technically their position was that of slaves. Bondage was a condition from which no one was exempt: including scholars and poets — Turks, Arabs, Gauls, Jews, Persians and Ethiopians. There have been many occasions to write about the Turkish slaves, their arrogance, their jealousies, their intrigues and their services. Some other prominent groups in medieval India were Afghans, Persians, and the Black slaves of Africa — Abyssinians or Ethiopians. A word only may be said here about each of these collectanea of 'imported' slaves, because we shall be referring to them in various contexts again and again.

From the eleventh century onwards, the Afghans started coming into India as soldiers of fortune in the armies of various invaders beginning with Mahmud of Ghazni. Muhammad Ghauri in his last expedition brought ten thousand Afghan horsemen with him.[7] In the time of Sultan Iltutmish, the Khwarizmi Prince Jalaluddin, fleeing before Chingiz Khan, brought many Afghan soldiers with him. Some of these took service under Iltutmish.[8] Balban appointed thousands of Afghans for garrisoning difficult outposts.[9] Saiyyad Khizr Khan, because of his unpopularity as Timur's nominee and lack of support in Hindustan, gave important assignments to men of Lodi, Sherwani, Niyazi, Jalwani and many other tribes of Afghans from Roh.[10] The Turkish sultans considered the Afghans to be good soldiers, but men devoid of culture. Their queer ideas of unbridled freedom, and their traditional attachment to their tribal leaders were not conducive to discipline and harmony. Sultan Bahlul Lodi handled his turbulent Afghan nobles with studied tact; whenever he wrote a *farman* to his Amirs, he always addressed them as "Masnad-i-Ali" (Your Exalted Lordship).[11] When Sikandar

[7] Niamatullah, *Makhzani-i-Afghana*, trs. N.B. Roy, 11.
[8] Olaf Caroe, *The Pathans*, 135.
[9] Barani, 57-58.
[10] Niamatullah's *History of the Afghans*, 14.
[11] Abdullah *Tarikh-i-Daudi*, 12-14; Rizqullah Mushtaqi, *Waqiat-i-Mushtaqi*, 4 (a).

Lodi made an attempt to show them their place, he had to face hard opposition. His son and successor Ibrahim lost his throne because of their intrigues, recalcitrance and disloyalty. All the same till the coming of the Mughals, the Afghan rulers surrounded themselves with their Afghan co-tribals and favoured them with important appointments.

The Persians and Central Asians (Iranians and Turanians) were generally appointed on higher posts in administration. Minhaj Siraj says that people from Persia and adjoining countries came to India in various capacities. Fakhr-ul-Mulk Isami, who had been Vazir at Baghdad for thirty years but then had suffered some disappointment, arrived in Hindustan and was appointed Wazir by Iltutmish. A great scholar of Iltutmish's reign was Amir Ruhani; he had come from Bukhara to Delhi during the upheaval of Chingiz Khan. Qazi Hamiduddin Nagori had also come from abroad. Muhammad Aufi, the author of the famous *Jami-ul-Hikayat* had also come to Delhi during Iltutmish's reign.[12] As noted earlier, because of the Mongol upheaval, there arrived in the court of Iltutmish and Balban not less than forty princes with their followers from Iraq, Khurasan, Mawaraun Nahr and adjoining countries.[13] These followers comprised masters of pen and of sword, scholars and Mashaikh, historians and musicians. In the royal procession of Sultan Balban 500 Sistani, Ghauri, Samarqandi and Arab soldiers with drawn swords used to march by his side. Similar was the case with other sultans of Delhi. All this indicates that a large number of foreigners had come to India during the Sultanate period. During the rule of the Mughals specially, they rose to heights of glory. Bairam Khan who helped in the reestablishment of the Mughal dynasty in India was a Persian. In the court of Jahangir and Shahjahan Persian nobles wielded great influence because of the support of queens like Nur Jahan and Mumtaz Mahal. The eminent po-

[12] Farishtah, I, 66-67.
[13] Minhaj, 598-99; Farishtah, I, 73.

sition of Iranis and Turanis ever remained well entrenched.

The fate and fortune of the black Africans was not that good. For a general term they may be called Habshis or Abyssinians. A few, but only a few, rose to high positions like Malik Yaqut the Personal Attendant of Sultan Raziyah, but the contemptuous attitude of Turks towards him shows the position of Africans in the early years of Muslim rule in India. Later on some rose to become the Sharqi kings of Jaunpur and some kings in Bengal and the Deccan. But the majority of them were treated as lesser Muslims. Barbak Shah of Bengal (1460-74) maintained a large number of Abyssinians as protectors of his throne. He recruited 8,000 Habshis and gave them high positions in his government.[14] The sultans of Gujarat and the Deccan also invited groups of Abyssinians and gave them "positions of respect and trust."[15] Male and female Abyssianian slaves were brought as presents for the Mughals.[16] Habshi women were employed as harem guards in Malwa and other Muslim kingdoms. But the largest concentration of Habshis was in the Deccan where they formed even powerful political groups.[17] The Quran and Sharia show no awareness of racial or colour prejudice. In the early seventh century, neither slavery nor bitter ethnic and national rivalries seemed to generate what the modern world would define as racism. By the late seventh century, however, blackness of skin was becoming a symbol that evoked distaste and contempt. Bernard Lewis points to the overwhelming evidence that racial slavery, as the modern world has come to know it, originated in medieval Islamic societies. Light-skinned Arabs, Berbers and Persians invented the long-distance slave trade that transported millions of sub-Saharan captives either by camel caravans across the deserts or by slave ships from East Africa to the Persian Gulf. Arabs led the

[14] Barbosa, II, 147.
[15] Farishtah, II, 298; Lach, *Asia in the making of Europe*, I, 401-05.
[16] *Tuzuk*, I, 167.
[17] For details Lal, *Indian Muslims*, 50-61.

way in classifying the diverse peoples who lived from the Horn of Africa on the east to the state of Ghana in the west as "blacks" — a single lowly group especially submissive to slavery because, as the famous fourteenth century Arab historian Ibn Khaldun put it, they "have little [that is essentially] human and have attributes that are quite similar to those of dumb animals"! Some Muslim writers ranked the Nubians and especially the Ethiopians somewhat higher than the despised Zanj, a vague term applied to the Bantu-speaking labourers imported from East Africa. In short, medieval Muslims came to associate the most degrading forms of labour with black slaves. In fact, the Arabic word for slave, 'abd', came to mean only a black slave.[18]

Black Slaves in India

These slaves were brought to India in very large numbers. Their position was generally that of inferior species. Sometimes they were not trusted. A case in point is seen during Akbar's conquest of Gujarat. After the fall of Ahmedabad all officers of Sultan Mahmud Gujarati came to make submission to Akbar. These included Aitmad Khan "the slave and Prime Minister of Sultan Mahmud Gujarati"[19] (who was originally a Hindu slave),[20] Mir Abu Turab, Saiyyad Ahmad Bukhari, Malik Ashraf, Ulugh Khan Habshi, Jajhar Khan Habshi, and other amirs and chiefs of Gujarat "too numerous to mention". Abul Fazl writes that Emperor Akbar desired to include the Habshis (Abyssinians) among the royal slaves on the same terms as they had been slaves of Sultan Mahmud. But Akbar's officers were suspicious of them. Aitmad Khan too became surety for all Gujarati slaves except the Abyssinians.[21] Therefore, for reasons of security, Akbar

---

[18] Bernard Lewis, *Race and Slavery in the Middle East*, OUP, 1990. Also Koenraad Elst, *Indigenous Indians*, 378-81.

[19] Badaoni, II, 141.

[20] *Ain.*, II, 385.

[21] Nizamuddin, *Tabqat-i-Akbari*, trs. E.D.,V, 342-43.

ordered the headmen of the Habshis to be made over to the great officers of the court.[22]

D.B. Davis in his *Slavery and Human Progress* attempts to estimate the number of blacks that would have been sold as slaves and imported into India. According to him "the importation of black slaves into Islamic lands from Spain to India constituted a continuous large-scale migration that in total numbers may well have surpassed, over a period of twelve centuries, the African diaspora to the New World".[23] The absence of a large population of black survivors can be explained by their high mortality rate; by assimilation with other peoples; and by the fact that many male slaves had been castrated. Even so in central part of India and on the western coast, there are communities of blacks who are descendants of African slaves. On some Western Coast Islands also there live descendants of black slaves. The Jinjeera Island, so called because of mispronunciation by Marathas of Jazeera meaning island, or Zanzeera meaning land of Zanj or Blacks, is their main abode. It is also called Habsan or the land of Africans or Habshis. In the seventeenth century these islanders, called Sidis of Jinjeera, served as admirals of the Mughals and were at constant war with the Marathas.

In short but broadly speaking, the foreign nobles consisted of Turks, Arabs, Mughals, and Persians. The others were Hindustanis (Indian-born), Deccanis, Blacks and Muwallads (offsprings of African fathers and Indian mothers). In some measure foreign Muslim scorn for blacks is confirmed by a similar attitude towards the brown Indians. Black slaves did not get any education, so blacks came to be regarded as stupid. Amir Khusrau talks of Hindus in a similar vein; Barani recommends that Indians should not be given more than elementary education. Still compartmentalization was not that complete. Instances of gratitude to a benefactor

[22] Abul Fazl, *Akbar Nama*, III, 10-11.

[23] David Brion Davis, *Slavery and Human Progress*, Oxford, 1984, 45-56.

or compromise with self-interest were not unknown, but were not frequent. Party spirit too was stronger than patriotism. If the foreign Turks and Persians felt superior and monopolised higher positions, a Black could found a ruling kingdom at Jaunpur and a Hindu convert a ruling dynasty in Gujarat. But all nobles, foreign or Indian, exerted in the cause of Islam, undertook campaigns and captured captives. These captives were employed on all kinds of government and private jobs.

CHAPTER VIII
EMPLOYMENT OF SLAVES

Muslim regime in medieval times drafted slaves in every sphere of activity. Slaves were needed in thousands for any large enterprise which, in modern technological age, would be accomplished by a few machines or even gadgets. There was no dearth of slaves either. Muslim victories in India had provided kings and nobles with innumerable slaves. From government affairs to domestic errands slaves were employed on every work.

On Building Construction

The first thing the Muslim Sultanate of Delhi started on was construction of impressive buildings. It aimed at overawing the people of the land with the greatness and might of the new Islamic regime. This could be achieved by constructing huge Muslim edifices with the wealth obtained from war and materials from Hindu buildings after destroying them. Architecture was considered as the visual symbol of Muslim political power with which the Turks wished to impress and overawe the conquered people. It denoted victory with authority. Wherever the Muslim conquerors marched or ruled in Central Asia or India, they constructed edifices both gigantic and delicate. The important fact to note in this connection is that slaves were drafted to construct the buildings.[1]

And so thousands of slaves were drafted to construct the edifies (many even now extant as monuments), so as to complete the work in the shortest possible time. Surely, the task could be accomplished only by pressing into service thousands and thousand of slaves captured in early victories who were made to do the job. The congregational mosque at Delhi named, purposefully, as the Masjid Quwwatul Islam

[1] *Cambridge History of Islam*, I, 471.

(Might of Islam), was commenced by Aibak in 592/1195 within two years of its conquest.[2] It was built with materials and gold obtained by destroying 27 Hindu and Jain temples in Delhi and its neighbourhood. A Persian inscription in the mosque testifies to this.[3] The mosque at Ajmer erected by Qutbuddin Aibak soon after its occupation and known as the *Arhai din ka Jhonpra,* was also built from materials obtained from demolished temples. The Qutb Minar, planned and commenced by Aibak sometime in or before 1199 and completed by Iltutmish,[4] was also constructed with similar materials, "the sculptured figures on the stones being either defaced or concealed by turning them upside down." "*In this improvisation,*" rightly observes Habibullah, *"was symbolised the whole Mamluk history"* (emphasis added).[5]

How many slaves were needed to accomplish the task on these three and the other buildings of Qutbuddin Aibak and Iltutmish such as mosques, *madrasas*, mausoleums, *qasrs* and tanks (e.g. Hauz-i-shamsi) in and outside Delhi? It is difficult to determine but easy to conjecture their numbers, for these two sultans had embarked on constructional activity on a very large scale. It is known that Alauddin Khalji, another great builder, had 70,000 slaves working on his buildings, as attested to by the contemporary chronicler Ziyauddin Barani.[6] Alauddin built "masjids, minars, citadels and tanks". But his Qutb Minar alone was an edifice more than equal to all his undertakings. Thus the men working on the buildings of the first two sultans were probably not less than those of Alauddin Khalji; they may have been probably more. These slaves were to dismantle standing temples, very carefully, stone by stone, carry the carved columns, shafts and pillars to the new sites of construction, and raise the new structures.

---

[2] Minhaj, 520 n.
[3] It is reproduced in Thomas, *Chronicles of the Pathan Kings of Delhi*, 22-23.
[4] Sir John Marshall in C.H.I., III, 578 n1.
[5] A.B.M. Habibullah, *The Forundation of Muslim Rule in India*, 375.
[6] Barani, 341.

Although Hasan Nizami says that temples were demolished with the help of elephants and one elephant could haul stones for which 500 men were needed,[7] yet it has to be recognised that not many mechanical devices were available. Most of the work was done by human hands and muscles. The task was delicate and the slaves were freely flogged for any damage to stone slabs thus carried. The *korrah* (whip) of Bernier was not an invention of Shahjahan's time; it had been there all along during Muslim conquest and rule.

Hindu masons and architects were expert builders, they created wonderful specimens of architecture. About the temples of India, Alberuni says that his own people "are unable to describe them, much less to construct anything like them". Indian builders would never have liked to destroy their own splendid creations and dismantle their own sacred temples, to build in their instead mosques and minars for foreign invaders and rulers. But they had no choice. All Turkish slaves from abroad had become masters in India as kings, nobles, army officers and even soldiers, lording over the native workers who had been reduced to the position of slaves. Furthermore, Hindu masons and labourers turned slaves under the new dispensation had to do the work in record time. Barani in his enthusiasm hyperbolically says that during Alauddin's reign a palace could be built in 2-3 days and a citadel in two weeks.[8]

It was considered a matter of pride for a newly crowned king to build a city of his own to give name and fame to himself and his dynasty. The old city of Iltutmish was abandoned by Balban who built the Qasr-i-Lal or the Red Palace, and Kaiqubad built the city of Kilughari. "It is their custom," writes Ibn Battuta, "that the king's palace is deserted on his death... and his successor builds a new palace for himself."[9]

---

[7] *Tajul-Maasir*, E.D., II, 222.
[8] Barani, 341.
[9] Ibn Battuta, 77.

The slaves had often to do double the work, destroy Hindu buildings and construct new ones from the materials of earlier ones. In those times people lived in congested localities for reasons of security. A city used to get dirty and uninhabitable after a few years because of lack of means of disposing off garbage and filth. Ibn Battuta and Babur[10] affirm that all was destroyed because of moisture. It is because of this reason also that it was thought better to found and shift to a new town where everything was clean and tidy. Hindu slaves toiled as scavengers and cleaners in old cities. They toiled with blood and sweat to create new ones.

Muhammad Tughlaq and Firoz Tughlaq were as keen as Aibak, Iltutmish and Alauddin about founding new cities, raising new buildings and repairing old edifices of earlier Muslim rulers. Shams Siraj Afif counts Firoz's builders among the 180,000 (or about 2 lakh) slaves of Firoz Tughlaq,[11] but the break up for various duties would point to there being separate contingent of masons and builders with 12,000 slaves as stone-cutters alone. Even the shifting of the two Ashokan pillars to Delhi required the services of a few thousand men (*chandin hazar admi*). No wonder the invader Timur (1399 C.E.) found in India exquisite Muslim buildings, and enslaved thousands of craftsmen and builders many of whom he took with him to Samarqand to construct edifices similar to the Jama Masjid built by Firoz Shah and the Qutb Minar built by Aibak.[12] But after his departure from India new slaves soon replaced those taken away by Timur, and every sultan and noble embarked on building enterprises as usual.

Besides the Sultanate, new independent Muslim states sprang up all over the country throughout the fifteenth century. In all of them feverish architectural activity was carried

---

[10] *Babur Nama*, II, 519-20.

[11] Afif, 271. For short list of his buildings, 329-33.

[12] Percy Brown, *Indian Architecture (Islamic Period)*, 26; Harold Lamb, *Tamerlane the Earth Shaker*, London, 1929, 272. Mulla Sharaf testifies that stone-cutters from Hindustan worked on Timur Beg's Stone Mosque, *Babur Nama*, II, 520. For detailed references see K.S. Lal, *Twilight*, 40.

on with the help of local slaves. At the centre, Sultan Sikandar Lodi is credited with constructing mosques in almost all important cities including Lahore, Karnal, Hansi, Makanpur (District Kanpur) besides many in Delhi and Agra.[13] In addition to the tombs in Lodi Gardens in Delhi, there are also so many other nameless tombs belonging to the Lodi period. Sikandar Lodi, like Firoz Tughlaq before him, is credited with constructing a canal in 1492-93[14] and a Baoli in Rajasthan. In "Mathura and other place" like Allahabad and Banaras he turned temples into mosques, and established Muslim Sarais, colleges and bazars in Hindu places of worship.[15] Like Firoz Tughlaq, Sikandar was also a great repairer and conserver of old Muslim monuments. An inscribed frieze at the entrance doorway of the Qutb Minar credits him with repairing this edifice in 1503 (909 H).[16]

We have spoken about only some of the architectural works of just five sultans of Delhi — Aibak, Iltutmish, Alauddin Khalji, Firoz Tughlaq and Sikandar Lodi — and noted that thousands and thousands of slaves were required for their construction. It is unnecessary to repeat that all Muslim rulers were great builders and the number of slaves engaged on building cities, mosques, Sarais, tombs of every sultan and noble and Sufi Shaikh in Delhi and other cities of the Sultanate ran into thousands. Same was the case with the buildings of the provincial and independent kingdoms into which the Sultanate of Delhi broke up.

"There was a strain of artistic feeling which ran through the successive generations of the ruling Moghul house in India," observed E. Maclagan in 1932. This artistic feeling found its greatest manifestation in their architecture. And

---

[13] *Arch. Sur. Report*, XVII, 105.

[14] *Proceedings of the Asiatic Society of Bengal*, 1872, 48.

[15] Nizamuddin, *Tabqat-i-Akbari*, I, 335-35; Farishtah, I, 186; *Makhzan-i-Afghani*, fol. 67 a; trs. Dorn, 66.

[16] *Epigraphia Indica*, 1919-20, 4; Carr Stephen, *Archaeology and Monumental Remains of Delhi* (Calcutta, 1876), pp. 59-60; J. A. Page, *A Guide to the Qutab Delhi*, 21.

those who built had unbounded command of both money and slaves. Babur writes that "680 men worked daily on my buildings in Agra... only; while 1491 stone-cutters worked daily on my buildings in Agra, Sikri, Biana, Dulpur (Dholpur), Gwalior and Kuil (Aligarh). In the same way there are numberless artisans and workmen of every sort in Hindustan."[17] Some workers were wage-earners, for says he at another place, "Gifts were made to the stone-cutters, and labourers and the whole body of workmen in the way customary for master-workmen and wage-earners of Agra."[18] But as discussed elsewhere slaves were preferred to servants and wage-earners, and the *Korrah* was the surest leveller of artisan, handicraftsman, servant and slave. From the days of Babur to those of Shahjahan during whose "august reign, when... lovely things reached the zenith of perfection," money in millions and slaves in thousands were employed on erecting the hundreds of huge Mughal buildings still extant.[19]

The example of kings was universally imitated by their principal nobles. The opulent grandees in the provinces esteemed it an honour and obligation to adorn towns and cities of the regions under their control with magnificent buildings. The law of escheat encouraged them to spend lavishly. Pelsaert perhaps has the last word on it. "I have often ventured to ask great lords," says he, "what is their true object in being so eager to amass their treasures, when what they have gathered is of no use to them or to their family (because of escheat)... I have urged they would share it with the poor, who in this country are hundreds of thousands, or indeed innumerable [including of course the slaves]... Their answers have been based on the emptiest worldly vanity..." Buildings they constructed with great zest — gardens, tombs, and palaces — "they build them with so many hundreds of thou-

[17] *Babur Nama*, II, 520.
[18] Ibid., 634.
[19] *Badshah Nama*, I, 221. Also C.H.I. IV, 554.

sands[20]... Once the builder is dead, no one will care for his buildings, but every one tries to erect buildings of his own, and establish his own reputation alongside that of his ancestors. If all these edifices were attended to and kept in repair, the lands of every city, and even village, would be adorned (covered)[21] with monuments; but as a matter of fact the roads leading to the cities are strewn with fallen columns of stone."[22]

In short, the Turkish and Mughal sultans and nobles were ever busy on a building spree without any thought of preserving the edifices. The strain of their artistic feeling was borne by the blood and toil of the silent slaves.[23]

In the Army

Another cadre which absorbed the services of large number of slaves from the beginning of Muslim rule was the Army. Without a strong army there could be no conquest, no Muslim rule in India. Ziyauddin Barani declares that "Kingship is the army and the army kingship,"[24] that is, the one was concomitant to the other. Extension of Muslim rule in India was not possible without conquest and so the Sultanate was, by its very nature, committed to maintaining a large army.

Soldiers in permanent service and the king's bodyguards called Jandars, were largely drawn from his personal slaves' *ghilman* and *mamalik*.[25] Foreign slaves were purchased from all countries and nationalities. There were Turks, Persians, Seljuqs, Oghus (also called Iraqi Turkmen), Afghans, Khaljis etc., in the army of Ghaznavids and Ghaurids. "To sustain the

[20] W.H. Moreland is the translator of Pelsaert's *Jahangir's India* and the author of *India from Akbar to Aurangzeb*. He says that this paragraph of Pelsaert has some problems of translation, Pelsaert, 56n., and hundreds of thousands may be taken as referring to either money or labourers.

[21] 'Adorned' in Pelsaert, 56, 'covered' in *Akbar to Aurangzeb*, 197. The two words convey very different impressions.

[22] Pelsaert 55-56; *Akbar to Aurangzeb*, 197.

[23] For the estimated cost of some Mughal edifies see *Akbar to Aurangzeb*, 196-197.

[24] Barani *Fatawa-i-Jahandari*, 22.

[25] Bosworth, *The Ghaznavids*, 98.

new principalities, slaves, imported as youths from peripheral regions were trained at the court of their masters to be a fighting and administrative elite loyal to them alone and thus comrades in arms."[26] This tradition of obtaining slaves by all methods and from all regions, was continued by Delhi sultans. These foreign slaves may be called, for the sake of brevity, by the generic term Turks and Afghans. Muhammad Ghauri in his last expedition brought ten thousand Afghan horsemen with him.[27] In the time of Iltutmish, Jalaluddin Mangbarni of Khwarism, fleeing before Chingiz Khan, had brought contingents of Afghan soldiers. In course of time many of them took service under Iltutmish.[28] Balban appointed three thousand Afghan horse and foot in his campaigns against the Mewatis,[29] and thousands of others for garrisoning difficult forts like Gopalgir, Kampil, Bhojpur, Patiali and Jalali.[30] In his royal processions hundreds of Sistani, Ghauri, Samarqandi and Arab soldiers, with drawn swords, used to march by Balban's side. Like the Afghans, the Mongols (again a generic term ethnically),[31] were enslaved or persuaded to join the forces of the Khaljis. They were called neo-Muslims under Alauddin Khalji. Persian element in the rank of officers and men was also prominent. Purchased Abyssinian slave-soldiers and officers became prominent under Raziyah. By the time of Firoz Shah Tughlaq indigenous slaves began to replace foreigners. As an example, "when the Sultan went out in state the slaves, accompanied him, in distinct corps—first the archers, fully armed, next the swordsmen, thousands in number (*hazar hazar*), the fighting men (*bandgan-i-aword*), the *bandgan-i-mahili* riding on male buffaloes, and slaves from the Hazara,

[26] Ira Marvin Lapidus, *Muslim cities in* the Later Middle Ages, Harvard, Massachusetts 1967, 6, 44.
[27] *Makhzan-i-Afghani*, N.B.Roy's trs. entitled Niamatullah's *History of the Afghans*, Santiniketan, 1958, 11.
[28] Olaf Caroe, *The Pathans*, London, 1958, 135.
[29] Minhaj, 315.
[30] Barani, 57, 58.
[31] *Ibid.*, 218; Farishtah, I, 94.

mounted on Arab and Turki horses, bearing standards and axes. All these thousands upon thousands, accompanied the royal retinue. About 40,000 were everyday in readiness as his personal guards.[32] Under Saiyyad and Lodi rulers, Afghans of all tribes and clans flocked into India like ants and locusts.[33]

Indian slaves were obtained as presents, part of tribute from subordinate states, or enslaved during campaigns. Once broken and trained into loyalty and service they were easily drafted into the army. Most Hindus belonged to the infantry wing and were called Paiks. Some of these were poor persons who joined the army for the sake of securing employment. Others were slaves and war captives. In war small boys were preferred as captives and they were the easiest to capture. For instance, in his campaigns in Katehar, Balban massacred mercilessly, sparing boys only of the age of eight or nine.[34] The age factor is significant. As these boys grew up, they could hardly remember their parentage or nativity, and remained loyal only to their master. In other cases also the situation was about the same. The slave was usually a prisoner of war, and according to Islamic usage his life was at the mercy of his captor. So when a conqueror or invader chose to spare the life of a slave and take him in his employment, it was an act of special benevolence for which the slave felt obliged to him.[35] Many other Paiks were recruited from the open market. Prince Alauddin Khalji, as governor of Kara, recruited 2,000 Paiks with the revenue he was supposed to send to Delhi, and marched with them on an expedition to Devagiri (1296).[36]

The Paiks were allotted sundry duties to perform. They fed, groomed, and looked after the horses of the cavalrymen who had a superior status. Alauddin Khalji had 70,000 caval-

[32] Habibullah, 119; Afif, 271; E.D., III, 342.
[33] Lal, *Twilight*, 126, 328-29.
[34] Barani, 58-59.
[35] Ashraf, op. cit., 189.
[36] Barani, 222; Farishtah, I, 95.

rymen besides other ranks.[37] Thousands of slaves were needed to look after them. Similar was the case with elephant stables. These pilkhanas had thousands of elephants and *mahouts,* and *ghulams* and Paiks were on duty to feed and nourish them.[38] The number of slaves for maintaining them and other animals can only be imagined.[39]

During a campaign, the slaves cleared the jungles and prepared roads for the army on march. During halts and on arrival at the destination the slaves and Paiks set up the camp and fixed tents, sometimes on land the total circumference of which was twelve thousand five hundred and forty six yards (about ten kilometer square).[40] They built Gargach and Sabat. Gargach was a covered platform on wheels for reaching the base of the fort under protection. Sabats were platforms raised from the ground to reach the top of the fort during assault. War drums and standards were placed in front of tents of load-carrying slaves who were kept under protective surveillance by mounted soldiers.[41]

The Paiks were often so stationed as to bear the first brunt of the enemy's attack, but they could not leave their posts because "horses are on their right and left... and behind (them) the elephants so that not one of then can run away."[42] But the Paiks were also great fighters. That is how Alauddin's army of invasion of Devagiri (1296) had 2000 Paiks. Most Persian chroniclers write about Paiks as being good soldiers lending strength to the Muslim army in Hindustan. Duarte Barbosa, a Portuguese official in India, writing in 1518 says this about them: "They carry swords and daggers, bows and

---

[37] Barani, 262; Khusrau, *Qiran-us Sadain,* Aligarh text, 1918, 35, 47; Afif. 318, 339-40; Farishtah, I, 200.

[38] Minhaj, 83; Barani, 53, 333; Khusrau, *Khazain-ul Futuh,* Habib trs. , 161; Afif, 163, 167 ff; 486.

[39] Even a ruler of an independent kingdom, Sultan Mahmud Sharqi of Jaunpur, marched against Delhi (1452) with a thousand elephants. Farishtah, I, 157; II, 308; Lal, *Twilight,* 135.

[40] Khusrau, *Khazain-ul-Futuh,* trs., Habib 63, during Kafur's siege of Warangal in 1310.

[41] *Adab-ul-Harb,* Trs. Rizvi, *Adi Turk Kalim Bharat,* 259-60.

[42] Alqalqashindi, *Subh-ul-Asha,* trs. Otto Spies, 76.

arrows. They are right good archers and their bows are long like those of England.... They are mostly Hindus."[43] Their most important weapon was Dhanuk or Dhanush.[44] During the time of the Khaljis (1290-1320), the Paik element had become prominent in Alauddin's army because he had wrested political power from the Turkish slave-rulers and could not entirely depend on Turkish soldiers. When Sultan Alauddin was about to encounter the Mongol invader Qutlugh Khwaja, Malik Alaulmulk, the Kotwal of Delhi, tried to dissuade him from taking any precipitate action and one of his arguments was that "our army is composed principally of the soldiery of Hindustan."[45] Their presence in large number was disliked by the fanatical Alim and historian Ziyauddin Barani who was against the recruitment of non-Muslims in the army.[46] Indeed among the Hindus there were sometimes such high officers as Malik Naik. According to Amir Khusrau it was under Malik Naik, the Akhurbeg-i-Maisara (Master of Horse of the Left Flank), a 'Hindu *banda*', that thirty thousand horsemen were sent against the Mongols — Ali Beg, Tartaq, and Targhi.[47] Alauddin's greatest general was Malik Kafur Hazardinari. Later in the day we come across names like Bahadur Nahar, Sarang Khan, Shaikha Khokhar and Mallu Khan, probably all converted Hindu warriors.

Loyalty of the Paiks

In an atmosphere of intrigue, suspicion and treachery, in which kings were overthrown and dynasties subverted by Turkish slaves or slaves turned nobles, the Paiks were known for their devotion and loyalty. Whether captured as small boys or grown ups in war or directly recruited as troopers,

[43] *The Book of Duarte Barbosa*, I, 181.
[44] Barani, *Tarikh*, 593, also 52.
[45] *Ibid.*, 255-57.
[46] *Fatawa-i-Jahandari*, 25-26.
[47] *Khazain-ul-Futuh*, trs. Habib., 26-27; *Deval Rani*, Persian Text, 320.

the Paiks in all situations remained mostly loyal to their masters. The foundation of this loyalty was the attachment of man to man, first by the relationship of the chief to his captive whose life had been spared, and if the warrior master succeeded in conquest and setting up a dominion, by the relation of suzerain to vassal. This adherence of loyalty to salt is a basic fact of Hindu tradition. There are many instances where the Paiks came to the rescue of their masters when danger threatened the latter's lives. For example, when Sultan Alauddin was marching to attack Ranthambhor (1301 C.E.), he halted at Tilpat for a few days during which Sulaiman, also known as Ikat Khan, planned to assassinate him. Ikat Khan had thought that just as Alauddin had obtained the throne by murdering his uncle Jalaluddin, so he could also kill his uncle and occupy the throne. That is why he had attacked the king. But the latter's loyal Paiks hedged around him from all sides and in their native shrewdness began to lament aloud that the Sultan was dead. The foolish and inexperienced Ikat Khan, partly because he was unable to lay hands on the Sultan and partly because he was in a hurry to seize the throne, readily believed the welcome wailings of the Paiks and dashed off towards the Camp and seated himself on Alauddin's throne. In the meantime, Alauddin's personal bodyguard Paiks dressed his wounds and he regained consciousness. He arrived in the Camp posthaste, ascended an eminence, and showed himself to the people. And Ikat Khan was beheaded.[48]

After Alauddin's death, his favourite slave, General and Wazir, Malik Kafur, wished to gather all power in his own hands and towards that end began to order the execution of one prince after another. He sent four Paiks by the names of Mubshir, Bashir, Salih and Munir to blind the Sultan's son Mubarak Khan. But when the Paiks approached him in his prison cell Prince Mubarak reminded them of their loyalty

[48] Barani, 273-75.

and duty which they owed to the sons of the late king. Impressed by Mubarak's appeal they not only left him untouched, but also murdered Kafur and thus facilitated Mubarak Khan's ascension to the throne.[49] Similarly, Rai Bhairon Bhatti, the personal attendant of Firoz Shah Tughlaq, came to his rescue when his own kith and kin made plans to murder the Sultan.[50] But there was no hard and fast behavioural pattern. The king was supreme but if the Paiks developed loyalty towards a nobleman who was inimical to the sultan, they could as well kill the king. That is how Sarwar-ul-Mulk, the Wazir of Sultan Mubarak Shah Saiyyad (1421-34), got the latter killed with the help of a group of Paiks.[51] On the other hand, the loyalty of Hindu officers and soldiers has become legendary.

In short, Indian slaves in the Muslim army performed all and sundry duties. They served as servants to cavalrymen. They cleared the jungles and laid roads during campaigns. They manufactured weapons, they fought in battles for their masters. Even so they were ever kept reminded of their inferior status so far as their remuneration was concerned. And this was determined according to Islamic law. In the booty collected during war, the State's share was one-fifth, while four-fifth went to the combatants, but the share of a horseman was twice that of a footsoldier.[52] As a Zimmi, the Hindu Paik had no share in the booty. Zimmi women and children cannot wage *jihad* and they too had no claim. But they were all to be paid something "in order to encourage them to fight and inferiority of their station be rendered manifest to them."[53]

---

[49] Ibid., p.377; Isami *Fatuh-us-Salatin,* 342-43. Farishtah, I, 124 mentions two Paiks only, Mubshir and Bashir.

[50] Afif, 102-104.

[51] Yahiya, 234-35; Nizamuddin, *Tabqat-i-Akbari,* I, 267; Farishtah, I, 169.

[52] *Hedaya,* Hamilton, 174.

[53] Ibid,. 178.

Employment in Karkhanas

Large numbers of slaves were drafted to work in the royal Karkhanas. The Karkhanas (literally workshops) of the Delhi sultans and Mughal emperors were both manufactories and storehouses where articles of delicacy were produced, sometimes in bulk, and imports from far off regions and foreign countries like China, Iraq and Alexandria, were received and stored. Shams Siraj Afif gives a detailed account of the Karkhanas of Firoz Shah Tughlaq although such workshops existed during the reigns of former as well as later sultans also. According to J.H. Krammers, "Industrial production in Muhammadan countries had developed in a particular way; it was chiefly characterized by being completely under the control of the rulers... and by its organization of the craftsmen in guilds. At the time of Islamic prosperity it had made possible a development of industrial skill which brought the artistic value of the products to an unequalled height. In the first place should be mentioned the products of the textile industry..."[54]

Under Firoz Tughlaq (1351-88) there were thirty six Karkhanas *directly under the Sultan.* In these were manufactured and stored articles of gold and silver and brass and other metals, textiles, wines, perfumes, armours, weapons, horse and camel saddles and covers of elephants, leather goods and clothes. But the Karkhanas also looked after "the elephant, horse and camel stables, the kitchen, the butlery, the candle department, the dog-kennels, the water-cooling department and other establishments... the wardrobe, the *'Alam-khana* or insignia, the carpet stores, and the like... About two lakhs of *tankahs* were expended in the carpet department, and 80,000 tankahs on the 'Alam Khana."[55] Each of these departments was under the charge of a senior Amir or Khan and lakhs of *tankahs* were sanctioned as recurring

[54] Krammers, in *Legacy of Islam*, 104.
[55] Afif, 337-43.

and non-recurring expenditure for each of the Karkhanas.

Thus some sort of capital investment was there and the guilds were formed by slaves trained as artisans (*kasibs*) by expert mechanics and handicraftsmen. 12,000 slaves worked in the Karkhanas of Firoz Tughlaq and were given a salary from 100 to 10 *tankahs* according to each one's competence. These slaves formed some sort of guilds and produced excellent articles. "There was no occupation in which the slaves of Firoz Shah (or for that matter any other sultan) were not employed." We cannot and need not study about all the departments in detail. Here we will confine ourselves to a brief account of two departments, those of wardrobe and weapons. These will suffice to give an idea of the institution of Karkhanas which employed a very large number, if not the bulk, of the royal slaves.

Textiles and Robes

According to Shahabuddin Al Umri "every year the Sultan (Muhammad Tughlaq) distributes 200,000 complete dresses: 100,000 in spring and 100,000 in autumn (among nobles)... Dresses are also distributed to the monasteries and hermitages (*khanqahs* and *dargahs*). The Sultan keeps in his service 500 manufacturers of golden tissues, who weave the gold brocades worn by the wives of the Sultan, and given away as presents to the amirs and their wives."[56] Ibn Battutah's list of the presents he carried from Muhammad bin Tughlaq to the Mongol emperor of Cathay also helps us appraise the development of textile industry in India manned by slaves. These presents comprised 100 pieces of cotton fabric called *bairami*, of matchless beauty priced at 100 *dinars* per piece; 100 pieces of silk called *juz* of variegated tints; 104 pieces of *Salahiya*, 100 pieces of *Shirinbaf*, 100 pieces of *Shanbaf*, 500 pieces of *muraz*, a kind of woollen fabric of various colours, 100 pieces of *Katan-i-Rumi*, 100

[56] *Masalik*, E.D., III, 578.

gowns without sleeves, a tent with six pavilions, four golden candlesticks and four embroidered with silver, four gold basins and six of silver, and ten dresses of honour embroidered. Also sent were ten quivers one of which was studded with pearls, and 10 swords the scabbard of one of which was inlaid with pearls and jewels.[57] Ziyauddin Barani's list of such items of textiles also indicates their prices under Alauddin Khalji, that of Abul Fazl under the Mughals.[58]

Slaves as Makers of Weapons

Slaves also manufactured weapons and their accessories including armour for men and covering of gilded iron for elephants.[59] As is well known, the most important element in the army was heavy cavalry. Mounted soldiers were armed with the bow for engaging in combat from a distance and with one or more weapons for hand to hand fighting, like the lance, the spear, the mace, the lasso. Fakhr-i-Mudabbir gives primacy to the bow and the sword as the most effective weapons of the horseman. Both these weapons were of different varieties. Among them all, the Hindu sword was the best and most lustrous (*gawhardartar*). Their export to such distant areas as Ummayad Spain and Seljuq Anatolia too is attested. He also declares that there is no better lance than the Indian.[60] From the time of Iltutmish to that of Firoz Shah great development had taken place in the manufacture of weapons and engines of war like Arrada, Manjniq and Maghrabi. These were stone and missile throwing machines. Haqqaha were rockets. The *Sirat-i-Firoz Shahi* mentions some very interesting "equipments, outfits and instruments for waging war". In the midst of a hotch-potch of assortment of items like traps, nets, noose and snare, "we find a brief

[57] Ibn Battutah, Def, and Sang., IV, 295, cited in I. Prasad, *Qaraunah Turks*, 138-39.
[58] Barani, *Tarikh*, 316-18; *Fatawa-i-Jahandari*, 35; Ain. I, 93-102.
[59] Thomas, *chronicles*, 78-79; *Masalik*, E.D., III, 577.
[60] *Adab-ul-Harb*, trs. Rizvi, *Adi Turk Kalin Bharat*, Aligarh, 1956, 258; Simon Digby, *War Horse and Elephant in the Delhi Sultanate*, Oxford, 1971, 15-20.

reference to such instruments as... Bandiqa (venetian cross-bow for throwing stone balls); Faraqha Falakun (slings made of rope for throwing stones); Kaman Guruha (large mounted crossbow); Harf-i-Kilk (arrow with inverted sharp points); Julahiq (balls of stone thrown by balists); Zand-i-Atish (incendiary fire-steel) etc.[61] All these weapons and equipments were manufactured by hundreds and hundreds of slaves, and were kept stored in the royal Karkhanas.

Work in Palace and Court

For invaders and conquerors, the establishment of a regular government takes some time. It is achieved through an evolutionary process. Its set up is completed in the course of decades. In medieval times this process was delayed by dynastic upheavals and arrival of fresh conquerors. But not too much. Most Muslim law-books and administrative manuals were ready when the Turks conquered Hindustan and stayed on to rule over it. And as in the case of construction of edifices and service in the army, slaves were required in large numbers for the working of the administrative machinery. Slaves were the hewers of wood and drawers of water in every sphere of life.

The government departments which needed the largest number of slaves were the Diwan-i-Wazarat, Diwan-i-Arz, Diwan-i-Insha, the Diwan-i-Rasalat. The detailed list of ministries, departments and offices is too large to mention. Thousands of slaves were required in the Revenue Department, thousands of others in the Postal Department as carriers of official communication and still others as spies. For shortage of space and paucity of detailed information about the employment of slaves in the households of nobles and other important Muslim elites, we shall confine our study of this aspect only to the Sultan's palaces for they "are exclusively

[61] 'A study of the rare Ms. Sirat-i-Firoz Shahi', by S.M. Askari, *Journal of Indian History,* Vol. L II, April, 1974, part I, 127-146, esp. 139.

occupied by the Sultan, his wives, concubines, eunuchs, male and female slaves and *mamaliks*".

How many slaves were on duty in the King's palace? It is difficult to surmise. One can only say — in thousands and thousands. At the gate there was the *nawbat* or the royal band played by a large number of instrument players in relay service — trumpets, drums, flagesletters, pipes etc. Hundreds were needed for carrying royal *alams* or standards, for wielding of fans to keep away flies from the royal person and wafting breeze, for carrying of *Chatr* (parasol) and *Durbash* (royal baton), and for attendance near the throne. The head of the Household staff, *Sarjandar* and *Sarsilahdar* or Commander of the Royal Bodyguard and head of the Royal Armour-bearer, required other hundreds of slaves to help them carry out their assignments. Among other officials in charge of domestic attendance were *Sar-abdar* (or *Aftabchi* of the Mughals) who looked after the washing and toilet arrangements of the Sultan, the *Kharitadar* who looked after the royal writing case and *Tahwildar* who looked after the purse. Each of these officials had subordinate slaves and servants. The *Chashnigir* (the predecessor of the *Bakawal* of the Mughals) supervised the royal kitchen with hundreds of subordinate slaves working under him. *Sar-Jamadar* was in charge of the royal wardrobe, the *Saqi-i-Khas* of wines and other drinks. The *Mashaldar* supervised the lighting arrangements of the palace, and the provision of lamps, candlesticks, lamp-stands etc. All these functionaries had a regular staff of subordinates comprising mainly of slaves.[62]

The scores of subordinates or slaves required to "run" the Muslim government in India ran into hundreds of thousands. The Muqti and later the Subedar lived like a miniature king, the paraphernalia of his court and household was patterned on that of the King. The Iqtadars and subordinate officers

---

[62] For detailed reference for the Sultanate period see Afif, 271; for the Mughal period Lal, *Mughal Harem*.

tried to emulate the higher nobles and the number of slaves continued to rise. In the heyday of the Sultanate period, Shihabuddin Al Umari has this to say about the time of Muhammad bin Tughlaq. At the cost of this prince there are maintained 1,200 physicians; 10,000 falconers who ride on horseback and carry birds trained for hawking; 300 beaters go in front and put up the game; 3,000 dealers in articles required for hawking accompany him when he goes out hunting; 500 table companions dine with him. He supports 1,200 musicians excluding his slave musicians to the number of 1,000 who are more especially charged with the teaching of music, and 1,000 poets of all the three languages, Arabic, Persian and Indian. According to one informant who based his account on the report of the royal cook, 2,500 oxen, 2,000 sheep, and other animals and birds were slaughtered daily for the supplies of the royal kitchen.[63] How many slaves were required to cater to all these services and amusements can easily be conjectured. In the Mughal times the numbers of slaves as part of the ever-expanding paraphernalia went on growing. Some numbers are available but details are not possible to give.[64]

The number of men employed in connection with sports and amusements was in aggregate very large. A numerous staff was employed specially for hunting and shooting, another for hawking, another for pigeon-flying. All Muslim rulers and nobles had pigeon-boys — Alauddin Khalji alone had 50,000 of them.[65] Provision was made for training the fighting instincts of a variety of animals "down to frogs and spiders."[66] The stables swarmed with animals and men. The number of animals in the stables may be judged from the fact that Sher Shah employed 3,400 horses for royal postal communications in the Kingdom, and maintained about 5,000

[63] Trs. in E.D., III, 578-80.
[64] Lal, *Mughal Harem*, 60-64
[65] Afif, 272.
[66] Moreland, *India at the Death of Akbar*, 88.

elephants on an average.[67] An elephants in the royal use had seven men to attend on it. Terry tells how Jahangir assigned four attendants to each of the dogs brought to him as presents from England.[68]

Slaves and Servants

The Imperial camp employed between 2000 and 3000 servants in addition to a guard of cavalry; there was one tent in particular which required 1000 men for a week for its erection."[69] As I have said elsewhere, in Akbar's time "each camp establishment required for its transport 100 elephants, 500 camels, 400 carts and a hundred bearers. It was escorted by 500 troopers. Besides, there were 100 *farrashes,* 500 pioneers, 100 water carriers, 50 carpenters, tent makers, and torch bearers, 30 workers in leather, and 150 sweepers."[70] Akbar's "*zanana* contained more than 5000 ladies, each of whom had separate apartments; they were attended by an adequate staff of servants, and watched in successive circles by female guards, eunuchs... and porters".[71] The Emperor set the standard in such matters, and everyone who occupied or aspired to a position at Court followed that example so far as his means allowed. Ten to twelve servants were attached to every lady of importance. Some princesses had as many slave-girls as a hundred.[72] Supplies for the Royal Household were obtained from distant sources, apparently regardless of the amount of labour expended. Wherever the Emperor might be, water for his use was brought from the river Ganga, a practice prevailing from the time of Muhammad Tughlaq if not earlier. Ice came daily by post carriages and by runners from snowy mountains. Fruit was supplied regularly from Kashmir and Kabul, and even from more distant

---

[67] Ashraf, 155 on the authority of Abbas Khan Sarwani's *Tarikh-i-Sher Shahi.*
[68] Moreland, *India at the Death of Akbar,* 88, n. Terry, 141.
[69] Ibid.
[70] Lal, *Mughal Harem,* 64; Ain., I, 49. Also Bernier, 359.
[71] Moreland, *India at the Death of Akbar,* 87-88.
[72] *Tarikh-i-Salim Shahi,* 51; Pelsaert, 64; Lal, *Mughal Harem,* 32.

places, such as Badakshan and Samarqand. Relay service on all these and many other such items required hundreds and thousands of slaves. The Emperor's personal officers modelled their establishments on similar lines, "one employing 500 torch-bearers, another having a daily service of thousand rich dishes, and so on".[73] Each fighting man of any consequence in the Turki and Mughal army had in the field an average of two or three servants. That the fashion was not confined to the entourage of the Emperor is shown by della Valle's statement that at Surat servants and slaves were so numerous and so cheap that "everybody, even of mean fortune, keeps a great family, and is splendidly attended". Pyrard says that the Zamorin of Calicut travelled with about 3000 men in his train, and that on the coast generally the prominent men had always a large following. He tells of the state maintained at Goa by the Bijapur envoy, who was accompanied about the town by a crowd of servants, pages, bearers, grooms, and musicians, and adds that all the great men of the Deccan indulged in similar display. Thevenot, writing of a later period (C. 1667) gives a corresponding description of the life in Golkunda. About North India in Jahangir's time, Pelsaert writes, "Peons or servants, are exceedingly numerous in this country, for everyone — be he mounted soldier, merchant or King's official — keeps as many as position and circumstances permit. Outside the house, they serve for display, running continually before their master's horse; inside, they do the work of the house." like the *bailwan*, the *farrash*, the *masalchi*, the *mahawat* etc.[74] "It will be understood," writes W.H. Moreland, "that the profusion of servants, which attracts attention in India at the present day (early twentieth century), is no modern phenomenon, but is in fact an attenuated survival of the fashions prevailing in the time of Akbar and doubtless dating from a

[73] Moreland, *India at the Death of Akbar*, 88-89.
[74] Pelsaert, 61-62.

much earlier period,"[75] indeed from the time of Qutbuddin Aibak when every Muslim householder or soldier began to possess a number of slaves.[76] Such exploitation in the Mughal period provided droves of *khidmatgars* to British officers and men when they established and ran their Raj in this country."[77] They found its impoverished people, ready to be used as Coolies to be sent abroad and exploited this nation as smartly as the Turks and Mughals had done in the medieval period.

---

[75] Moreland, *op.cit.*, 89.
[76] *Tarikh-i-Fakhruddin*, 20.
[77] Lal, *Legacy*, 298.

Chapter IX
GHILMANS AND EUNUCHS

The treatment meted out to the slaves depended upon the temperament, whim and caprice of the master. Some masters were kind hearted and treated their slaves kindly, many others cruelly, a few abominably. But one class of slaves who were very well looked after were *ghilman* and *mamalik*. The eunuchs also, because of the nature of their duties, received sort of a special treatment.

Ghilman va Mamalik

Muslim sultans were very fond of handsome young slaves whom they kept close to their persons as pages, service-boys, bodyguards, special troops and as gay companions. Infatuation for such slaves was a bane of the life of Muslim royalty and nobility in particular, although they considered it to be a fashion. P.K. Hitti has this to say about them, "*Ghilman*, who might also be eunuchs, were the recipients of special favours from their masters, wore rich and attractive uniforms and often beautified and perfumed their bodies in effeminate fashion. We read of *ghilman* in the reign of al-Rashid; but it was evidently the caliph al-Amin who, following Persian precedent, established in the Arabic world the *ghilman* institution for the practice of unnatural sexual relations. A judge of whom there is record used four hundred such youths. Poets did not disdain to give public expression to their perverted passions and to address amorous pieces of their compositions to beardless young boys."[1]

Muslim rulers and nobles in India were not lagging behind in these 'perverted passions.' Muhammad Hindu Shah Farishtah in his *Tarikh* and Khondamir in his *Dasturul Wuzra* relate the following incident about Mahmud

---

[1] *The Arabs*, 99.

Ghaznavi. Sultan Mahmud had a passion for slaves possessing handsome faces. His Wazir Abul Abbas Fazl bin Ahmad followed his example. "Fazl, on hearing the reputation of the beauty of a boy in Turkistan, deputed a confidential person to purchase that boy (whose countenance was beautiful as that of the planet Venus), and bring him to Ghazni, according to the mode of conveyance usually adopted for females. When an informer represented to the king these circumstances, his most august Majesty demanded that slave (who was as white as silver) from the minister... The minister made evasive replies, and pertinaciously refused to part with the slave, notwithstanding His Majesty's absolute power. The king one night visited the minister at his house (without prior notice), where the minister entertained him with respect and hospitality due to the dignity of a sovereign. When the slave (who looked as beautiful as a virgin of paradise) came into the presence of the king, high words passed between him and his minister, and so greatly was the king's anger kindled, that he issued orders to seize the minister and plunder his house. Soon after this the king departed for Hindustan, and certain evil-disposed *amirs* tortured the minister so severely with the rack that he lost his life." After him the old Khwaja Ahmad bin Hasan Maimandi was appointed to the office of Wazir.[2]

Sultan Mahmud's "court was guarded by four thousand Turkish good looking and beardless (*ghulam turk washaq*) slave-youths, who, on days of public audience, were stationed on the right and left of throne,— two thousand of them with caps ornamented with four feathers, bearing golden maces, on the right hand, and the other two thousand, with caps adorned with two feathers, bearing silver maces, on the left... As these youths attained into man's estate and their beards began to grow, they were attached to a separate corps, and placed occasionally under the com-

[2] Khondamir, E.D., IV, 149-50; Farishtah, I, 38.

mand of rulers of provinces."[3] Shams Siraj Afif's description of acquisition and distribution of handsome slave boys by Sultan Firoz Tughlaq points to similar arrangement.

The number of royal slaves (*bandgan-i-Khas*) was usually very large. They were invariably good looking, bought or captured at early age. Many foreign purchased slaves were also similarly chosen. Out of these, a few became favourites of the sultans and sometimes rose to the highest positions in life like Kafur Hazardinari under Alauddin Khalji and Khusaru Khan under Qutbuddin Mubarak Khalji. During Alauddin Khalji's invasion of Gujarat, his generals had brought immense booty from there including Raja Karan's consort Kamla Devi and the handsome slave Malik Kafur Hazardinari. The Sultan fell in love with both. In the words of Farishtah, he converted Kamala Devi to Islam and married her, and treating Kafur as a favourite "tied the sacred thread (*zunnar*) of his love in his own waist."[4] Khusrau Khan was brought from Malwa under similar circumstances. The rise of these catamites was due as much to their 'beauty' and nearness to the king as to their ambition and conspiratorial genius. So long as Alauddin held a firm grip on the administration, Malik Kafur served him with loyalty and won victories on his behalf in lands far and near. Once the king's health declined and he became dependent upon his dear slave-noble, the latter managed or at least attempted to poison him.[5] After Alauddin's death he gathered all political power into his own hands. Mubarak Khalji in his turn fell in love with his favourite Khusrau Khan. Like Malik Kafur, Khusrau Khan also provided pleasure to Qutbuddin and at the same time marched with armies to preserve and extend his master's dominions. But when an opportunity came handy he killed his patron.

Mubarak Khalji lost his life because of his degenerate

[3] Minhaj, 83-84 and n.
[4] Farishtah, I, 103.
[5] Barani, 369.

nature. In 1318 his favourite slave and Wazir Khusrau Khan led an expedition to the south where he seized much booty. As had happened in the case of Prince Alauddin, the wealth of the Deccan inflamed the ambition of Khusrau Khan and he began to plan to occupy the throne of Delhi. His plans fructified soon enough because of the Sultan's depravity. Qutbuddin was blinded by the infatuation he had for Khusrau Khan, and unable to bear his separation any longer sent for him from the Deccan. Khusrau Khan was taken in a palanquin post-haste from Devagiri to Delhi where he arrived in a week's time. One day Khusrau engaged the king in his intimate company and got him killed.[6] The custom of taking favourite slaves in palanquins seems to have been common so that Sultan Sikandar Lodi (1489-1517) could boast that "If I order one of my slaves to be seated in a palanquin, the entire body of nobility would carry him on their shoulders at my bidding."[7] This statement incidentally conveys an idea of the importance of handsome favourite slaves and also reflects on the status of nobles under autocratic Muslim rulers.

Instances of love of *ghilman* abound in the history of medieval India and hence we need not narrate many of them or dilate upon them. Suffice it here to note that love of slave-boys sometime made kings blind and provided not only Turkish or foreign slaves but also Indian slaves with opportunities to strive to grab the crown through the well-known methods of intrigue, poison and sword. Indian-born converted slaves were never considered equal to their foreign counterparts. They were always looked down upon by the foreign Muslims. But handsome favourites fell into a different category. Besides ambition and intrigue there were some other reasons for their reckless acts. The masters were often

[6] Barani, 390-408; Isami, 353-63; Farishtah, I, 125.

[7] *Tarikh-i-Daudi*, passage trs. by N.B.Roy, in his *Niamatullah's History of the Afghans*, 134.

sodden and depraved.[8] They used their *ghilmans* for unnatural carnal acts. The humiliation engendered by such acts made the slaves sullen and revengeful. These slaves also derived encouragement from the examples before them. If Balban could poison Sultan Nasiruddin and Alauddin Khalji openly kill his benefactor Jalaluddin Khalji, why could Malik Kafur not try to kill his master? If Malik Kafur could strive for the throne, why not Khusrau Khan? The abuse was so widespread that Barani writes with a sense of delight that Ghiyasuddin Tughlaq was free from this vice and he did not allow "handsome, beardless boys" to come near him and looked upon all immoral persons as his enemies.[9] According to Ibn Battuta one of the reasons for estrangement between the Sultan and his son Muhammad was the Prince's extravagance in purchasing slaves.[10]

But all slaves, all *ghilmans*, could not attain to such high positions because they were there in thousands and they could not all be equal. Alauddin had a corps of 50,000 personal slaves, Muhammad Tughlaq 20,000 and Firoz Tughlaq 40,000.[11] Muhamad Tughlaq maintained such large numbers of them that he set apart a day of the week to manumit some of them and to confer them in marriage.[12] Such was the situation throughout the medieval period, although the detailed description of Shams Siraj Afif about the reign of Firoz Tughlaq gives the impression that Firoz excelled all the kings of the Delhi Sultanate in collecting and maintaining beautiful slaves. Afif needs to be quoted at some length.

"The Sultan was very diligent in obtaining slaves, and towards that end he issued a *farman* to his *amils* and *jagirdars* to capture slaves whenever they were at war, and to pick out and send the best for the service of the court.

---

[8] *Ibid.*, pp. 302-307.

[9] Barani, 443.

[10] Ishwari Prasad, *Qaraunah Turks* 39-40, citing Ibn Battuta, Defd. and Sang. III, 212-14.

[11] Afif, 270, 272; Qureshi, *Administration*, 67n.

[12] Afif, 268-72. Also Ibn Battuta, 63.

When the feudatories went to the court, each one according to his ability took with him beautiful slaves, dressed in clean attire, elegant caps, turbans and socks, in short, ornamented in the most splendid style. They also, when they paid annual visits brought, together with other things, slaves for the Sultan... This regulation remained in force for forty years throughout the reign. The chiefs who brought many slaves received the highest favour, and those who brought few received proportionately little consideration. When the chiefs perceived the Sultan's eagerness for slaves, and that their efforts to get them were highly appreciated, they exerted themselves in providing them, and the numbers brought every year exceed description.

"Some of the slaves spent their time in reading and committing to memory the holy book, others in religious studies, others in copying books. Some were placed under tradesmen and were taught mechanical arts, so that about 12,000 slaves became artisans (*kasib*) of various kinds. Altogether, in the city and in the various fiefs there were 180,000 slaves. In fact there was no occupation in which the slaves of Firoz Shah were not employed. When the slaves became too numerous, some of them were given into the charge of Amirs and Maliks. These nobles treated them like children, providing them with food and raiment, lodging them and training them, and taking every care of their wants..."[13]

It would be pertinent here to add the observation of Major Raverty. "For the information of the general reader uninitiated in Oriental lore, I would mention that the words Mamluk and Ghulam, signifying 'slave', must not be understood in the sense 'slave' conveys in our language. These slaves were sometimes captives, but more often boys of Turkish origin were purchased by kings and their great nobles from traders — slave-dealers — and trained for the highest offices. They were sometimes adopted by their mas-

[13] Afif, 267-273. Large portions trs. in E.D., III, 340-42.

ter, and were frequently made governors of provinces and leaders of armies..."[14]

Captured or purchased, Indian slaves may not always fit in with this description, but in all cases provision was made for the *ghilman* and *mamalik* in a liberal manner with salaries, provisions, stipends and jagirs. In the time of Muhammad bin Tughlaq, according to Al Umari, "the slaves of the Sultan each receive a monthly allowance for their maintenance of two *mans* of wheat and rice, and a daily allowance of three seers of meat, with all *the* necessary accompaniments. Besides, he received ten *tankahs* per month, and four suits of clothes every year."[15] Under Firoz Tughlaq, "those who were stationed in the city (capital) were given cash salary, some a hundred *tankahs,* others fifty, or thirty or twenty-five. But no one was paid less than 10 *tankahs.*" The Sultan took special care of his slaves, writes Afif. There was a distinct muster-master (*majmu'-dar*) of the slaves, and a Ministry of Slaves (Diwan-i-Bandgan) which was established as a separate and distinct unit from the Diwan-i-Wazarat or Ministry of Finance.[16]

This 'pampering' of slaves by sultans and nobles aroused jealousy all around. To jealousy was added ethnic rivalry. Kindness on the part of the master was reciprocated with loyalty by the slaves. Often this proved to be harmful to the slaves in the long run. After the death of Alauddin Khalji many of his slaves were murdered in cold blood.[17] After the death of Firoz Tughlaq a similar fate awaited his loyal slaves. The newly crowned Prince Muhammad gave the slaves of Firoz three days to leave Delhi. Those who escaped, survived. Others, and particularly those who spoke the 'Purbi and Bengali' language, were done to death. These 'impure' rebels had put the crown into commission and behaved like

---

[14] Minhaj, 168 n 2. Also Ibn Khaldun trs. in Bernard Lewis, *Islam*, 98.
[15] E.D., III, 577.
[16] Afif, loc. cit.
[17] Lal, *Khaljis*, 288.

virtual king makers — such was the impression of warring princes who succeeded Firoz. The fault of these slaves seems to be that they were firstly not *asl* (or pure) Muslims and secondly they were loyal to Firoz Tughlaq and his progeny.[18] This is Farishtah's version. Whatever the real reason, after Firoz's death, "the heads of these his favoured servants were cut off without mercy, and were made into heaps in front of the Durbar."[19] "For a decade after Firoz's death the princes manoeuvred, the nobles intrigued and the people suffered."[20] Each new sultan — and they came to power in kaleidoscopic succession — wanted his own cadre of nobility, his own set of slaves, and destroyed those of the earlier ones. In short, slaves were made slaves for no fault of theirs and they were massacred for the fault of being slaves to their masters.

Eunuchs

Many if not most of the slaves were eunuchs. A Muslim king was unthinkable without his harem; a harem was inconceivable without eunuchs. Eunuchs were the guards and guardians of the harem. The seraglio of the size of the Mughal harem could be a security hazard for its inmates and even for the king, if not properly supervised by eunuchs. They guarded the gates of the palace, checked and regulated ingress and egress of persons male and female. They also served the inmates of the seraglio even while keeping surveillance over them.[21] Harem was the largest Department under Muslim rule. There was no sphere of court and administration which was not concerned with the harem in one way or the other. Therefore thousands and thousands of eunuchs were needed to serve the Muslim king and his harem. Their cadre was hierarchical. Senior eunuchs were known as Nazirs and Khwaja Saras. Each one of them had a

---

[18] Farishtah, I, 153.
[19] Afif, 273; Farishtah, I, 153.
[20] Lal, *Twilight*, 12.
[21] Manucci, II, 352; Finch in Foster, *Early Travels*, 16, 265.

number of junior eunuchs under him.[22]

It is a very significant fact of Muslim history that some of the greatest nobles in the Sultanate of Delhi and the Mughal Empire were eunuchs. Imaduddin Rayhan, the chief minister under Sultan Balban, Kafur Hazardinari, the army commander and vice-regent of Alauddin Khalji, and Khurau Shah the favourite of Qutbuddin Mubarak Khalji who rose to be king, were all eunuchs. Khwaja Jahan Malik Sarwar, a black eunuch, was appointed Wazir of Sultan Mahmud, a successor of Sultan Firoz Tughlaq. In 1394 he was sent as governor of Jaunpur with the title of Malik-us-Sharq (Master of the East). Within a short time he brought under his control the vast region stretching from Kol (Aligarh) on the west to Tirhut in Bihar in the east and became known as Sultan-us-Sharq. On his death his adopted son Qaranful (the Clove i.e. Black) took the regal title of Mubarak Shah and issued coins in his own name.[23] Under the Mughals many important eunuchs, who were known as Nazirs and Khwaja Saras, rose to the position of Mansabdars, commanders of armies and governors of Subahs. The chief Nazirs or Khwaja Saras generally enjoyed the title of Aitmad Khan or Aitbar Khan (the Trusted Lord). One Aitbar Khan, who served under Babur and Humayun, was appointed Governor of Delhi by emperor Akbar.[24] Another Aitmad Khan was made commander of one thousand and entrusted by Akbar to improve the finances of the state. He took part in the conquest of Bengal in 1576 and was later appointed Governor of Bhakkar. Another Aitmad Khan in Akbar's service went on a pilgrimage to Mecca and brought a huge stone which was said to contain an impression of the foot of the Prophet.[25] He was appointed Governor of Gujarat and held the command of four thousand.[26] Aitbar

---

[22] Manucci, II, 350.
[23] Yahiya, *Tarikh-i-Mubarak Shahi,* 156; Badaoni, Ranking, I, 348; Farishtah, I, 154. Lal, *Twilight,* 9, 68-69.
[24] *Ain.*, I, 442.
[25] *Ain,* 207, 570; Badaoni, Text, 311.
[26] *Maasir-ul-Umara,* I, 93-100.

Khan, the chief eunuch of Jahangir, was the Governor of Agra city. A eunuch, Firoz Khan, was conferred a mansab of 1500/600 by Jahangir.[27] Bakhtawar Khan (d. 1698), the superintendent of eunuchs under Aurangzeb, held the rank of 1000. He was a great scholar and historian. He prepared an abridgement of *Tarikh-i-Alfi* and *Akhbar-ul-Akhyar* and wrote the *Mirat-ul-Alam* also known as *Mirat-i-Jahan Numa*.[28] During the time of the Later Mughals three eunuchs, Mian Khushfahan, Mian Arjmand and Mian Mahabat ruled the state on behalf of Mughlani Begum (1754-1756).[29]

According to Manucci, the chief Nazir of the seraglio "is highly esteemed by the King. He has a large allowance, has charge of the treasury, is master of the wardrobe, decides on the details and the pattern of Sarapas (robes) to be prepared; in short, it is he who has charge of all the Mughal expenditure of the clothes, the linen, and the precious stones, of the jewelry, of everything that goes into or comes out of the palace."[30] Manucci gives a list of about forty Nazirs of the time of Aurangzeb, each of whom had a separate title bestowed upon him by the king. By their service to the kings and queens, the eunuchs could wield great influence and amass large amounts of wealth.[31] Some indeed were so trustworthy and powerful that they kept even grown up princes under strict discipline.[32]

The senior eunuchs or Khwaja Saras had a number of junior eunuchs under them. According to Manucci, "there is always one set above the rest who directs and looks after everything that goes on in the Mahal."[33] Of the subordinate eunuchs, some worked as messengers in the harem. Others were posted at the doors to keep a watch on those who

---

[27] Tuzuk, II, 83.
[28] E D, VII, 150.
[29] Sarkar, *Fall of the Mughal Empire*, I, 440.
[30] Manucci, II, 350-51.
[31] Barbosa, II, 147.
[32] Hamiduddin Bahadur, *Ahkam-i-Alamgiri*, English trs. by Jadunath Sarkar, Calcutta, 1912, 71-72.
[33] Manucci, II 350.

came or went out of the palace and saw to it that no unauthorised person entered the seraglio.[34] Some others looked after the education of princes. Bernier writes that Mughal princes "instructed from infancy to the care of women and eunuchs, slaves from Russia, Circassia... Gurjustan (Georgia), or Ethiopia, whose minds are debased by the very nature of their occupation; servile and mean to superiors, proud and oppressive to dependants these princes... leave the walls of the seraglio quite ignorant."[35]

The main business of the eunuchs was to guard as well as to keep an eye on the activities of the harem ladies. Since they were always present in the seraglio, they also served and helped them in various ways. The eunuchs guarded the secrets of their mistresses. They smuggled drugs and wines for them into the harem. The ladies sometimes even arranged through the eunuchs to invite men into the harem; Manucci avers that eunuchs were helpful in smuggling men into the women's apartment.[36] In exchange for such delicate and risky services the eunuchs could get from them "whatever they desired", for they could blackmail their client ladies. Naturally some women of the harem even allowed the eunuchs to enjoy them according to his ability.[37] They served princes and their beloveds as go-between.[38] It is such errands of secrecy that sometimes made the eunuchs powerful, arrogant and even vainglorious.[39]

In short, there was hardly any area of Muslim rule in which the eunuchs were not required to play an important role. They fought battles and conquered kingdoms, they held high administrative posts, they were appointed governors and commanders of armies. They rendered invaluable service in the affairs of the harem. They formed dependable

[34] Bernier, 267; Manucci, II, 352, 357.
[35] Bernier, 144-45.
[36] Manuncci, II, 80.
[37] Pelsaert, 66; Bernier, 131; E.D., VI, 493-516.
[38] Lal, *Mughal Harem,* 158-59, 184-85, 187-88.
[39] Saqi Mustaad Khan, *Maasir-i-Alamgiri,* 73.

escorts of ladies and trustworthy jailers of very important persons like princes and kings. Aitbar Khan who was earlier in the service of Babur and Humayun, once chaperoned Akbar's mother and other Begums from Kabul to Hindustan.[40] In 1565 the eunuch Aitmad Khan escorted the daughter of Miran Mubarak Shah, the King of Khandesh, to the harem of Akbar.[41] Aitbar Khan, the favourite eunuch of Jahangir, was placed in charge of the rebel prince Khusrau during his incarceration. Another eunuch-noble with the same title was appointed by Aurangzeb as the jailer of Shahjahan in captivity.

With so many eunuchs needed for so many odd duties to perform, their number in the Muslim king's harem was very large. Delve deep into the life-story of any important noble and he turns out to be a eunuch. Boys and men in thousands were emasculated to serve the Muslim cities as domestics and guards in the harem primarily, although there was no work which was not assigned to them. In the Middle Ages there were many slave markets in Muslim cities in India and outside, and trade in slaves and eunuchs was a regular commercial activity. Many slaves and eunuchs were imported at high price from outside[42], many others were bought within the country. But most of the eunuchs comprised of slaves captured during wars and then castrated.

The practice of converting men into eunuchs was very common in Bengal. "In Hindustan," writes Jahangir, "especially in the province of Sylhet, which is a dependency of Bengal, it was the custom for the people of those parts to make eunuchs of some of their sons and give them to the governor in place of revenue (*mal-wajibi*)... This custom by degrees has been adopted in other provinces and every year some children are thus ruined and cut off from procreation.

[40] Ain., I, 443.
[41] A.N., II, 351-52.
[42] Bernier, 134-36, 426.

This practice has become common."[43] Bengal in the time of Jahangir was a very large province. Large tracts of Northern Hills, the Sarkar of Orissa and large parts of Bihar were included in it.[44] If the practice of making eunuchs had become common outside Bengal also, then it seems it had spread almost all over the empire. Jahangir issued *farmans* abolishing the practice and hoped for the best. But a system in which revenue was collected in the form of eunuchs, could not be changed through a few orders. Said Khan Chaghtai, a noble of Jahangir possessed 1,200 eunuchs.[45] Besides, eunuchs formed a profitable commercial commodity and, as we shall see in the chapter on Slave Trade, the price of a eunuch in the market was three times that of an ordinary slave. Therefore, some areas, notably Bengal, were regular providers of eunuchs for the Muslim upper classes in Delhi, Isfahan and Samarkand.[46] In 1668 Aurangzeb also prohibited castration of young boys "throughout the empire".[47] It appears that in forbidding eunuch-making, Jahangir was apprehensive of decline in Muslim demography while Aurangzeb was prompted by religious motives. Yet, in spite of their orders, young men continued to be turned into eunuchs and Jahangir and his successors themselves went on accepting eunuchs as gifts for duties in the harem.[48] In Aurangzeb's time in the city of Golkunda (Hyderabad), in the year 1659 alone, 22,000 individuals were emasculated."[49]

The need for turning so many boys and men into eunuchs and also obtaining them from outside is obvious. The safety, security and surveillance of a large number of beautiful women in the seraglio could not be left only to female matrons. And normal healthy men could not be trusted to

[43] Jahangir, *Tuzuk*, I, 150-51.
[44] Ibid., 207 and n.
[45] *Tuzuk*, I, 13, 168; *Tarikh-i-Salim Shahi*, 16; *Maasir-ul-Umara*, II, 403.
[46] Elst, *Indigenous Indians*, 375-76.
[47] Saqi Mustaad Khan, *Maasir-ul-Alamgiri*, 48; Sarkar, *Aurangzeb*, III, 61.
[48] Tuzuk, I, 247.
[49] Elst, *op.cit.*, 376 quoting Michel Erlich, *Les Mutilations Sexuelles*, Paris, 1991, 59.

serve in the harem in which resided so many sex-starved young women.[50] So the safest thing was to make men who were on duty in the harem harmless. The king also lived in the harem, and nobles and servants personally attending on him also had to be eunuchs. The cruelty entailed in this system was nobody's concern in a despotic regime. On the other hand, it was very advantageous to the master. Once a man was made eunuch, his sensibility for manhood was dwarfed, his spirit of assertiveness destroyed, and he was perforce turned into a loyal and devoted slave; it did not matter to the master if his loyalty and devotion were fruits of compulsion. So the practice of making eunuchs went on and on under Muslim rule. If eunuchs were denied "the greatest pleasures attainable in this world,"[51] they were compensated by sometimes performing great feats of bravery, by showing great loyalty to the master or by just piling up great wealth.

It is not the task of the historian to pity the eunuchs or condemn those who emasculated them. But pernicious was the system in which man could exploit man to this extent. It is another matter that most eunuchs perforce reconciled themselves to their lot, though cruelty and crime could go no farther than deforming and desexing of man by man. Many, people suffered because of the medieval Muslim slave system, but undoubtedly the eunuchs suffered the most.

---

[50] Lal, *Mughal Harem,* 179-80.
[51] Manucci, II, 78-79.

CHAPTER X
SLAVE TRADE

It is nowhere mentioned in medieval chronicles how slaves, captured in war, were sorted out and separated for the purpose of being sold, drafted into the army, given as gifts to princes and nobles or set apart for domestic service. All that is known is that slaves were disposed of on all these counts and many more. It appears that the sorting was done on the basis of the looks of the females, physical fitness of the males, intuition of the master, as well as the specific work that a slave was deemed fit to do. An early example is about the capture of Brahmanabad by Muhammad bin Qasim. Of the prisoners captured a selection was made from the slaves and other spoils, "in order to detach the usual one-fifth share of the State. The number of the selected slaves came to about 20,000. The rest were distributed among the troops."[1] But the criterion of selection has not been specified. Another instance is about Amir Timur who invaded India in 1399, and took a large number of prisoners. He writes "I ordered that all the artisans and clever mechanics, who were masters of their respective crafts, should be picked out from among the prisoners and set aside, and accordingly some thousands of craftsmen were selected to await my command. All these I distributed among the princes and *amirs* who were present, or who were engaged officially in other parts of my dominions (to take care of them). I had determined to build a *Masjid-i-Jami* in Samarkand, the seat of my empire, which should be without rival in any country; so I ordered that all builders and stone-masons should be set apart for my own especial service."[2] But such details are not available in most cases.

---

[1] *Chachnama*, Kalichbeg, 163.
[2] *Malfuzat-i-Timuri*, trs E.D., III, 447.

Sale of Slaves

The majority of Indian slaves comprised captives made during wars. These slaves formed property of the State. At the time of Muhammad bin Qasim's invasion of Sindh the head of the State was the Caliph and prisoners taken in Sindh were regularly forwarded to him. Kufi, the author of the *Chachnama,* rightly sums up the position. Out of the total catch, four-fifths was the share of the soldiers, "what remained of the cash and slaves was... sent to Hajjaj (the Governor of Iraq)" for onward transportation to the Khalifa.[3] In such a situation any special acquisition had to be paid for in cash. Muhammad bin Qasim who wished to possess Raja Dahir's wife Ladi, avers the *Chachnama,* "purchased her out of the spoils, before making her his wife."[4] But the price he paid is not mentioned. Similarly, when Hajjaj sent 60,000 slaves captured in India to the Caliph Walid I (705-715 C.E.), the latter "sold some of those female slaves of royal birth",[5] but again their price has not been specified.

Mahmud of Ghazni carried away large numbers of captives from India in every campaign and sold most of them. Jayapala the defeated Hindu Shahiya King of Kabul was publicly exposed at some slave market in Khurasan by the order of Mahmud who "commanded that he might be ransomed for the sum of eighty *dirams*". Raverty suggests that "the word 'thousand' must have been left out. If not, Mahmud did not set much value on his captive."[6] As Jayapala was old, the price he could fetch in open auction probably could not be more than 80 *dirhams.* Or, as Hodivala points out, the object of exposing Jayapala to public derision was evidently to compel him into surrendering to his victor's demands and purchase his release on his captor's own terms, which was fixed at "200,000 golden *dinars* and 250 elephants; and the

[3] *Chachnama,* trs. Mirza Kalichbeg Fredunbeg, 86.
[4] Ibid., 176.
[5] Ibid., 154.
[6] Minhaj, 82, n.7.

necklace taken from Jaipal was valued at another 200,000 gold *dinars*."[7] Therefore, 80 *dirhams* as the price of an old king signifies nothing.

In one instance specifically Al Utbi gives an idea of the gain from the sale of captives. According to his narrative, Mahmud, after his campaign in Mathura, Mahaban and Kanauj (1018-19), returned to Ghazni with, besides other booty, 53,000 captives and each one of these was sold for two to ten *dirhams*. From this statement it would be safe to infer that the lowest price at which an Indian captive was sold was two, and the highest ten *dirhams*. It would also be safe to conclude that slaves were captured by invaders to be sold to make money; for Utbi adds that "Merchants came from different cities to purchase them so that the countries of Mawarau-n-nahr, Iraq and Khurasan were filled with them".[8] Earlier, in the expedition to Thaneshwar (1015), according to Farishtah, "the Muhammadan army brought to Ghaznin 200,000 captives, so that the capital (Ghaznin) looked like an Indian city, for every soldier of the army had several slaves and slave girls".[9] Similarly, in the Kashmir Valley (1014 C.E.), according to Utbi, the captives taken "were so plentiful that they became very cheap..."[10] But he does not say how cheaply they were sold.

The mention of price at one place is hardly sufficient to estimate the money value of Indian slaves sold in foreign lands in the eleventh century. What was the value of two to ten *dirhams* in those days is also not known. Abul Fazl traces the history of *dirham* from the time of Caliph Umar, but his detailed and rather confusing account only shows that the earliest *dirhams* of the Ghaznavid period were struck at Ghazni and Lahore. It was a silver coin of great variations in

[7] Ibid., 80-81 and n. 5. Also Al Utbi, *Tarikh-i-Yamini*, E.D., II, 26; Hodivala, 192; Nazim, 'Hindu Shahiya Kingdom of Ohind', in J.R.A.S., 1927, 494; Isami, *Futuh-us-Salatin*, text ed. by Agha Mahdi Husain, 38.

[8] Utbi E.D., II, p.39. For detailed references see Lal, *Growth of Muslim Population*, 214.

[9] Farishtah, I, 28.

[10] For detailed references Lal, op. cit., 213 and Ubti E. D.,II, 50 and n.1.

weight and value as was the case with the *dinar*, a gold coin.[11] Yet, the sale of thousands of slaves after every campaign, as the figures of captives carried away by Mahmud shows,[12] brought good profit to the invader. No wonder that besides treasure, captives also used to be regularly carried away from India during the Ghaznavid occupation of Punjab for making extra money through their sale. This lucrative business continued, and a scion of the house, Sultan Ibrahim (1054-1099), once carried away one lakh captives to Ghazni.[13]

During the first hundred years of Muslim rule, that is, under Aibak, Iltutmish and Balban (1206-1290), slaves of both sexes were captured in droves during military expeditions, but they were mostly distributed among kings, nobles and soldiers for sundry duties.[14] Large number of workers were needed by these early sultans for clearing jungles, making roads, as auxiliaries in the army, for construction of buildings, as errand runners by administrators, tent fixers and workers in camp establishments. Slaves were needed for arranging supplies for households of all kinds of foreign Muslims from kings and nobles to commoners, constructing small residential dwellings or grand and imposing State buildings etc. Slave girls were needed in plenty for providing pleasure and other services. All this work was done by captives turned slaves. It appears that because of their being detailed on these jobs, very few slaves were left available for sale. That is why there is no specific mention of their sale during this period. But sale of captives was a common practice. For example, it is mentioned that Sultan Nasiruddin, son of Iltutmish (1246-66), had no "purchased" (*laundi va khadima*) slave girl, that his wife cooked for him and he

---

[11] *Ain.*, I, 36, 38. Thomas, *Chronicles of the Pathan king of Delhi*, 13-14. Also note by Ranking in Badaoni, trs., I, 18.

[12] Minhaj, 105n.

[13] Farishtah, I, 49.

[14] Fakr-i-Mudabbir, *Tarikh-i-Fakhruddin Mubarak Shah*, 20; Minhaj, Text, 175; Farishtah, I, 66-7 1.

earned his livelihood by selling copies of Quran written by himself. "This story, however, is very stale indeed," adds Raverty, "as stale as the days of one of the early Khalifas", for this very sultan could present *forty head of slaves* to his nobleman Minhaj Siraj for being sent to his dear sister in Khurasan.[15]

During the reign of Sultan Alauddin Khalji the Sultanate grew strong (1296-1316).[16] He conquered extensively and in every campaign slaves were captured in large numbers. These were sold in various ways — on the spot,[17] in the markets of Delhi, and of other cities. Sometimes even women and children of Mongol invaders were captured and sold like Hindu slaves in Delhi and other cities of India.[18]

Sale Price of Slaves

Alauddin Khalji's Market Control has become famous in medieval Indian history. He fixed the price of every commodity, including slaves. The sale price of slaves was like this. The standard price of a working girl was fixed at from 5 to 12 *tankahs,* and that of a good looking girl suitable for concubinage from 20 to 30 and even 40 *tankahs*. The price of a man slave (*ghulam)* usually did not exceed 100 to 200 *tankahs*. The prices of handsome boys were fixed from 20 to 30 *tankahs;* the ill-favoured could be obtained for 7 to 8. The price of a child slave (*ghulam bachchgan naukari)* was fixed at 70 to 80 *tankahs.* The slaves were classified according to their looks and working capacity. In the case of bulk purchases by traders who had ready money and who had the means to carry their flock for sale to other cities,[19] prices were fixed accordingly.

Who got the profit form such sales? If Alauddin Khalji

---

[15] Minhaj, 675 & n 5, 686 & n 7; Farishtah, I, 74.
[16] Khusrau, *Nuh Sipehr*, E. D., III, 561; Barani, 297-98; Isami, 569-70; Afif, 38.
[17] cf. Vidyapati, *Kirtilata,* 42, 72.
[18] Farishtah, I, 116, *daran sal zan va farzand mughlan ra dar Dihli va sair-i-bilad hindostan batariq-i-asiran hindi farokhtand.*
[19] Barani, 314-15.

followed the example of contemporary rulers in West Asian countries, then the profit went to him, that is, the sultan or the government. This was also customary. It is stated by Isami in his *Futuh-us-Salatin* that when Mahmud of Ghazni defeated Raja Jayapala of the Hindu Shahiya dynasty, he "carried him to the distant part of the kingdom of Ghazni and delivered him to an agent (*dalal*) of the *Slave Market* ...(and) at the command of the king Mahmud they [the Brokers of the Market, *muqiman-i-bazar* in the original] sold Jaipal as a slave for 80 *Dinars* and deposited the money realised by the sale in the Treasury". Hodivala adds that "it would be difficult to get better evidence than this of the ruler making the profit.[20] In some of the West Asian countries in the Middle Ages, according to Ira Marvin Lapidus, the rulers used to take over wholesale trade, in grain and also probably in other commodities, so that profits from sale accrued to them rather than to the private traders. Ibn Khaldun also says that "The slave merchants bring them to Egypt in batches... and government buyers have them displayed for inspection and bid for them, raising the price above their value."[21] It was equally true of Alauddin. He treated the merchants themselves as slaves. As per his orders, no middlemen or brokers were allowed to visit the slave-market and examine the "goods", so that the profits of the traders were curtailed while those of the Sultan swelled. No wonder then that at his demise the Sindhi (Multani) merchants took out processions to rejoice at the death of Alauddin.[22]

No rule about the sale price could be laid in special cases when the catch was big or a very beautiful slave ("man or woman/boy or girl") of very high price, say 1000 to 2000 *tankahs* was brought for sale in the market. Sometimes it created a very piquant situation as nobody dared to buy him/

[20] Hodivala, 192-93.

[21] In *Ibar*, trs. by Bernard Lewis in *Islam*, 98; Ira Marvin Lapidus, *Muslim Cities in the Later Middle Ages*, 52ff.

[22] Barani, 306, 385.

her, lest the king should come to know that so and so was rich enough to pay so high a price for a slave/concubine. Even then slaves were sometimes purchased for high amounts. The poet Badr Chach claims to have bought a slave named Gul-Chehra (Rose Face) for 900 *tankahs*.[23] The title Hazardinari (of a thousand gold coins) for Malik Kafur shows that a skilled slave could have cost anything. It may therefore be contended that except in the reign of Alauddin when prices were fixed, prices of slaves and concubines were uncertain, varying according to fortunes of war and famine, looks of the person, bargaining talent of the auctioneers, shrewdness of the buyer[24] and fluctuations in the market through influences of demand and supply. For instance, when Muhammad Ghauri and Qutbuddin Aibak mounted a combined attack on the Khokhars of the Salt Range (Koh-i-Jud), "great plunder was taken and many captives, so that five Hindu [Khokhars] captives could be bought for a *dinar*".[25] Captives were so plentiful that they were also sent "to sell in Khurasan, not long after."[26] On the other hand, if the supply was short and demand great, the prices went shooting high. Narrating the events of the reign of Sultan Qutbuddin Mubarak Khalji (1316-20), the son and successor of Alauddin Khalji, Ziyauddin Barani says that the strict regulations of Alauddin were all thrown to the winds by the new Sultan, and Qutbuddin and his nobles gave themselves up to a life of debauchery and licence. In such circumstances the "demand for beautiful girls and beardless boys made them a scarce commodity, and their prices rose to 500 and sometimes even to one thousand and two thousand *tankahs*."[27] So, in the early fourteenth century the lowest average price of a slave mentioned by chroniclers was about eight *tankahs*,

[23] Ashraf, *Life and Conditions of the People of Hindustan*, 236, quoting *Qasaid-i-Badr Chach*, Kanpur, 1877, 39.
[24] Ibid., 235-36.
[25] Hasan Nizami, *Taj-ul-Maasir*, E. D., II, 235; Minhaj, 484 n.
[26] Minhaj, 487 n.
[27] Barani, 384; Lal, *Khaljis*, 290.

the highest 2000 *tankahs*. Slaves in Hindustan were cheap during the Khalji period because of the price-control of Alauddin Khalji and also because coined money was in short supply. So that, writes Ziyauddin Barani, "a camel could be had for a *dang* (small copper coin), but wherefore the *dang* ?"[28] In view of this some sort of barter should have been practised.

Low Price of Indian Slaves

Ziyauddin Barani reckons regulations regarding sale of "horses, slaves and quadrupeds" under one category. T.P. Hughes quoting the *Hidayah* says that slaves, male and female, are treated merely as articles of merchandise, and "very similar rules apply both to the sale of animals and bondsmen."[29] A milch buffalo cost 10-12 *tankahs*; a working girl was cheaper. The price of a good quality horse was 90-120 *tankahs*, that of a *ghulam* was 100 on an average. A handsome boy could be had for 20 to 30 *tankahs*.[30] It is therefore a matter of some satisfaction that under the Khaljis the value of humans in terms of price was not less than that of horses and buffaloes.

The contemporary chronicler Barani boasts that the cheapness of prices in Alauddin's time was not witnessed after his reign.[31] But the trend towards low prices was universal and spread over a long period. Writing about the days of Sultan Muhammad bin Tughlaq (1325-51), Shihabuddin Al-Umari writes: "The Sultan never ceases to show the greatest zeal in making war upon the infidels... Every day thousands of slaves are sold at a very low price, so great is the number of prisoners... (that) the value at Delhi of a young slave girl, for domestic service, does not exceed eight *tankahs*. Those who are deemed fit to fill the parts of domestic and concu-

[28] Barani, 312.
[29] *Dictionary of Islam*, 598.
[30] Barani, 314-15.
[31] Ibid., 312; Farishtah, I, 113.

bine sell for about fifteen *tankahs*. In other cities prices are still lower..." Probably it was so because Ibn Battuta while in Bengal says that a pretty *Kaniz* (slave girl) could be had there for one gold *dinar* (or 10 silver *tankahs*). "I purchased at this price a very beautiful slave girl whose name was Ashura. A friend of mine also bought a young slave named Lulu for two gold coins."[32] It is very difficult to establish a relationship between the prices of Delhi market and those of the provinces. Umari continues, "but still, in spite of low price of slaves, 20000 *tankahs*, and even more, are paid for young Indian girls. I inquired the reason... and was told that these young girls are remarkable for their beauty, and the grace of their manners."[33]

The cheapness of price of young slaves is indirectly attested to by Ibn Battuta also. Such was their influx that at one place he writes, "Once there arrived in Delhi some female infidel captives, ten of whom the Vazir sent to me. I gave one of them to the man who had brought them... My companion took three young girls, and I do not know what happened to the rest."[34] Thousands of slaves were captured in the minor yearly campaigns of Firoz Tughlaq and obviously sold, for, says the contemporary chronicler Shams Siraj Afif that "in places which are sacked and looted the captives are selected as per royal regulations. Those fit for royal service (alone) are sent to the court."[35] The others were sold. It was under such a system that one of Firoz's slaves Bashir Sultani could buy with money 4,000 slaves (*mal kharida*) for his personal service.[36]

From the fifteenth century onwards, we have some more information about the sale of slaves and their prices at home and abroad. Babur writes in his Memoirs that "there are two

---

[32] Battuta, Mahdi Husain, 235; *Quaunah Turks*, 155 n.
[33] *Masalik-ul-Absar*, E.D., III, 580-81.
[34] Battuta, 123, also 63.
[35] Afif, 267-68, also 119-20.
[36] Ibid., 444.

trade-marts on the land-route between Hindustan and Khurasan; one is Kabul, the other, Qandhar. (Route to Kabul was from Lahore, to Qandhar from Multan)... Down to Kabul every year ...from Hindustan, come every year caravans... bringing slaves (*barda*)" and other commodities, and sell them at great profit. "In Kabul can be had the products of Khurasan, Rum, Iraq and Chin (China); *while it is Hindustan's own market* (emphasis added)." There was also barter prevailing with regard to the disposal of slaves. For example, William Finch writing at Agra in about 1610 says that "in hunting the men of the jungle were on the same footing as the beasts" and whatever was taken in the game was the king's *shikar*, whether men or beasts. "Men remain the King's slaves which he sends yearly to Kabul to barter for horses and dogs." Many other writers tell it besides Finch.[37] Barter was in vogue not only in the days of Jahangir but it was practised throughout the medieval period.

The Ain-i-Akbari

The *Ain-i-Akbari* and other similar works giving data about the wages of servants and labourers, in consequence indirectly giving the value of slaves as a market commodity. W.H. Moreland observes that some of the men employed on various works were free, while others were slaves, but the functions assigned to the two classes were to a great extent interchangeable and, therefore, for our purpose it is relevant to treat them as a single group, and the price of slaves may be estimated on the basis of wages paid to the free labourer. In Mughal India, in the reign of Akbar (sixteenth century), and as seen by Bernier (seventeenth century), "Freemen were hired at rates which sufficed for a little more than a bare existence.... a servant with no special qualifications cost about 1 1/2 rupees monthly at Akbar's court, and perhaps 2

[37] *Babur Nama*, I, 202, emphasis added. Finch in Foster, *Early Travels*, 154; Moreland, *India at the Death of Akbar*, 27-28n.

on the west coast... Pyrard puts the price of a slave-girl at the equivalent of about 50 rupees in Goa, which was a very busy market for such commodities, but the rate must have varied between very wide limits, depending as it did partly on the qualities of the individual and partly on fluctuations in the supply."[38] This price of 40 to 50 rupees for a slave paid by the English was the average, "the earlier reference shows that the Dutch demand had raised prices to about this level from the former standard of Rs. 15 to 20."[39] The wages of free men, that is, labourers and not slaves, were equally low. But the proportion of slaves, who were valued as property, was more considerable than that of servants, who can be computed only as an expense. It was more to the interest of rulers, nobles, merchants and manufactures to purchase than to hire their workmen. In the countryside, slaves were employed as the cheapest and most laborious instruments of agriculture. But medieval slavery was more necessary for urban service. So rural populations were made captives and brought for work in cities. Rural slaves and servants were not bought on the market but reproduced themselves through demographic increase. In the cities themselves there was no dearth of them. Pelsaert and so many other foreigners noted that men stood in the market to be hired and "most of the great lords reckon 40 days to the month, and pay from 3 to 4 rupees for that period."[40] "Akbar sanctioned the following daily wages for workers and artisans — 2 *dams* (copper coins, 140 to the *Rupia*) for ordinary labourers, 3 to 4 *dams* for superior labourers, 3 to 7 *dams* for carpenters and 5 to 7 *dams* for builders."[41] In several instances the lowest grades of servants were entitled to less than two rupees monthly, "while the bulk of the menials and of the ordinary foot-sol-

[38] Moreland, *India at the Death of Akbar*, 87, 90.
[39] Moreland, *From Akbar to Aurangzeb*, 77 n.; Mukerjee, *Economic History*, 75-76.
[40] Pelsaert, *Jahangir's India*, 62.
[41] Lal, *Legacy*, 292. The wages given by Abul Fazl have been indicated by Blochmann in shillings and pence and changed by Moreland into Rupia and dams. *Ain.*, 235-36; Moreland, *India at the Death of Akbar*, 191.

diers began at less than three rupees... The minimum for subsistence at the Court is probably marked by the lowest grade of slaves who were allowed one dam daily, equivalent to three-quarters of a rupee monthly in the currency of the time... These instances appear to justify the conclusion that early in the seventeenth century foreigners could secure capable servants for somewhere about three rupees a month. What this represents in real wages is uncertain (but) the rates struck the Europeans as extraordinarily low..."[42]

The inescapable conclusion deduced from the wages of labourers and applied to the prices of slaves is that these were very low throughout. There are not many references available about the actual price of slaves and therefore this section is closed with the information that "in the month of November (1947), Hindu and Sikh girls brought by Pathan raiders from Kashmir were sold in the bazars of ghulam,"[43] for rupees 10 or so each in the wake of the partition of the country, 1947-48.

Import of foreign slaves

As compared to Hindu slaves, who were often captured and sold in droves, the price of foreign slaves was high. They used to be Muslims, were always considered as talented, and in some cases essentially an item of luxury. Foreign slaves were purchased from merchants coming from lands beyond the river Sindh for as much as 500 to 1000 dinars. Both in the *Hidayah* and the *Fatawa-i-Alamgiri* the price of a slave repeatedly mentioned, although in the form of examples, is mostly 1000 dirhams.[44] For example Qutbuddin Aibak purchased two accomplished Turkish slaves for one lakh *jitals* or 2,000 *tankahs* (at 48-50 copper *jitals* to one silver *tankah*).

---

[42] Moreland, *India at the Death of Akbar*, 192-93.

[43] S.Gurbachan Singh Talib, *Muslim League Attack on Sikhs and Hindus in the Punjab 1947*, New Delhi, Reprint 1991 (first published 1950), 201. Also 80.

[44] *Ashraf-ul-Hidayah*, Deoband, VIII, 13, 228, 232; *Hedaya*, Hamiltion, II, 187; *Fatawa-i-Alamgiri*, Deoband XII, 30, 67.

Similarly, Iltutmish purchased Qamaruddin Timur Khan for 50,000 *jitals* or 1000 *tankahs*.[45] And the transaction was concluded after great haggling and bargaining. In this context the sale of Iltutmish to Qutbuddin Aibak makes an interesting and instructive reading. As seen earlier, a slave merchant Jamaluddin Muhammad had brought Iltutmish to Ghazni to sell him to Sultan Muizzuddin. "At that period, no Turk superior to him in comeliness, commendable qualities... intelligence and sagacity, had they brought to that capital." The Sultan inquired about his price. The merchants or their brokers mentioned the price of two slaves together — one Iltutmish and another Ibak, as the "sum of a thousand *dinars* of pure Rukni gold for each." But the merchant Jamaluddin Muhammad declined to sell Shamsuddin for that amount. An angry Sultan then commanded that no one should purchase him, and that the sale should be prohibited. Jamaluddin Muhammad took Iltutmish back to Bukhara, which was a renowned centre of slave trade in the Middle Ages.[46] When he returned to Ghazni after four or five years, Qutbuddin Aibak showed an inclination to buy Iltutmish and requested Muizuddin for permission to do so. The Sultan replied: "Since a command has been issued that he should not be purchased at Ghaznin, let them take him to the city of Delhi and there he can be purchased." The merchant accordingly brought him to Delhi and Iltutmish and the other slave were bought by Qutbuddin Aibak for the sum of one hundred thousand *jitals*.[47]

Haggling and bargaining was possible in individual cases. In bulk purchases price was settled for the whole lot at one go. Merchants from Turkey, Syria, Persia and Transoxiana used to approach Muslim kings with their consignments.[48] Foreign slaves of both sexes were in great demand

[45] Minhaj, 601-603.
[46] *Camb. History of Islam*, I, 482.
[47] Minhaj, 599-603; Farishtah, I, 64-66.
[48] C.H.I., IV, 104.

in India. Males were needed for heavy duties, females for concubinage and keeping surveillance on other harem inmates. Niccolao Manucci writes that when in 1661-62 an embassy was sent by the king of Balkh, "the envoys brought several Tartar and Uzbeg women with them for sale. Aurangzeb purchased some of them. They were placed in the list of numerous Kashgar, Qalmaq, Pathan and Abyssinian women. They were chosen because they are warlike and skilful in the use of lance, arrow and sword,"[49] and therefore could serve as efficient guards of the harem. For concubinage fair women from East European countries were preferred. For example, Udaipuri-Mahall, the concubine of Aurangzeb, was a Georgian slave girl.

Importation of foreign slaves went on right up to the eighteenth century. In the fifteenth century, the Ottoman capture of Constantinople in 1453 gradually diverted the immense flow of slaves from the Crimea, the Balkans and the steppes of western Asia to Islamic markets. Later on, the southward expansion of Russia, culminating in the annexation of Crimea in 1783, gradually shut off the supply of white slaves to the Islamic markets. As Africa became almost synonymous with slavery, the world forgot the eagerness with which Tatars and other Black Sea peoples had sold millions of Ukrainians, Georgians, Circassians, Armenians, Bulgarians, Slavs and Turks.[50] In Africa, in the nineteenth century in the Sudan region there were farms that specialized in breeding black slaves for sale like cattle or sheep. Other enterprising merchants in upper Egypt reaped large capital gains by purchasing prepubescent boys at a price of about three hundred piastres apiece, having them castrated by Coptic monks, and then selling them as eunuchs for one thousand piastres each.[51] "Islamic civilization did indeed

---

[49] Manucci, II, 42-43.
[50] Bernier, 134-36; 144-45; 426.
[51] David Brion Davis, in his review of Bernard Lewis's *Race and Slavery in the Middle East* in *The New York Review*, October 11, 1990.

practise castration of slaves on an unprecedented scale. Several cities in Africa were real factories of eunuchs; they were an expensive commodity as only 25% of the victims survived the operation."[52] In short, black or white, castrated or otherwise, the price of foreign slaves was high as, besides other factors, it also covered the cost of their transportation.

Slavery was recognised by Prophet Muhammad. It was considered lawful in Islam. Regular trade in slaves began with the Ummayad Caliph Muawiya.[53] In the days of the Abbasid Caliphs it gained in impetus and extent. Slave trade spread so rapidly that no one was safe from being enslaved in the heyday of Muslim power, and black and white slaves were traded throughout the Muslim world. Brigandage was commonly resorted to in order to obtain slaves. "The *Hudud al-Alam* (a tenth century Persian document) describes the Sudan (the land south of the desert separating it from the Maghreb) as follows: no region is more populated than this. The merchants steal children there and take them away. They castrate them and take them to Egypt, where they sell them. *Among them [the Sudanese] there are people who steal each other's children to sell them to the merchants* when they come."[54] Turks, Negroes, Ethiopians, Abyssinians, Berbers, Slavs and many others were sold in "thousands". White slaves were costlier than the black. Egypt and Syria supplied a large number of them and Italian ports formed transit points for export. In the tenth century the most valuable commodity that was carried from Volga to Central Asia was slaves. They were brought to the Oxus region, more particularly Samarkand. There the best were put in the market for sale,[55] and the trade was very profitable.

T.W. Arnold's observations on this slave-taking in East European and African countries is relevant in the Indian con-

---

[52] Elst, *Indigenous Indians*, 375.
[53] Ameer Ali, *The Spirit of Islam*, 267.
[54] Claude Mellasoux, *The Anthorpology of Slavery*, 143.
[55] Ruben Levy, *An Introduction to the Sociology of Islam*, I, 117-18.

text. He writes that "though the lot of many of the Christian captives was very pitiable one, others who held positions in the households of private individuals, were often no worse off than domestic servants in the rest of Europe. As organised by the Muhammadan Law, slavery was robbed of many of its harshest features, nor in Turkey at least does it seem to have been accompanied by such barbarities and atrocities as in the pirate states of Northern Africa.... The condition of the Christian captives naturally varied with the circumstances of their own capabilities of adapting themselves to a life of hardship; the aged, the priests and monks, and those of noble birth suffered most, while the physician and the handicraftsman received more considerate treatment from their masters, as being servants that best repaid the money spent on them. The galley slaves naturally suffered most of all." In East Africa the Arabs were "given up wholly to the pursuit of commerce or to slaves-hunting.... Naturally the feeling of both chiefs and people was hostile to the Muhammadans, who were hated and feared as slave-dealers."[56] For the Muslims, on the other hand, slaves were stolen through acts of violence and then converted into commodities. "Slave is the most fundamental form of property."[57]

Slave trade was carried on both by sea and land routes. Import of slaves from Africa and Western Asia was of substantial importance. "In the centuries preceding the year 1500 Arabs and Persians had acquired a position of predominance in the sea-borne trade of the whole of Indian Ocean from Mozambique to the Straits of Malacca."[58] They had settlements at seaports on both sides of India, and we meet with Muslims at practically every Indian seaport. One of the commodities in which they traded was slaves. They sold these slaves to Indian rulers and nobles in such large numbers that

---

[56] Arnold, *Preaching of Islam* , 172-73, 345-46.
[57] Meillassoux, *The Anthropology of Slavery,* 8.
[58] Moreland, *India at the Death of Akbar* , 23-26.

the complexion of the government looked foreign. Indian sultans imported slaves throughout the medieval period for service in many fields, more particularly in administration and army and saving their kingdoms from indigenous popular risings, for, as Moreland remarks, even "Akbar's court was essentially foreign, and even in his later years the Indian element, whether Hindu or Moslem, constituted only a small proportion of the whole."[59] Abyssinians were in much demand, and we read of them frequently in the chronicles of the times. A regular traffic existed in the inhabitants of Mozambique, and there was also an import trade from Persia and countries lying beyond. Not only the sultans of Delhi or the Mughal emperors, but even the sultans of the Deccan states imported slaves to keep their rule established. Golkunda was connected with three great ports of Goa and Surat on the west coast and Masulipatam on the east.[60]

For northern India, the land route was equally important if not more. There were slave markets in all important Muslim cities in the medieval world. It may be pertinent to recollect that Subuktigin had been purchased by Alptigin at Bukhara and Qutbuddin Aibak had been purchased by Qazi Abdul Aziz Kufi in the slave market of Nishpur. All rulers of Delhi and Agra used to import foreign slaves. Sultan Shamsuddin Iltutmish once sent a Muslim merchant to Samarqand, Bukhara and Tirmiz to bring some slaves from those places. The trader purchased for the Sultan one hundred slaves and Balban was one of them. Chinese traders also once brought forty slaves and presented them to the Sultan. The list of Shamsi slaves given by Minhaj Siraj mostly comprised purchased slaves.[61]

[59] Ibid., 24.
[60] R.K.Mukerjee, *Economic History of India* , 99 and map facing 110.
[61] Minhaj, 213-324; Isami, *Adi Turk Kalin Bharat*, 302; Battuta, 171; Moreland, *The Agrarian System of Moslem India;* 217-18.

Internal Trade

In India the Muslims established a number of slave trade centres. Besides Delhi and cities in Bengal there is mention of Badaon in Uttar Pradesh and Mandor in Rajasthan.[62] But of course from the narrative of the chroniclers it appears that slave markets existed in almost all important places in the country, for slaves were also sold in fairs held in major cities. In this inhuman business the Hindus were not interested. Firstly, they were themselves at the receiving end, they themselves were the victims. And secondly, as W.H. Moreland points out, "We may infer from della Valle's statements that the principal Hindus at Surat — perhaps the most humane people that ever lived — disapproved entirely of slavery." Now few people are as good traders as Gujaratis. They would have excelled if they had taken to slave-trading. But catching and selling of slaves did not fit in with the Hindu psyche. Although, commenting on the statement of della Valle, Moreland says, "but I do not think that this remark can be extended to Hindus generally... though in Akbar's time at least it did not secure the approval of all Hindus.... The existence of slavery is testified to by the travellers Abdur Razak, Conti and Barbosa."[63] It would be safe to presume that it prevailed in the Deccan, because it prevailed farther north in the country whence the Deccan dynasties had sprung and we may believe Nikitin's statement that in his time there was a trade in 'Black people' in Bidar."[64] But the trade was carried on by Muslims and not Hindus, for Moreland adds that in 1643, "a Nayak, or chief, rejected a Dutch request for leave to buy up to 1000 slaves yearly on the ground that the sale of human being was not only a scandal but a sin."[65] All accounts point to the fact that Hindus, otherwise great traders

[62] Minhaj, 232, 237, 268; Battuta, 325.

[63] Major 29, 30, 31; Barbosa, 309, 358; della Valle, 157, as cited by Moreland, *India at the Death of Akbar*, 91.

[64] Moreland, *India at the Death of of Akbar*, 91.

[65] Moreland, *From Akbar to Aurangzeb*, 79.

and merchants throughout India's history, did not indulge in slave trade.

But the Portuguese in this matter followed the custom of the Muslims. "Linschoten recorded that they never worked, but employed slaves, who were sold daily in the market like beasts, and della Valle notes that the 'greatest part' of people in Goa were slaves."[66] The Portuguese not only employed Indian slaves for domestic and other duties, but they also regularly brought slaves from Abyssinia and Mozambique for sale at good price in Goa and Surat. They dominated the Indian seas where they pirated non-chalantly, captured slaves and sold them in the markets of Hugli, Tamluk, Pipli, St. Thome, Ceylon and Goa. Pyrard (1608-11) observed that goods of all the world must pass Ormuz and pay tribute to the Portuguese.[67] It so happened that their Governor in Hugli, Manoel Travers, infuriated Shahjahan when as a prince, he was in rebellion and in a helpless position. Travers seized some of the prince's richly laden boats and carried away some of Mumtaz Mahall's slave girls. When Shahjahan became king he ordered the Mughal governor of Bengal to chastise the Portuguese. After a sanguinary battle on the famous river port Hugli in 1632 they were expelled from Bengal.[68] As a matter of fact the people of India hailed the other European adventurers as liberators from Portuguese tyranny, their forcible conversions and their obnoxious slave trade.[69]

The Dutch also indulged in slave trade. In this regard the views of Coen, the great Dutch Governor-General, are worth noting. In 1623, he advised his successor, not merely the prosecution of Asiatic trade, "but the investment of all available capital in principal means of production ('many thousands of slaves')... so that the returns for our native country be made out of the gains of the inland trade and the ordinary

---

66 Moreland, *India at the Death of Akbar*, 91.
67 R.K.Mukerjee, *Economic History of India*, 116; C.H.I. IV, 191.
68 Lahaori, E.D., VII, 31-35, 42-43; Manucci, I, 182; Bernier, 177; C.H.I., IV, 192.
69 Mukerjee, op.cit., 103.

revenues".[70] From about 1620 the Dutch requirements from India were, first, a large initial supply of slaves, and then a steady stream of reinforcements to make good the losses. For example, Dutch families in the Spice Islands needed a sufficient number of slaves, "mostly of Indian origin" besides those who had experience of working on the spice fields. Many imported slaves, "Bengalders, Arakandars, Malabars, etc.," were greatly affected by sickness owing to the change of climate on arrival in the Islands and losses had to be made up. "There is nothing to suggest that the Dutch merchants practised either force or fraud, and we find them buying regularly from Indian dealers after obtaining the permission of the authorities."[71] In 1661 a ship belonging to the Sultan of Golkunda carried 300 slaves to Achin and slave trade was regarded by Muslims as well as the Dutch, "precisely as any other branch of commerce".[72]

The Portuguese and the Dutch were followed by the British. The export of slaves and indentured Indian labour by the British to various parts of the British Empire when it was in the making, is beyond the scope of this study. But the genesis of endeavours and achievements of the European nations in the field of making and exporting Indian slaves was a continuation of the practice by the Muslims in medieval times. It is even said that the profits accruing to the Muslims from slave trade tempted many foreign nations to join in the race. However, in contrast to the foreign imported slaves, whose market price was rendered high by cost of transportation and deaths in transit, the price of Hindu slaves, sold abroad remained low. For example, Hindu Kush (Hindu-killer) mountain is so named because thousands of enslaved Hindus died in crossing it. But their numbers were so large that the price of survivors remained low in foreign markets.

---

[70] Moreland, *From Akbar to Aurangzeb*, 63.
[71] Ibid., 77.
[72] Ibid., 79.

Chapter XI
RULES REGARDING MANUMISSION AND SALE OF SLAVES

It has been seen in the preceding pages that a very prominent feature of Muslim polity, society and economy in this country was its slave system. Muslim history throughout the country and indeed in this world is incomplete without its slaves. The two main sources of obtaining slaves were by capture and purchase. The two main means of their disposal were by manumission and sale. We shall here briefly discuss the problems and rules associated with these two aspects.

Manumission of slaves was a pre-Islamic Arab custom for earning religious merit. It was recommended by prophet Muhammad also. His advice finds mention in both the Quran and the Hadis. Manumission was widely practised in India for various reasons and causes. For instance, many are the blessings to those who fast during Ramzan, but if neglected intentionally the offender must expiate his guilt by the manumission of one male slave *(ghulam)* for every day that he broke the fast.[1] Or, when the emperor Shahjahan was ill, his daughter liberated several slaves, made them walk round her father, and then sent them away to carry his infirmities with them.[2] It is not mentioned whether these slaves were just sent away or released according to the rules of manumission, but since Islam is stickler about rules, it is probable that appropriate procedure was followed while freeing them.

After the compilation of the Quran and the Hadises, many schools of jurisprudence developed with many manuals of commentaries and interpretations on these two main source-scriptures. Named after their founders Abu Hanifa (c. 699-767), Abu Abdulla Muhammad bin Idris (c. 767-820),

[1] Herklots, *Islam in India,* 112.
[2] Manucci, I, 217. Also Meer Hassan Ali, *Observations,* 215.

Ahmad bin Hanbal (c. 780-855) and Malik bin Anas (715-795). and called the Hanafi, Sha'afai, Hanbali and Maliki, the four famous schools of Islamic jurisprudence developed in the eighth-ninth century. In the twelfth century Shaikh Burhanuddin Ali (530-593 H/1135-1196 C.E.) of Marghinan in Transoxiana wrote the famous *Hidayah* or the Guide, a well-known work of Sunni law. It is based on the Quran, the Hadis and the four schools of Muslim Jurisprudence mentioned above. Throughout medieval India Muslim Ulema, jurisconsults and judges (Qazis) depended on these scriptures and law books for deciding cases about slaves. Besides, during Muslim rule, spreading over several centuries, numerous judgements, *Zawabits* (Regulations) and commentaries appeared concerning matters of law and were referred to as precedents. Their large numbers were bound to create confusion and sometimes lead to decisions convenient or otherwise to particular parties and situations. Emperor Aurangzeb therefore decided to consolidate the main canons of Sunni law in one book. This resulted in the coming into being of his voluminous magnum opus entitled the *Fatawa-i-Alamgiri*. Bakhtawar Khan, a nobleman of Aurangzeb's court, has this to say about the *Fatawa-i-Alamgiri*. "As it is a great object with this Emperor that all Muhammadans should follow the principles of the religion as expounded by the most competent law officers and the followers of the Hanafi persuasion and as these principles, in consequence of the different opinions of the *kazis* and *muftis* which have been delivered without any authority, could not be distinctly and clearly learnt, and as there was no book which embodied them all.... His Majesty, the protector of the faith, determined that a body of eminently learned and able men of Hindustan should take up the voluminous and the most trustworthy works which were collected in the royal library, and having made a digest of them, compose a book which might form a standard canon of the law, and afford to all an easy and available means of ascertaining the proper and authoritative interpretation. The chief conductor of this difficult undertaking was the most learned man of the time, Shaikh Nizam, and all the members of the society were handsomely paid, so that up to the present time (early years of the reign) a sum of about two hundred thousand rupees has been expended in this valuable compilation, which contains more than one hundred thousand lines. When the work, with God's pleasure, is completed, it will be for all the world the standard exposition of the law, and render every one independent of Muhammadan doctors."[3]

Fatawa-i-Alamgiri thus forms the most important source book for Muslim law in India. It was compiled in the later Mughal period, gathering information from books and judgements of Qazis through all the centuries of Muslim rule. And more importantly it was written in Indian environment. Besides citing from the treatises and scriptures from the Quran to the *Hidayah*, it quotes as its sources almost all great authorities like Imam Abu Hanifa, Imam Abu Yusuf, Imam Muhammad, Imam Karkhi, Fatawas of Qazi Khan, *Fateh-ul-Qadiri, Sharah Ziadat-ul Utabi, Akhtiyar-i-Sharai Mukhtiyar, Muhit-i-Surkhi,* etc., etc. The *Hidayah* and the *Fatawa-i-Alamgiri* thus form the most authentic volumes for the study of Muslim slavery in medieval India. Its corpus deals with all aspects of Muslim law concerning the life of Muslims including the two aspects under discussion — upkeep and manumission, sale and purchase of slaves — in great detail.[4]

[3] *Mirat-i-Alam* also known as *Mirat-i-Jahan Numa,* E. D., VII, 159-60.

[4] We have depended on two versions of the *Hidayah*: 1. The Urdu translation done at Deoband by Maulana Jamil Ahmad Sukrodvi, Muddaris of Dar-ul-Ulum; it is entitled *Ashraful Hidayah*. It was published in 1980s, only vols. 1 to 5 and 8 to 9 were available to us. 2. The English translation of the work done by Charles Hamilton in 4 vols. in 1791; it is entitiled "*The Hedaya* (or Guide) — A commentary on the Mussulman laws". Hamilton gives a valuable Discourse, iii-Lxxxviii, and an Introductory Address, ix-xii, at the beginning of vol. I.

There are two Urdu translations of *Fatawa-i-Alamgiri*. The one by Allama Maulana Syed Amir Ali and publilshed by Hamid & Co Delhi in 10 vols. in 1988 is very well printed and beautifully bound. The other has been done by Maulana Mufti Kafi-ul-Rahman of Deoband. It is printed in 42 parts of about 100 pages each. The years of publication are not given. The translation of Deoband has been found to be better than that of Delhi in many ways.

Manumission

Rules regarding manumission of slaves are given in the *kitab al-'Ataq*, and about sale in *kitab al-Biyu'*. But there is no book or chapter whether on *Nikah* (marriage) or *Talaq* (divorce), barter or oath, sale or purchase, mortgage or transfer of property, offspring and progeny, in which slaves or slave girls do not find a prominent and lengthy mention.[5] This only shows that Muslim society was incomplete without slaves and the slave system permeated every sphere of Muslim life.

Manumission is of four kinds —*wajib* (obligatory), *mubah* or *halal*), in accordance with Shara), *Mustahaj* (a pious act), and *Haram* (prohibited). Manumission can be done orally or in writing, but it has to be done in accordance with rules and in proper form and proper words. Captured slaves, if kafirs, could not be freed.[6] To be kafir is a disqualification (*aib*) both in *ghulam* (male slave) and *bandi* (female slave). The Muslim detests the company of kafirs "because the object, in the purchase of a female slave, is cohabitation and generation of children."[7] T.P. Hughes on the authority of the *Hidayah* says: "The Imam, with respect to captives, has it in his choice to slay them because the Prophet put captives to death and also because slaying them terminates wickedness; or, if he choose, he may make them slaves, because by enslaving them the wickedness of them is remedied, and at the same time the Muslims reap an advantage; or, if he please, he may release them so as to make them freemen and Zimmis... but it is not lawful so to release the idolaters of Arabia, or apostates... If captives become Muslims, let not the Imam put them to death; ... but yet he may lawfully make them slaves, after their conversion..."[8] But kafir *ghulam* was not all useless. He could do work which was *infra dig* or

---

[5] *Fatawa-i-Alamgiri* , Delhi trs. by Amir Ali, II, 125-277; 278=620. IV, 195-544.
[6] *Fatawa-i-Alamgiri* , XII, 5-8.
[7] *Hedaya* , Hamilton, II, 409.
[8] Hughes, 597.

prohibited for Muslims.[9] Once a slave converts, there is provision for his freedom. If a slave apostatizes, he cannot be freed until he returns to Islam. "An exposition of the faith is to be laid before an apostate; who, if he repent not within *three days* is put to death." A female slave or free woman who apostatizes is not to be killed, but she "must be daily beaten with severity until she return to the faith."[10] A Musalman slave, purchased by an infidel, becomes free after entering an infidel territory. The slave of an infidel, upon becoming Musalman, acquires the right to freedom.[11]

A recognised method of getting manumission was through the custom of *tadbir*. It was so called when a master told his slave, "you are free after my death." After this declaration a slave was known as *mudabbir*. A slave who was declared *mudabbir* by this master stood manumitted after the death of the latter. It appears that there was keenness on the part of the master, when he had grown old, to grant freedom to the slave. But the bondsman, also grown old, did not necessarily care to seek freedom in declining age. Grant of manumission in advanced age was more beneficial to the master than to the slave. The former could get rid of him; the latter could hardly find a buyer who would look after him at the fag end of his life. Slaves who were captured or purchased young, sometimes so young as to wet their beds — and there is mention of such cases in Islamic law books[12] — would have felt relieved at their being declared *mudabbir*. They could have enjoyed their freedom because they might be still young when the master died. But most *mudabbirs* used to grow old in the service of the owner, in all probability too old to be bought and usefully employed by a new master. Therefore *mudabbiri* held no charm for him. He could have some hope if the master died early. He some-

---

[9] *Ashraful Hidayah,* Deoband, VIII, 138-39.
[10] *Hedaya,* Hamilton, II, 225-26, 228.
[11] *Ibid.*, 190-91.
[12] *Ashraful Hidayah* , Deoband, VIII, 134.

times wished it to be so, and initiated or joined in a conspiracy to remove the master from the scene while he was still young. For this he would have cultivated the habits of exhibiting loyalty outwardly and practising hypocrisy by secretly harbouring hostility. But loyal or disloyal, old and incapacitated slaves were generally done away with by the new king or master. On the other hand, old slaves were also reluctant to join the new distrusting dispensation. As seen earlier, medieval Muslim society and polity is full of such cases.

There was provision for partial manumission of a slave in Islamic law. For instance, a slave could be exempted from doing a particular type of work from a specific date.[13] A slave could be freed to the extent of one-half, one-third, or one-sixth. That is, if he is made one-third free, he will repay two-third of his price for getting total manumission.[14] If the slave was shared by two masters, rules of manumission were different in his case.[15] The slave on emancipation becomes *atiq* (freed man) or *mawla* (client) of his late master, who becomes his *wali* (patron).[16] Slaves cannot marry without the consent of the proprietor.[17] A master can permit a slave to marry more than one wife, but not more than two wives at the same time, according to most of the doctors.[18] Marriage between slaves with the consent of the master is valid. If contracted without his permission, it is null.[19] The marriage of an infidel couple is not dissolved by their jointly joining the faith. If only one of them converts, a separation takes place automatically.[20] Apostates are incapacitated from marrying.[21] If either the father or the mother be Musalman their children

[13] *Hedaya*, Hamilton, I, 422-23; *Fatawa-i-Alamgiri*, Deoband, XII, 11-12.
[14] Hamilton, I, 437; *Fatawa-i-Alamgiri*, Deoband, XIII, 10, 20-21; *Ibid.*, Delhi, VI, 445.
[15] *Ashraful Hidayah*, VIII, 104.
[16] Reuben Levy. *An Introduction to the Sociology of Islam*, I, 116.
[17] Hamilton, I, 161.
[18] *Fatwa-i-Alamgiri*, Deoband; Hughes, 600. VII, 34.
[19] Ibid., Delhi, II, 243 ff.
[20] *Hidaya*, Hamilton, I, 174-76.
[21] Ibid., 176.

become Musalman invariably.[22]

Every slave girl could be used as a concubine. As quoted from the *Hedayah* earlier, "the object in the purchase of a female slave, is cohabitation and generation of children." Therefore for our purpose words like slave girl (*bandi)* and concubine should be considered synonymous.[23] In a *bandi* physical fitness, correct menstruation and absence of physical and mental defects were the main considerations at the time of purchase. Odour in the mouth or armpits of a *bandi* was considered a defect as she was meant to be kissed and caressed, but not so in a *ghulam* who was required to do manual work.[24] Bernard Lewis quotes many Muslims who describe blacks as "ugly, stupid, dishonest, frivolous and foul-smelling" and black women with the same epithets — "the blacker they are, the uglier their faces... there is no pleasure to be got from them, because of the smell of their armpits and the coarseness of their bodies." Similarly, a blind, half-blind, squinted, deaf or dumb *bandi* or one having extra or less fingers was considered defective. If the breasts are large or vagina wide or baggy (which does not give requisite pleasure), whether in a *bakira* (virgin) or a *taiba* (non-virgin), the purchaser has a right to return her to the seller and claim refund of money.[25] A desire to do a little make-up, speak or walk daintily is excusable, but too much sexiness, deliberate lowering of voice, blandishments and walking with a provocative gait or swaying the hips are definite defects in a slave girl.[26] In short, whoredom and bastardy is not desirable in a slave girl; it was not considered so bad in a *ghulam* unless it was so excessive as to interfere with his normal duties.[27]

The sale of an *am-walad* (mother of child), that is, a

---

[22] Ibid., 177.
[23] *Fatawa-i-Alamgiri*, Deoband, XII, 14-15.
[24] *Ashraful Hidayah*, VIII, 137; *Hedaya*, Hamilton, II, 408.
[25] *Fatawa-i-Alamgiri*, Deoband, XXIV, 5-6, 26-27.
[26] *Ibid* ., 7.
[27] *Ashraful Hidayah*, Deoband, VIII, 138; *Hedaya*, Hamilton, II, 409.

slave girl who conceives from her master and gives birth to a child, is 'null' and therefore wrong. The offspring of the master by a slave girl was considered to be free. The woman also gained in status through *istawad*, that is, right of the child. Henceforth the slave girl was called *am-walad* and used to become free after the death of her master. As the Prophet has said, "Her child hath set her free" (that is, her child is a cause of freedom to her). So an *am-walad* cannot be sold as she is free upon the master's death.[28] It is also not correct to lend, mortgage, or give on wages an *am-walad* slave girl, but if some stranger shares bed with her, the income is of the master. If he marries her off to someone, the amount of *mehr* (dower) also belongs to the master. To give her in marriage to a stranger is the right of the master.[29] His control over the *bandi* is total. Parts of the slave girl's body could be freed individually and collectively. If the master told his *bandi* that her *farj* (private part) is free or that her back or neck or head is free, she is freed according to some jurists but not according to others.[30] A master may withhold permission from his female slave to dwell in the house of her husband.[31] If one buys a pregnant *bandi*, the unborn would form part of the transaction. If she is collected in loot then the offspring is also counted as slave together with the mother and counted as property of the master.[32] There are rules laid down to determine if a *bandi* is pregnant at the time of purchase or capture.[33] If the master makes his slave girl *mudabbir*, then her pregnancy and progeny also become *mudabbir*. If the pregnancy alone is manumitted, then only the offspring becomes free, not the *bandi*.[34] Even after a bandi is declared *mudabbir* or free after the master's death

[28] *Hedaya*, Hamilton, I, 479, 482.
[29] *Ashraful Hidayah*, Deoband, XIII, 23.
[30] *Fatawa-i-Alamgiri*, Deoband, XII, 6, 8. Also *Hedaya*, Hamilton, I, 421-23.
[31] *Hedaya*, Hamilton, I, 161.
[32] *Fatawa-i-Alamgiri*, Deoband, XII, 18; XIII, 22.
[33] Ibid., XIII, 12.
[34] *Fatawa-i-Alamgiri*, Deoband, XII, 18, 21; XIII,12.

he can continue to cohabit with her during his life-time.

Sale/Purchase

It may be mentioned at the outset, even at the cost of repetition, that the slave was the property of the master. "The slave forms the most fundamental form of property which, as in the case of every property, is a source of profit."[35] The master is empowered to endow his slave with almost all privileges and responsibilities of freeman, preserving at the same time his property in him inviolate, which rendered him an attached dependent rather than a mere servile instrument.[36] This we have seen being universally practised in the case of early Turkish slaves who were treated well by their master merchants and sold at good profit.

In the *Hidayah,* rules about sale and barter of slaves are mentioned under the category of any other property or commodity like land, trees, clothes, fruit, grain and beasts.[37] The price of a slave depended on physical strength and good looks and such other considerations like if he was shared between two or more masters or a *bandi* was shared between two men.[38] In the case of partnership in a female slave, she becomes the property of the man who has carnal relationship with her with the consent of the other.[39]

There were elaborate rules in this regard so as to avoid contentious sales.[40] For example if a number of slaves were sold out of a big group, those to be taken out were determined by odd or even numbers of the slaves possessed by the seller master.[41] A deception with respect to the sex of the slave invalidates the sale which stands cancelled (*akala*).[42]

---

35 Foreword by Paul E. Lovejoy to Claude Meillassoux, *The Anthropology of Slavery*, 8.
36 *Hedaya*, Hamilton, I, xxxvi.
37 *Ashraful Hidayah,* Deoband, VIII, *kitab-ul-Biyu*,81-83.
38 *Fatawa-i-Alamgiri*, Deoband, XII, 26, 31-33.
39 *Hedaya*, Hamilton, II, 331-32.
40 *Ashraful Hidayah*, VIII, 149, 155-65, 178, 181, 187; Hamilton, II, 386-90, 419-20.
41 *Hidaya,* Hamilton, I, 456-64, 538. *Fatwa-i-Alamgiri,* XV, 57-71.
42 Ibid., 425, 465.

Sale of a *mudabbir*, an *am-walad* or a *mokatib*, is null.[43] A man purchases a slave. He finds some defect in him and beats and tortures him. In case the signs of torture are visible on his person the buyer is not entitled to return him to the seller and receive compensation. If he flogs or slaps him two-three times but there are no signs of such infliction on his body he will have the right to return the slave to the seller.[44] A *ghulam* or *bandi* who has absconded is not to be purchased at any cost but has to be restored to the master. "An absconded slave may, in every instance, be reclaimed by the proprietor."[45] There is a whole set of rules detailed in *Kitab-ul-Abaq* determining action about absconded slaves.[46] Repeated mention of such rules leads to the inference that flight of slaves was not uncommon.[47]

Slaves who could not be broken or made to submit, sometimes took revenge. In most cases they conspired to do away with the master. They could steal or even do such irritating things as soiling the bed by urinating.[48] The all powerful master could strike back mercilessly. "The power which a Muslim possesses over the persons of his bondsman or bondsmaid is unlimited." For example, a master is not slain for the murder of his slave.[49] "Amputation of a slave for theft was a common practice recognized by law."[50] That is how even physically defective and mutilated slaves were put up for sale in the market. If a master killed his *ghulam*, it was taken that the latter had died a natural death.[51] That is why slaves by and large remained loyal to the master and followed the rules laid down for them. For example, when Imadul Mulk Bashir Sultani, the slave noble of Firoz Tughlaq,

---

[43] *Ashraful Hidayah*, VIII, 193-98; Hamilton, II, 468.
[44] *Fatwa-i-Alamgiri*, XXIV, 26.
[45] *Hidaya*, Hamilton, II, 189; *Fatwa-i-Alamgiri*, XXV, 22-31.
[46] *Fatwa-i-Alamgiri*, Delhi, by Amir Ali, III, 485-501.
[47] For example, *Fatwa-i-Alamgiri*, XXIV, 11.
[48] Ibid., 11-13.
[49] Hughes, 599; Hamilton, IV, 282.
[50] *Hidaya*, Hamilton, II, 423-27; *Ashraful Hidayah*, VIII, 178, 181.
[51] *Ashraful Hidayah*, VIII, 149.

became old and decrepit, he first got a letter of manumission for himself written by the Sultan, and only after that he freed his four thousand purchased slaves.[52]

Sale of slaves was so common in medieval India that it is referred to by Persian chroniclers throughout the period. Manumission too was common although it is not mentioned as often. It is a good thing in Islam that there are elaborate rules guiding their lives. There are some hundreds of rules about the treatment and obligations, manumission, sale and purchase of *ghulam* or *bandi*. All transactions were done in accordance with the rules laid down by the Doctors of Islam. But a bad aspect is that the rules went on multiplying and becoming complicated with passage of time. From the eighth to the seventeenth century rules became so numerous and so complicated because of *fatwas* and judgements of Doctors that it became necessary "to afford to all an easy and authoritative interpretation and standard canon" by launching the project *Fatawa-i-Alamgiri*. These rules could take care of all situations, serious or sober or even pornographic.[53] Rules in the *Kitab-ul-Talaq* form an excellent treatise on sex-education. Still a plethora of rules contained contradictions leading to various interpretations. Owners of slaves and the Qazis could do a lot of manipulation in sale and manumission. Naturally, the slave, generally poor and exploited, was at the receiving end against the all-powerful master. For us these rules and laws have an importance of their own. It is on the basis of these historical and legal works compiled by medieval Muslims that an idea of the lives of slaves who could be sold, bartered, lent, mortgaged and used in so many ways, can be formed.

[52] Afif, 444-45.
[53] *Fatwa-i-Alamgiri*, XI, *Kitab-ul-Talaq*, 26-27.

CHAPTER XII
SEX SLAVERY

In the preceding pages it has been seen how women and children were special targets for enslavement throughout the medieval period, that is, during Muslim invasions and Muslim rule. Captive children of both sexes grew up as Muslims and served the sultans, nobles and men of means in various captives. Enslavement of young women was also due to many reasons; their being sex objects was the primary consideration and hence concentration on their captivity.

Psychology regarding Sex

Islam originated in the Arabian peninsula which is by and large stony and sandy. There is no luxuriant herbage, there are no lofty trees or winding rivers. Muhammad used to say that "three things gladden the eye of the gazer: green fields, running water, and fair faces."[1] Since green fields and running water were denied to the medieval Arab, he concentrated on deriving comfort and society mainly in fair faces. This phenomenon became prominent in the course of Islamic history throughout the world.

In the campaigns launched by Muslims, it was easy to capture women, more so after their menfolk had been massacred. The Prophet's one great aim was propagation of his religion and as Margoliouth observes, "Abu Bakr (the chief campaigner for Muhammad's creed) probably was aware that women are more amenable to conversion than men.... slaves than freemen, persons in distress than persons in prosperity and affluence."[2] Women slaves turned concubines could increase Muslim population by leaps and bounds when cap-

---

[1] Margoliouth, *Muhammad,* 149.

[2] Margoliouth, 97. For role of women in spreading Islam see also Arnold, *Preaching of Islam,* 234.

tured in large numbers.[3] Hence there was particular keenness on enslaving women from the very beginning of Islam.

This was also encouraged by the injunctions of the Quran. Muslims are allowed four wives besides they are allowed to cohabit with any of their female slaves. Surah iv:3 says, "Then marry what seem to be good to you of women"; Surah iv:29, "Take what your right hand possesses of young women", and Surah xxxiii:49, "Verily we make lawful for thee what thy right hand possesses out of the booty God hath granted thee." Muslims are allowed to take possession of married women if they are slaves. Surah iv:28 declares, "Unlawful for you are... married women, save such as your right hand possesses", that is, female slaves captured in war. Manucci's observation on the seventeenth century India is significant in this regard. He says that "all Muhammadans are fond of women, who are their principal relaxation and almost their only pleasure."[4]

From the teachings of the Quran quoted above, it will be seen that while Muhammad restricted the number of lawful wives, he did not restrict the number of slave girls and concubines.[5] All female slaves taken as plunder in war are the lawful property of their master, and the master has power to take to himself any female slave married or single. T.P. Hughes adds that "there is absolutely no limit to the number of slave girls with whom a Muhammadan may cohabit, and it is the *consecration* of this illimitable indulgence which so popularizes the Muhammadan religion amongst uncivilized nations, and so popularizes slavery in the Muslim religion".[6]

Then there was the life and thought of the Prophet himself. Muslims try to imitate, as far as possible, the life-style of Muhammad. He is the model, the paradigm of every pious

---

[3] Arnold, 365.
[4] Manucci, II, 240; also 336-338, 391-93. 467; Lal, *The Mughal Harem,* 164 and n. 49, 50, 51.
[5] Hughes, *Dictionary of Islam,* 464.
[6] Ibid., 600.

Muslim.[7] There is nothing unusual in this phenomenon. The followers of Mahavira, Buddha, Christ or Guru Govind Singh live, as far as in them lies, the life that their Masters lived. Their teaching was mostly oral but their words were lovingly collected by devoted men as guides to their own personal conduct. So did the followers of Muhammad collect the *hadises* and tried to imitate his way of life. Company of women had a very important place in Muhammad's life. William Muir writes that "Aisha used to say: 'the Prophet loved three things—women, scents, and food; he had his heart's desire of the two first, but not of the last".[8] This is put by Margoliouth as "the three things about which he cared were scent, women, and prayer..."[9] According to these aphorisms and sayings attributed to the Prophet, the place of women was prominent in his mind, a preoccupancy in his psyche.[10] It is well-known that his matrimonial affairs gave him the means of establishing a princely harem.

Besides the urge of following in his ways, Muhammad's idea of Paradise inspired the Muslims even more in craving for the company of women. The Paradise in the Quran provided "Rest and passive enjoyment; verdant gardens watered by murmuring rivulets, wherein the believers... repose (quaffing) aromatic wine such as the Arabs loved from goblets placed before them or handed round in silver cups replendent as glass by beautiful youths... 'Verily! for the Pious is a blissful abode; Gardens and Vineyards, and damsels with swelling bosoms, of an equal age, and a full cup...' These damsels of Paradise are introduced as '*lovely large-*

[7] A devout Muslim Uwayah Qarni lived in the valley of Urfa. He told Umar and Ali that "when I learnt that a tooth of the Prophet had been martyred (in the Battle of Uhud) I broke one of mine. Then I thought that perhaps some other tooth of his had been martyred. So, I broke all my teeth... It is only after that that I felt at peace" (Shykh Fariduddin Attar, *Tazkirat-ul-Auliya*, trs. into Urdu by Maulana Zubair Afzal Usmani, Delhi, n.d., 16, and quoted by Sita Ram Goel, *Islam vis-a-vis Hindu Temples*, New Delhi, 1993, 59-60).

[8] William Muir, *Life of Mahomet*, 528.

[9] Margoliouth, 148. Also Gibbon, II, 694.

[10] Margoliouth, 351-52; also 449-50 writing on the authority of *Musnud*, iv, 422.

eyed girls resembling pearls hidden in their shells, a reward for that which the faithful have wrought .... 'Verily! we have created them (the houries) of a rare creation; We have made them virgins, fascinating, of an equal age.' "[11]

Abode in such a Paradise of "carnal image", says Gibbon, was the reward of the faithful in the next world. In this world Muhammad encouraged the Muslims to take slave women without restraint. From very "early period Muhammad admitted slave girls to be lawful concubines, besides ordinary wives. Bond-women with whom cohabitation is thus permitted are here specified by the same phrase as was afterwards used for female slaves taken captive in war, or obtained by purchase, viz. '*that which your right hand possesses.*' ...(It was) an inducement to fight in the hope of capturing women who would then be lawful concubines."[12] Margoliouth working with the same scriptural source materials, also avers that "It was then [early years of publicity of Islam] too, that coveting the goods and wives (possessed by Unbelievers) was avowed without discouragement from the Prophet."[13]

Special interest in Sex

In brief, the climatic conditions of Arabia the birth-place of Islam, Muhammad's life-style as a model for Muslims, and injunctions in the Quran and the Hadis, determined Muslim psychology about women. Islam permits polygamy with unbelievable liberality. A man can have four wives at any point of time, that is, if he chooses to have a fifth one, he can divorce one of the already at hand and keep the number within the legal limits of four. Besides, he can have as many slave girls or concubines as he pleases. It is related in the Hadis that Muhammad said that "when the servant of God marries, he perfects half his religion.... Consequently in Islam, even the ascetic orders are rather married than

[11] Quran, Lii.21ff; Lvi.11ff; Lxxviii.31ff. Cited in Muir, 74-75. Hughes, 449.
[12] Muir, 73-74n.; Hughes, 59. Also Gibbon, II, 678.
[13] Margoliouth, 149.

single."[14] In Islam there is provision for temporary marriage (*muta*), multi-marriages, divorce, remarriage of widows, concubinage — in short, there is freedom from all inhibitions and reservations in matters of sex. The insistence is on everybody marrying and celibacy is frowned upon. According to a tradition derived from Ibn Abbas and quoted by Ibn S'ad, popularly known as Katib al-Waqidi the Prophet's biographer, Muhammad said that "in my *ummah*, he is the best who has the largest number of wives."[15]

It has been repeatedly said Musalmans are allowed by the Quran and the Hadis to have four wives. The aphorisms and maxims current about this phenomenon indicate that all wives could not have been procured in the normal way; some would have been purchased, some others captured. One aphorism says, "One quarrels with you, two are sure to involve you in their quarrels; when you have three, factions are formed against her you love best; but four find society and occupation among themselves, leaving the husband in peace."[16] According to another, "Wives there be four: there's Bedfellow, Muckheap [dirty], Gadabout [idle] and Queen O' women. The more the pity that the last is one in a hundred."[17] Yet another says, "A man should marry four wives: A Persian to have some one to talk to; a Khurasani woman for his housework; a Hindu for nursing his children; a woman from Mawaraun nahr, or Transoxiana, to have some one to whip as a warning to the other three."[18] The mention of so many nationalities in the sayings show that obtaining wives and concubines through all kinds of means — capture, purchase, enslavement — was in vogue among medieval Muslims.

In later times, this encouragement to polygamy was taken advantage of by Muslim conquerors. That Muhammad

---

[14] Hughes, 313-14.
[15] Ram Swarup, *Understanding Islam through Hadis*, 57 and n.
[16] Burton, *Sindh Revisited*, I, 340.
[17] Bary, 81.
[18] *Ain.*, I, 327. All these three references have been given in Herklot, *Islam in India*, 85-86.

restricted the number of lawful wives but did not restrict the number of slave concubines, came handy to Musalmans. He "thus left upon the minds of his followers the inevitable impression that an unrestricted polygamy was the higher state..."[19] Hazrat Umar, the second Caliph, was the first to allow instant divorce (by the pronouncement of *talaq, talaq, talaq,* three times) called *talaq-i-bidat* (innovative form of divorce), "to meet an extraordinary situation brought on by wars of conquests". Those wars brought in such an influx of women that constant divorce became necessary to falicitate quick acquisition of fresh spouses by divorcing the old ones. "Victory over an enemy would seem to have been consummated only when the enemy's daughter was introduced into the conqueror's harem"[20] — a precept so enthusiastically practised by Muslim conquerors and rulers in India.

It is therefore no wonder that from the day the Muslim invaders marched into India to the time when their political power declined, women were systematically captured and enslaved throughout the length and breadth of the country. Two instances pertaining to two extreme points of time would suffice as examples. When Muhammad bin Qasim mounted his attack on Debal in 712, all males of the age of seventeen and upwards were put to the sword and their women and children were enslaved.[21] And after the Third Battle of Panipat (1761), "the unhappy prisoners were paraded in long lines, given a little parched grain and a drink of water, and beheaded... and the women and children who survived were driven off as slaves — twenty-two thousand, many of them of the highest rank in the land, says the *Siyar-ul-Mutakhirin.*"[22]

These two instances have been chosen from two points of time on either extremity of Muslim rule in India. And now

[19] Hughes, 464.
[20] Margoliouth, 177.
[21] W.Haig in C.H.I., III, 3; *Chachnama* Kalichbeg, 82-84.
[22] H.G.Rawlinson in C.H.I., IV, 424 and n.

onwards this pattern of mentioning only two examples, one from the earlier period and the other from the later, will be adhered to. There are reasons for adopting this model. Persian chroniclers were not scientific historians. They often give isolated and disjointed bits of information. This characteristic is also found in their references to issues pertaining to our area of study. For example, while most of the chroniclers give detailed information about the enslavement of women in times of war, only a few like Abul Fazl and emperor Jahangir write about how they were captured, lifted or seduced by nobles and officers in times of peace. Of the women captured in war, some were appropriated by the king, many were presented by the king to the nobles, and many others were sold. But all writers do not give satisfactory information on all these points for the whole of the medieval period. Ibn Battuta gives details of "presentation" ceremonies of slave captives in the time of Muhammad bin Tughlaq, and Bernier and Manucci in the time of Jahangir and Shahjahan. Detailed account of the Slave Markets and prices of slave girls are mainly given by the fourteenth century chronicler Ziyauddin Barani, although some others also refer to them but only casually. Many writers, especially European travellers, describe the treatment meted out to slave girls and girls turned concubines, but the accounts of Pelsaert and Manucci are the most detailed. Many women from Hindu rulers' families were forcibly married by Muslim kings throughout the medieval period and yet only Shams Siraj Afif narrates in detail of the marriage of Firoz Shah's mother to Malik Rajjab, a cousin of the king, and emperor Jahangir tells how he demanded daughters of Hindu kings.

In this background, it would be an unremitting task both in volume and repetition to give all anecdotes, facts and figures of enslavement and concubinage of captive women in the central and provincial kingdoms and independent Muslim states found mentioned in the chronicles. This would only lead to repetition resulting in the book becoming bulky. Therefore, two examples — one from the Sultanate period and the other from the Moghul times — would be enough as samples of the system that prevailed throughout. These will suffice to being out the panorama of Muslim indulgence in sex slavery in the medieval period.

The special interest of Muslims in sex slavery was universal and widespread and a plethora of evidence is available in contemporary Persian chronicles. In fact, Muslim historians derive extra delight in narrating anecdotes and stating facts about Muslim indulgence in sex and allied activities. Two incidents from the lives of the first two Sultans, Qutbuddin Aibak and Shamsuddin Iltutmish, may be mentioned here as examples.

On the arrival of Qutbuddin Aibak at Karman (situated between Kabul and Bannu), Tajuddin Yaldoz received him with great kindness and honour and gave him his daughter in marriage. A fete was held on the occasion and poetical descriptions in Hasan Nizami's *Taj-ul-Maasir* follow — "of stars, female beauty, cup-bearers, curls, cheeks, eyes, lips, mouths, stature, elegance, cups, wine, singers, guitars, barbets, trumpets, flutes, drums, of the morning, and the sun."[23] And again, when Aibak, some years later tried to remove Yaldoz form his kingdom, he marched to Ghazni and occupied the throne. But only for forty days, for during this period he was "wholly engaged in revelry", wine and riot, and the affairs of the country through this constant festivity were neglected, and the "Turks of Ghaznin and Muizzi Maliks" invited Yaldoz back to his capital. Aibak was incapable of opposing him and retired to Delhi.[24]

The following anecdote is related of Sultan Shamsuddin Iltutmish. He was greatly enamoured of a Turkish slave girl in his harem, whom he had purchased, and sought her ca-

[23] E.D., II. 221.
[24] Minhaj, 506, 526n.

resses, but was always unable to achieve his object. One day he was seated, having his head anointed with some perfumed oil by the hands of the same slave girl, when he felt some tears fall on his head. On looking up, he found that she was weeping. He inquired of her the cause. She replied, "Once I had a brother who had such a bald place on his head as you have, and it reminds me of him." On making further inquiries it was found that the slave girl was his own sister. They had both been sold as slaves, in their early childhood, by their half-brothers; and thus had Almighty God saved him from committing a great sin. Badaoni states in his work, "I heard this story myself, from the emperor Akbar's own lips, and the monarch stated that this anecdote had been orally traced to Sultan Ghiyasuddin Balban himself."[25]

Forcible Marriages

Forcible marriages, euphemistically called matrimonial alliances, were common throughout the medieval period. Only some of them find mention in Muslim chronicles with their bitter details. Here is one example given by Shams Siraj Afif (fourteenth century). The translation from the original in Persian may be summarised as follows. Firoz Shah was born in the year 709 H. (1309 C.E.). His father was named Sipahsalar Rajjab, who was a brother of Sultan Ghiyasuddin Tughlaq Ghazi. The three brothers, Tughlaq, Rajjab, and Abu Bakr, came from Khurasan to Delhi in the reign of Alauddin (Khalji), and that monarch took all the three in the service of the Court. The Sultan conferred upon Tughlaq the country of Dipalpur. Tughlaq was desirous that his brother Sipahsalar Rajjab should obtain in marriage the daughter of one of the Rais of Dipalpur. He was informed that the daughters of Ranamall Bhatti were very beautiful and accomplished. Tughlaq sent to Ranamall a proposal of marriage. Ranamall refused. Upon this Tughlaq proceeded to the villages

[25] Ibid., Reverty in 601n.

(*talwandi*) belonging to Ranamall and demanded payment of the whole year's revenue in a lump sum. The Muqaddams and Chaudharis were subjected to coercion. Ranamall's people were helpless and could do nothing, for *those were the days of Alauddin, and no one dared to make an outcry* (italics ours). One damsel was brought to Dipalpur. Before her marriage she was called Bibi Naila. On entering the house of Sipahsalar Rajjab she was styled Sultan Bibi Kadbanu. After the lapse of a few years she gave birth to Firoz shah.[26] If this could be accomplished by force by a regional officer, there was nothing to stop the king. In the seventeenth century, Jahangir writes in his Memoirs that after the third year of his accession, "I demanded in marriage the daughter of Jagat Singh, eldest son of Raja Man Singh (of Amer)."[27] Raja Ram Chandra Bundela was defeated, imprisoned, and subsequently released by Jahangir.[28] Later on, says Jahangir, "I took the daughter of Ram Chandra Bandilah into my service (i.e. married her)."[29]

The reason for including such cases of 'royal marriages' in the study of sex slavery is obvious. The language of the above citations shows that such wives, or such secondary wives, are always mentioned as having been taken into service or included among female servants, or as obtaining glory by entering the king's harem. This style of language is not used in describing the marriages of Nur Jahan or Mumtaz Mahall. Such wives were no more than concubines. Concubinage was very common among Muslim royalty and nobility. Among the Muslim rulers children born of concubines were considered equal to children by marriage, although this is not explicitly laid down in the Quran. The custom must have asserted itself in the first century of Islam.[30]

---

[26] Afif, 36-40. Trs in E.D., III, 271-73.
[27] *Tuzuk-i-Jahangiri*, I, 144.
[28] Ibid., 82-83, 87.
[29] Ibid., 160.
[30] Hamilton, *Hedaya*, I, Discourse, XVIII; Schacht, *Cambridge History of Islam*, II, 144.

The children of such a union belonged to the master and were therefore free but the status of the concubine was thereby raised only to that of 'mother of children'.[31] As an example, the case of Sultan Sikandar Lodi (1489-1517) may be cited. His mother Zeba was originally a Hindu by the name of Hema or Amba. Bahlul Lodi was attracted by her beauty while he was governor of Sarhind. He married her after ascending the throne of Delhi. He had nine sons. Zeba's son was not the eldest nor was she originally more than a Hindu concubine.[32] Although sons of concubines are very freely mentioned without any inhibition,[33] Hindu concubines themselves had little influence on the Muslim psyche. This is evident from the fact that while the mothers of Firoz Tughlaq and Sikandar Lodi were both originally Hindu, their sons became Muslim bigots.

There were some marriages which were not forced, but the wedded women were not accorded due regard even by their own people. In the homes of Muslim ruling classes such women were treated no better than slave girls or concubines. The cases of Rani Ladi and Deval Rani are appropriate examples. Muhammad bin Qasim had captured Rani Ladi, consort of Raja Dahir, during his invasion of Sind. Later on he married her. Thinking that she could wield some influence with her people, he sent her to persuade the people of Alor fort to cooperate with the powerful invader. But "the men standing on the top of the ramparts jeered at her saying: 'You have mixed with the *chandals* and defiled yourself. You prefer their rule to ours.' They then began to abuse her."[34] Deval Devi was the daughter of Raja Karan Baghela of Gujarat and his queen Kamala Devi. Kamala Devi was captured in the sack of Gujarat (1299), and married by Alauddin

[31] Hitti, *The Arabs*, 76.

[32] Ahmad Yadgar, *Tarikh-i-Salatin-i-Afghana*, Persian Text, 17, 31-34; Farishtah I, 179; *Tabqat-i-Akbari*, I, 298. For many other references see Lal, *Twilight*, 162-63.

[33] Niamatullah, *Makhzan-i-Afghani*, 51 (6); *Tuzuk*, I, 20.

[34] *Chachnama*, Kalichbeg, 176-77.

Khalji. According to the Islamic law, kafir women could be married to Muslims even while their husbands were alive,[35] for marriage is annulled by captivity.[36] Later on her daughter Deval Devi was also captured in another campaign (1308) and brought to Delhi.[37] There she was married to Alauddin's son Khizr Khan who had fallen in love with her.[38] After the assassination of Khizr Khan in the politics of succession, she was married by Qutbuddin Mubarak Khalji (1316-20) against her will.[39] With the murder of Qutbuddin at the hands of Khusrau Khan she was taken into the latter's harem. In short, this princess was treated as nothing more than a chattel or transferable property in the Khalji ruling house.[40] Although such 'wives' were treated more or less as slave girls or concubines, they sometimes brought with them scores of *bandis* for service in the harem. The best example for the Sultanate period is to be found in Malik Muhammad Jaisi's *Padmavat*. The story of Padmini may be allegorical, but the important fact is that Padmini and her companions and *bandis* are said to have been carried in 1,600 litters (actually Rajput warriors who rescued Ratan Singh) to the palace of Alauddin Khalji.[41] For the Mughals, it has already been said that Akbar had 5,000 women in his harem who in turn had their own entourage of *bandis*. To the conquering and ruling Mughals there was no dearth of such women.

Distribution of Slave Girls

Marriages brought servants and *bandis*, but the largest number of slave girls was collected during raids, campaigns and wars throughout the medieval period. We have briefly seen the achievements of Muslims in this regard from the

---

[35] Muir, *Life of Mahomet*, 365.
[36] Hughes, *Dictionary of Islam*, 59; Margoliouth, *Mohammed*, 407, 461.
[37] For details see Lal, *Khaljis*, 234-36.
[38] Ibid., 264-65.
[39] Hajiuddabir, *Zafarul Valih*, 841-44; Farishtah, I, 125.
[40] Barani, 410-11; Lal, *Khaljis* , 298-99.
[41] Lal, *Khaljis*, 102-110, esp. 103.

time of Muhammad bin Qasim onwards. It was a consistent policy to kill all males, especially those capable of bearing arms, and enslave their hapless women.[42] Al Biladuri writes that "the governors (who succeeded Qasim) continued to kill the enemy, taking whatever they could acquire..."[43] Most of the captives were distributed among nobles and soldiers. Two examples of this custom may be given, one from the Sultanate and the other form the Mughal period.

Muhammad bin Tughlaq became notorious for enslaving women and his reputation in this regard spread far and wide. Ibn Battuta who visited India during his reign and stayed at the Court for a long time writes: "At (one) time there arrived in Delhi some female infidel captives, ten of whom the Vazir sent to me. I gave one of them to the man who had brought them to me.... My companion took three girls, and — I do not know what happened to the rest."[44] On the large scale distribution of girl slaves on the occasion of Muslim festivals like Id, he writes: "First of all, daughters of Kafir (Hindu) Rajas captured during the course of the year, come and sing and dance. Thereafter they are bestowed upon Amirs and important foreigners. After this daughters of other Kafirs dance and sing... The Sultan gives them to his brothers, relatives, sons of Maliks etc. On the second day the *durbar* is held in a similar fashion after Asr. Female singers are brought out... the Sultan distributes them among the Mameluke Amirs....."[45] Thousands of non-Muslim women were distributed in the above manner in later years.[46]

Shahjahan attacked the Portuguese in Hugli in 1632, and captured many women. One such was Maria de Taides "one of the sisters living in the palace of king Sahajahan."[47] Maria

---

42 *Chachnama,* Kalichbeg, 83, 155, 161, 173-74; E.D., I, 164, 170-71, 203; Al Biladuri, E.D., I, 123. For massacres of Alauddin Khalji, *Khazain-ul-Fatuh*, Habib trs, 49.

43 Al Biladuri, op.cit. 127.

44 Ibn Battuta, 123.

45 Ibn Battuta, 63; Hindi tras., in Rizvi, *Tughlaq Kalin Bharat* part I, Aligarh 1956, 189.

46 Afif, 119-20, 180, 265.

47 Manucci, I, 202; II, 35; III, 179.

de Taides was later married to Ali Mardan Khan.[48] One Thomazia Martins also had been taken captive during the fall of Hugli. Many more like these were distributed among the nobles.

Jauhar during attack

How did the Indian women react to such a desperate situation? When Sindh lay prostrate before the armies of Muhammad bin Qasim, "Raja Dahir's sister Bai collected all the women in the fort (of Rawar) and addressed them thus: 'It is certain that we cannot escape the clutches of these Chandals and cow-eaters...As there is no hope of safety and liberty, let us collect fire-wood and cotton and oil (and) burn ourselves to ashes, and thus quickly meet our husbands (in the next world). Whoever is inclined to go and ask mercy of the enemy, let her go....' But all of them were of one mind, and so they entered a house and set fire to it, and were soon burnt to ashes."[49] Thereafter, throughout the medieval period, as soon as it was certain that there had been a defeat and the men had been killed, women perished in the fire of Jauhar (*jiva har,* taking of life). In some cases it was practised by Muslim women also,[50] because of the influence of Hindu practice. The Jauhar at Chittor during Akbar's invasion may be mentioned as an instance in the Mughal period. On the night of 23 February 1568, Rajput commander Jaimal's death had so discouraged the people of Chittor that they resolved to perform the rite of Jauhar. Flames broke out at various places in the fortress and the ladies were consumed in them. The Jauhar took place in the house of Patta who belonged to the Sisodia clan, in the house of Rathors of whom Sahib Khan was the chief, and the Chauhans whose chief was Aissar Das. "As many as three hundred women

[48] Saksena, B.P., *History of Shahjahan*, 89, 112-13, for the Portuguese captives of Hughli and female prisoners of the Bundela ruling family of Orcha.

[49] *Chachnama*, Kalichbeg, 153-55; E.D., I, 181.

[50] Yazdi, *Zafar Nama*, II, 130-32. Lal, *Twilight,* 32.

were burnt in the destructive fire."[51]

But all were not that brave or lucky to escape capture in this manner. During Jujhar Singh Bundela's resistance in Orcha in the time of Shahjahan, many women were captured and treated most cruelly. Jujhar Singh abandoned his fort of Chauragarh and hastened towards the Deccan. He put to death several of his women whose horses had foundered. The remaining ones made for Golkunda (December, 1634) but were taken by surprise. They had not the time to perform the full rites of Jauhar, but stabbed a number of women. The Mughals picked up the wounded women and made away with them.[52] It was in this fashion that women used to be captured and distributed for service in the harems of the Muslim elite.

Behaviour of Slave Girls

Slave girls may be divided under three categories on the basis of their character and conduct. One set comprised of the ambitious, cunning and crafty who tried to wield influence in the harem. Just the opposite were the simple, docile and submissive. In between were those who were keen to exercise ascendancy but through beauty and tact; they were otherwise loyal and lovable.

During the very beginning of Muslim rule in India the domineering and intriguing figure of Shah Turkan attracts our attention. According to Minhaj Siraj, the author of the contemporary chronicle *Tabqat-i-Nasiri*, "Shah Turkan was a Turkish hand-maid, and the head [woman] of all the Sultan's (Iltutmish's) *haram*."[53] She manipulated to prefix the title of Khudawand-i-Jahan to her name and rise to the position of "the greatest [of the ladies] of the sublime *haram*, and her

[51] *Akbar Nama*, II, 472.

[52] C.H.I., IV, 195.

[53] Minhaj, 630;631 and n.4. *Futuh-us-Salatin*, a historical work by Isami, composed in the 14th century, mentions casually that she was a Hindu slave girl. Mahdi Husain's acceptance of Isami's version lacks critical analysis. *Futuh*, trs. II, 247 and n.2. Also 249.

place of residence was the royal palace".[54] She used to confer lavish presents upon the nobles of the court in order to win support for her son for the throne. She caused royal orders and decrees to be issued in her name and tortured many favourite ladies of Iltutmish after his death.[55] For the later Mughal period, there is the classic example of Lal Kunwar and her lay-in-waiting Zohra, both concubines of the Mughal emperor Jahandar Shah (1712). Lal Kunwar was a vulgar, thoughtless, dancing girl from the streets.[56] She received a large allowance and imitated the style of Nur Jahan, the famous queen of Jahangir.[57] "All the brothers and relatives... of Lal Kunwar received *mansabs* of four or five thousand... and were raised to dignity in their tribe."[58] Naturally, talented and learned men were driven away from the court. Zohra was a melon seller and a friend of Lal Kunwar. At the latter's instance she was called into the harem by Jahandar Shah. She was highly ambitious and scheming like Lal Kunwar. She was, however, shown her place by the servants of Chin Qulich Khan, a retired general of Aurangzeb. The incident is interesting to narrate. Once Zohra was going on an elephant with her retinue, an insolent lot. Chin Qulich also happened to go that way and was met by her equippage. His men stepped aside, but Zohra called out: "Thou, Chin Kalich Khan, must surely be the son of some blind father, not to move out of the road." These words unhinged the general's temper, who made a sign to his people to chastise that vulgar woman's servants. After dealing with her servants and eunuchs, "they dragged Zohra herself from the elephant to the ground, and gave her several cuffs and kicks."[59] Arrogant and crafty women like Shah Turkan, Lal Kunwar and Zohra were rather common in the Muslim harems. Nor uncommon were

[54] Minhaj, 638.
[55] Nigam, *Nobility under the Sultanate of Delhi*, 28.
[56] C.H.I., IV, 328.
[57] Sarkar in Ibid., 226.
[58] Khafi Khan, 432-33.
[59] *Siyar-ul-Mutakhrin*, 33.

women who were not that uncultured although they were equally unscrupulous. Aurangzeb could imprison his brother Prince Murad through the active cooperation of one of his concubines,[60] and Udaipuri-Mahall, a Georgian slave girl and concubine of prince Dara Shukoh, willingly went over to Aurangzeb on the latter's ascension to power.[61]

On the other extreme were women of unquestioned fidelity. Akbar was told that because of the practise of monogamy among Christians, fidelity of their women was taken for granted. "The extraordinary thing is," he said to the Christian Fathers in retort, "that it occurs among those of the Brahman (i.e. the Hindu) religion. There are numerous concubines, and many of them are neglected and unappreciated and spend their days unfructuously in the private chamber of chastity, yet in spite of such bitterness of life they are flaming torches of love and fellowship." On hearing about such noble souls the seekers after wisdom were filled with surprise in the august assemblage.[62] Devotion of such women was well known. Jahangir narrates the story of Lal Kalawant — the singer also know as Miyan Lal[63] — "who from his childhood had grown up in my father's service... (He) died in the 65th or 70th year of his age. One of his girls (concubines) ate opium on this event and killed herself. Few women among the Musalmans have shown such fidelity."[64] Rupmati of Sarangpur, because of her love for her paramour Baz Bahadur "bravely quaffed the cup of deadly poison and carried her honour to the hidden chambers of annihilation,"[65] rather than be captured by Adham Khan. Before her, Deval Rani, though not so lucky, was an equally determined character. Loyalty of Hindu concubines was proverbial, but Muslim ones were not devoid of it. Akbarabadi-Mahall and

[60] C.H.I., IV. 215.
[61] Andre Butenschon, *The Life of the Mughal Princess,* 39, 194-95.
[62] A.N., III, 372.
[63] *Ain,* I, 681 and n.
[64] *Tuzuk,* I, 150.
[65] A.N., II, 213-14.

Fatehpuri-Mahall, shared Shahjahan's captivity in the Agra Fort and they were present by his beside when he breathed his last in January, 1666. Rana-i-Dil was originally a dancing girl before she became a favourite concubine of Prince Dara Shukoh. After his execution, Aurangzeb desired to possess her, but she refused.[66]

Extreme cases of shrewish and termagant women on the one hand and those known for sacrifice and devotion on the other were few. Muslim harems mainly contained attractive women with normal behaviour. In medieval times mutilation and castration were common punishments meted out to men in war and peace and their beautiful women were taken into the harems of the elites. Besides, "silver bodied damsels with musky tresses" were purchased in the slave markets of India and abroad. The harems were thus filled with an assortment of beauties from various countries and nationalities, although Indian women predominated. They were renowned for their beauty, delicacy and femininity. From the time of Amir Khusrau, many a poet in medieval India has extolled their beauty and charm. So also have the Europeans. Orme, along with many others, affirms that "nature seems to have showered beauty on the fairer sex throughout Hindustan with a more lavish hand than in most other countries."[67] Their faithfulness and devotion matched their charm. In the harem these amenable creatures were an asset and were welcome in ever larger numbers.

Concubinage

Slave girls had two main functions to perform, domestic service and providing sex if and when required. In medieval Muslim society sex slavery and concubinage were almost interchangeable terms. For the polygamous Muslim men of means slave girls and maids were as much in demand as

[66] Lal, *Mughal Harem*, 30.
[67] Orme's *Fragments*, 438.

kanchanis or dancing girls, concubines or even free born women. Whether they were purchased in the open market,[68] or captured during war, or selected during excursions, or came as maids of brides, in short whatever their channel of entry into the harem, the slave girls kept in the palace of the king or *mahals* of the nobles were invariably good looking. Their faces determined their place in the harem and in the heart of the master. Their being a little sexy was an additional attraction,[69] but those with bad breath and odour in the armpits were avoided as unpleasant smell was repugnant to kissing and caressing.[70] They used to be elegantly attired. Their garments were sometimes gifted to them by their masters or mistresses. It was a custom that the princesses did not wear again the dresses they put on once, and gave them away to their *bandis*.[71] Some favourite slave girls were taught to sing and play on musical instruments. Many of them were trained to recite verses, *naghmas* and *ghazals*. The habit of speaking elegantly in correct diction and immaculate pronunciation was so familiar to the females of Muslim society that maids too were readily distinguished by their refined language. Placed as they were, they knew how to win the hearts of their masters who gave them lovely and caressing names like Gulab, Champa, Chameli, Nargis, Kesar, Kasturi, Gul-i-Badam, Sosan, Yasmin, Gul-i-Rana, Gul Andam, Gul Anar, Saloni, Madhumati, Sugandhara, Koil, Gulrang, Mehndi, Dil Afroz, Moti, Ketki, Mrig Nain, Kamal Nain, Basanti etc., etc. Elaborating on their ethnic status Manucci adds that "All the above names are Hindu, and ordinarily these ...are Hindus by race, who had been carried off in infancy from various villages or the houses of different rebel Hindu princes. In spite of their Hindu names, they are however, Mahomedans."[72] As

---

[68] Barani, 314-15; Bernier, 426.
[69] *Ashraful Hidayah*, VIII, 138.
[70] Ibid., 137.
[71] *Bernier*, 258; Manucci, II, 341.
[72] Manucci, II, 336-38.

a rule, "being kafir is a defect in both *ghulam* and *bandi* as by nature the Musalman detests to associate with or keep company of a kafir."[73] Obviously, the number of such converted slave girls was so large that even Hindu names of all of them could not be changed to Islamic ones. For instance, while under Aurangzeb women and children of the Rajputs and Marathas[74] were regularly enslaved during raids and invasions, even nobles of lesser note indulged in reckless enslavement throughout. Sidi Yaqut of Janjira or Zanjira (Zanj is used for black African), once took a Maratha fort and seven hundred persons came out. Notwithstanding his word to grant quarter to the garrison "he made the children and pretty women slaves, and forcibly converted them to Islam... but the men he put to death."[75]

Francisco Pelsaert gives a succinct description of the sex-play of a nobleman in his harem. and the role of slave girls therein. He writes that "each night the Amir visits a particular wife, or *mahal*, and receives a very warm welcome from her and from the slaves (i.e. slave girls), who (are) dressed specially for the occasion... If it is the hot weather, they... rub his body with pounded sandalwood and rosewater. Fans are kept going steadily. Some of the slaves chafe the master's hand and feet, some sit and sing, or play music and dance, or provide other recreation, the wife sitting near him all the time. Then if one of the pretty slave girls takes his fancy, he calls her to him and enjoys her, his wife not daring to show any signs of displeasure, but dissembling, though she will take it out on the slave girls later on."[76] But the wife could not

---

[73] *Ashraf-ul-Hidayah,* Deoband, VIII, 138-39. P. Venkateshwar Rao Jr., in his review of Akbar Ahmed's, BBC BKs/Penguin, *From Samarkand to Stornoway living Islam,* in the *Indian Express Sunday Magazine,* June 27, 1993, observes: "He (Ahmed) hates Muslim wives whose children have Hindu names." But that is the legal position. A Musalman is expected to detest the company of a kafir, in spite of the efforts made for acquiring non-Muslim wives in medieval and modern times. But Ahmed's aim is, as he himself claims, to show "where Muslims are able to live by the ideal and where they are not".

[74] Khafi Khan, II, 300, 371.

[75] Ibid., II, 228, 261 ff, 498 ff.

[76] Pelsaert, 64-65.

get rid of her by dismissing or selling her. As per the Islamic law the mistress could quarrel with the husband, could even reproach him, but she could not free a slave girl or get rid of her.[77] Manumitting a *ghulam* or *bandi* was the privilege of the master only.

But except in exceptional cases, where the maid's beauty and blandishments so excited the jealousy of the mistress that she treated her severely, a slave girl's life was not of unmitigated suffering. In this scenario, the *bandis* were both maids and companions of their mistresses. The mistress in distress poured out her heart to her slave girl and the maid sought the advice of the former regarding her problems. Young and beautiful girls, whether ladies or maids, did wish to be married. And marriage was not shut out for either. A slave girl could be married with the permission of the master. If the master liked a maid, he just took her as his own wife.[78] Slave girls could be easily swapped by admiring masters. Prince Aurangzeb readily gave his concubine Chhatar Bai in exchange for Hira Bai with whom he had fallen passionately in love.[79] Begums like Mumtaz Mahall and Nur Jahan married off a large number of slave girls to deserving men.[80] But all were not so lucky and many of the slave girls had to wait in vain for matrimony. Manucci writes that some of them suffered from insomnia, hallucinations and hysteria, and marriage brought them back to "perfect health."[81] Manucci helped many maids to marry.

But all slave girls were not married. They were not captured, purchased or enticed to be married. They were there in the Muslim harems to do service and be enjoyed by the masters. They could be sold, distributed or exchanged.

---

77 *Fatawa-i-Alamgiri*, Delhi, III, *Kitab-ul-'Ataq* , 1-89; Deoband, XII, 23-98; esp. 15.

78 Gulbadañ Begum, *Humayun Nama*, Persian Text, 27, Englilsh trs., 112.

79 Hamiduddin Khan, Bahadur, *Ahkam-i-Alamgiri*, 36-38; Lal, *Mughal Harem*, 158-60.

80 Muhammad Hadi, *Tatimma-i-Waqiat-i-Jahangiri* (or Epilogue to Jahangir's Memoirs), E.D., VI, 339.

81 Manucci, II, 397-98.

Therefore most of them were unhappy. And they were never a scarce commodity; fresh arrivals or rivals were always replacing old ones. Hence the desire for self-preservation dominated their psyche. A change on the throne meant passing over to a new master, and if and when a ruler or noble lost power, slave girls sought shelter in fending for themselves. An example of this scenario given by us elsewhere pertains to the slave girls in the harem of Saiyyad Abdulla Khan of Saiyyad Brothers fame.[82] On the fall of Abdulla Khan from power, "when in 1720, the intelligence of his captivity reached Delhi, his women, of whom he had gathered a large number around him, were in dismay: some of noble birth, remained in their places, but a good many made the best of time, and before the arrival of the royal guard (who would have taken them away also in escheat), they seized whatever they could, and disguising themselves with old veils and sheet, they took their departure."[83] This is the version of Khafi Khan. Mir Ghulam Husain Khan, the author of *Siyar-ul-Mutakherin,* also throws light on some other facets of the situation and therefore he needs to be quoted at some length. "The ladies of Abdullah-Khan's family," writes he, "far from quitting the house, remained within their own apartments, and covering themselves from head to foot with the veil of decency and modesty, sat weeping in a circle, without anyone offering to move or to escape the dismal scene around them... But some of the inferior females availed themselves of the confusion to carry off whatever came to hand, and stole away in disguise, wearing dirty clothes and common veils. These had disappeared before the government officers thought of taking possession of the palace of the Saiyyads. Some of these women were taken up by the police officers, but others effected their escape... One Abdullah-Khan, of Cashan in Persia, to whom Abdullah-

[82] *The Mughal Harem,* 198.
[83] Khafi Khan, *Muntakhab-ul-Lubab,* text, II, 921 ff. trs. in E.D., VII, 515.

Khan, his old friend and master, had intrusted the care of his seraglio, no sooner heard of the disaster that had befallen his benefactor, entering the sanctuary of the women, seized and carried away whatever persons and effects he chose..."[84].

The above narrative correctly depicts the role of men and women slaves in a Muslim harem. Everything went off well in days of prosperity. When misfortune struck, the noble ladies suffered in silence, the ever-exploited slave girls fled without remorse, and the 'confidant' men slaves did not miss the opportunity to carry away women and indulge in unbridled sex slavery.[85]

Hijras

Early in the eighteenth century Muslim rule in India set on its path of decline. The harems of royalty and nobility began to suffer from a financial crunch. Many slave girls in these establishments, unable to bear the rigours of penury, left their palaces and mansions and took up quarters in the cities to fend for themselves. Thousands of eunuch guards of the harems also took to the streets when their services were dispensed with or starvation knocked at their doors.[86]

In their effort to provide means of livelihood for themselves many slave girls adopted the profession of dancing girls and prostitutes and hundreds of eunuchs, thrown out of employment, turned *bhands* and *hijras*. Prostitution is practised the world over, *hijras* are a people peculiar to India. Basically, and historically, they have come down or 'descended' from the medieval eunuchs.

A typical and complete *hijra* was Sultan Qutbuddin Mubarak Khalji (1316-1320). He occasionally dressed himself in female attire, embroidered with laces and adorned with

---

[84] Mir Ghulam Husain Khan, *Siyar-ul-Mutakherin*, revised from the translation of Haji Mustafa by Johns Briggs, 1832, and republished Allahabad, 1924, 183.

[85] Servants formed part of the establishment and so were included in escheat. Ibid., 188.

[86] Lal, *Mughal Harem*, 198,199.

gems, and went about dancing in the houses of the nobles like a typical *hijra.* Similarly, Hasan Kangu, the ruler of Malabar, often used to come to court (*darbar-i-am*) dressed in the fashion of females. He bedecked his arms and neck with jewellery and ornaments and used to ask his nobles to treat him to sexual passivity.[87] In short, the courts of Qutbuddin and Hasan Kangu presented licence and obscenity of the *hijras* in utter nakedness.

In the polygamous Muslim society some men possessed a plurality of women leaving many other men to remain unmarried. This led the latter to entice, abduct and enslave girls wherever possible as well as to make love to beardless boys (*amrads*) and *hijras*. Thus need combined with perversion contributed to the proliferation of *hijras*. This is amply reflected in a brief survey of life in Delhi in *Muraqqa-i-Dihli* (Album of Delhi) written by Dargah Quli Khan who visited the metropolis in 1738-39 and often walked through its streets. Like in the fourteenth, in the eighteenth century also one found in the city of Delhi boys dancing in a world of lecherous sinners soliciting their hearts' desire. *Amrads* were as much in demand as courtesans.[88] During and after the decline of the Mughal empire, *hijras* did not remain confined to cities like Delhi or Agra. They spread far and wide but especially where the scions or governors of the Mughals established independent states like in Avadh or Hyderabad. A good number of *hijras* are found in Lucknow and in Hyderabad, as well as in cities like Bombay where 'composite culture' and a respectable presence of Muslims obtains.

These unfortunate *hijras*, who have continued as a legacy of the Muslim slave system, still play a pernicious and parasitical role in Indian society. Their aggressive demand for benefaction makes them detested. There are many negative aspects of Muslim slave system of which probably the *hijra*

---

[87] Barani, 396; Afif, 261-62

[88] *Muraqqa-i-Dihli*, Persian text and trs. in Urdu by Nurul Hasan Ansari, 129-34, 192-205 respectively.

is the worst. But in medieval times *hijras* were as essential a part of Muslim society as any other section. In Delhi and its environs there are extant a number of mausoleums, called Gumbads, of the Saiyyad and Lodi period. It is an interesting fact that with Bare Khan Ka Gumbad (Dome and Tomb), Chhote Khan Ka Gumbad, Dadi ka Gumbad, and Poti Ka Gumbad, there is also the famous Hijre Ka Gumbad.[89]

[89] Percy Brown, *Indian Architecture (Islamic Period)* third ed. 28-29; Carr Stephen, *Archaeology and Monumental Remains of Delhi*, 196-97; *Archaeological Survey Report*, IV, 67ff; XX,155-58. Also Lal, *Twilight*, 230-31 for other references.

POSTSCRIPT

We began by quoting Thomas Patrick Hughes to say that "slavery of Islam is interwoven with the Law of marriage, the Law of sale, and the Law of inheritance... and its abolition would strike at the very foundation of the code of Muhammadanism".[1] The statement holds as good today as in the early years of Islam. The rules of Islam remain the same for all time, for Islam is changeless and unchangeable. As I.H. Qureshi puts it: "The Muslim jurists and theologians believe in the supremacy of the *shar* and hold that it is eternal and immutable in its essence. It is based on the Quran which is believed by every Muslim to be the Word of God revealed to His prophet Muhammad. Not even the Prophet could change the revelation..."[2] Muhammad could not change the revelation; he could only explain and interpret it. So do the Muslims do today. There are liberal Muslims and conservative Muslims, there are Muslims learned in theology and Muslims devoid of learning. They discuss, they interpret, they rationalize, but all by going round and round within the closed circle of Islam. There is no possibility of getting out of the fundamentals of Islam; there is no provision of introducing any innovation. So, Muslim slave system could not remain confined to the Middle Ages. Muhammad legitimized slavery in the Quran and therefore it is recognized to be in complete conformity with Islam. Slavery is considered an integral part of Islam.

That being so, Muslim holy men and men of jurisprudence, endowed the institution with supreme religious sanction. According to Bernard Lewis, "they were upholding an institution sanctioned by scripture, law, and tradition and one which in their eyes was necessary to the maintenance of the social structure of Muslim life." For example, in 1855 the

---

[1] *Dictionary of Islam*, 600.
[2] Qureshi, *Administration*, 42.

Ottoman Empire ordered the governors of its far-flung districts to ban the commerce in slaves. For rebellious Arabs in the Hijaz this was exactly the kind of anti-Islamic, Western-influenced measure they had been waiting for as case for throwing the Turkish rule. The Arab leader Shaykh Jamal issued a legal ruling "denouncing the ban on the slave trade as contrary to the holy law of Islam. Because of this anti-Islamic act, he said,... the Turks had become apostates and heathens. It was lawful to kill them without incurring criminal penalties or bloodwit, and to enslave their children." The Ottoman Turks succeeded in suppressing their southern rebels in mid-1856. But as a conciliatory measure to prevent further secessionist movements, the Turkish government granted a major concession to the slave traders who had long made the Red Sea and the Hijaz a central route for transporting African slaves to the Middle East. The Sultan's government exempted the Hijaz from its 1857 decree outlawing the trade in black slaves throughout the rest of the Ottoman Empire. As late as 1960, Lord Shackleton reported to the House of Lords that African Muslims on pilgrimages to Mecca still sold slaves on arrival, "using them as living travellers cheques."[3]

Till today, black slaves are being bought and sold in countries like Sudan and Mauretania. "The Islamic doctrine of slavery was closely linked with the doctrine of the inescapable struggle between believers and unbelievers... and Pagans were routinely sold into slavery if they had the misfortune of being captured by Muslims."[4] Right from the fifteenth century Muslims would go on furnishing black slaves to European slave traders. At least 80% of all the black slaves that were ever exported from Black Africa, went through

[3] For documentation regarding Lord Shackleton and the situation in 1960, see, Davis, *Slavery and Human Progress*, 317, 362. For Quotes form Bernard Lewis see Review of his book, *Race and Slavery in the Middle East* by Davis in the *New York Review*, October 11, 1990.

[4] Elst, *Negationism*, 101.

Muslim hands. A large part of the slaves transported to America had also been bought from Muslim slave-catchers.[5] "Slavery, as far as established by law, was abolished in India by Act V, 1843, but the final blow was dealt on January 1, 1862, when the sections of the Indian Penal Code dealing with the question came into operation."[6] The point to note, however, is that life of slavery is lived by millions of *burqa*-clad Muslim women kept behind bolted doors and by men who still believe in slavery as a part of their religious and social life. *Burqa* remains the symbol of slavery; its enforcement is now ensured by the dictates of militants. As-Said al-Ashwamy, renowned Egyptian writer and chief justice, on a recent visit to India, said, "insulating women if they don't wear the veil ensures that they wear it out of fear not faith... women now accept the position of being slaves."[7] "There is no doubt that many thousands of slaves are still serving in the wealthy palaces of Arabia," and now and then one hears about the condition of girls from Malaysia, Sri Lanka, India etc., married by Shaikhs and living in the Gulf countries as nothing better than slave girls.

[5] Elst, *Indigenous Indians*, 375, 381.
[6] Herklots, *Islam in India*, 112 n. 2.
[7] Detailed report in *The Times of India*, 10 December, 1993.

BIBLIOGRAPHY

Original Sources

Abdullah, *Tarikh-i-Daudi,* Bankipore Ms. Text, ed. by S.A. Rashid, Aligarh.

Abdul Hamid Lahori, *Badshah Nama,* Bib. Ind., 2 vols., Calcutta, 1898.

Abul Fazl, Allami, *Ain-i-Akbari,* 3 vols., Vol.I trs. by H. Blochmann and ed. by D.C. Phillot, Calcutta, 1939; Vol.II trs. by H.S. Jarret and annotated by Jadunath Sarkar, Calcutta, 1939; Vol.III trs. by Jarret and Sarkar, Calcutta, 1948.

Abul Fazl, Allami, *Akbar Nama,* Bib. Ind. Text, 3 vols., English trs. by Henry Beveridge, Calcutta, 1948.

Afif, Shams Siraj, *Tarikh-i-Firoz Shahi,* Bib. Ind., Calcutta, 1890.

Ahmad Yadgar, *Tarikh-i-Salatin-i-Afghana,* Bib. Ind., Calcutta, 1936.

Ain-ul Mulk Multani, *Qasaid Badr Chach,* Kanpur, n.d.

Alberuni, Abu Raihan Muhammad., *Alberuni's India,* Eng. trs. by Edward Sachau, 2 vols., London, 1910.

Al Biladuri, *Futuh-ul-Buldan* (written 9th cent. C.E.), trs. in E.D., vol.I.

Al Istakhri, *Kitab-ul-Aqalim* (written 951 C.E.), trs. in E.D., vol. I.

Al Kufi, *Chach Nama,* trs. in E and D, I. Also by Mirza Kalichbeg Fredunbeg, Karachi, 1900, Delhi reprint, 1979.

Al Qalqashindi, *Subh-ul-Asha,* trs. by Otto Spies as *An Arab Account of India in the 14th Century,* Aligarh, 1935.

Ali Muhammad Khan Bahadur, *Mirat-i-Ahmadi,* Calcutta, 1928; English trs. by Lokhandvala, 2 vols., Baroda, 1965.

Amin Qazvini, *Badshah Nama,* Ms. Raza Library, Rampur.

Amir Khurd, see Kirmani.

Amir Khusrau, Abul Hasan, *Deval Rani,* Aligarh, 1917.

Amir Khusrau, Abul Hasan, *Tughlaq Nama,* ed. by Hashim Faridabadi, Aurangabad, 1933.

Amir Khusrau, Abul Hasan, *Qiran-us-Sadain,* Aligarh, 1918.

Amir Khusrau, Abul Hasan, *Khazain-ul-Futuh,* see Habib under Modern Works.

Amir Khusrau, Abul Hasan, *Miftah-ul-Fatuh,* Aligarh Text, 1954.

Babur, Zahiruddin Muhammad, *Babur Nama or Tuzuk-i-Baburi,* trs. from Turki by Mrs. A.S. Beveridge, 2 vols., London, 1922; trs. from the Persian version by John Leyden and William Erskine as *Memoirs of Babur,* London, 1926.

Badaoni, Abdul Qadir Ibn-i-Muluk Shah, *Muntakhab-ut-Tawarikh,* ed. by Ahmad Ali, Persian Text, Bib. Ind., 3 vols., Calcutta, 1864-67; English trs. by George S.A. Ranking, Calcutta, 1898.

Baihaqi, Khwaja Abul Fazl, *Tarikh-i-Subuktgin* (written 1089 C.E), trs. in E.D., II.

Bakhtawar Khan, *Mirat-i-Alam* (written 1078H/1666 C.E.), trs. in E.D., VII.

Barani, Ziyauddin, *Tarikh-i-Firoz Shahi,* Bib. Ind., Calcutta, 1864.

Barani, Ziyauddin, *Fatawa-i-Jahandari,* English trs. by Afsar Begum and Mohammad Habib, Allahabad, 1960.

Barani, Ziyauddin, *Sana-i-Muhammadi,* trs. in *Medieval India Quarterly,* vol.I, pt.III.

Bihamad Khani, Muhammad, *Tarikh-i-Muhammadi,* British Museum Ms.; Rotograph copy in Allahabad University Library; English trs. by Muhammad Zaki, Aligarh, 1972.

Dargah Quli Khan, *Muraqqa-i-Dehli* (written 1739 C.E.) translated in Urdu and edited by Nurul Hasan Ansari, Delhi 1982.

Devalsmriti, Anandasrama Sanskrit Series, Poona; English trs. by M.N. Roy in *Journal of the Bihar and Orissa Research Society,* 1927.

Fakhr-i-Mudabbir, *Tarikh-i-Fakhruddin Mubarak Shah,* ed. by Sir Denison Ross, London, 1927.

Fakhr-i-Mudabbir, *Adabul Harb wa Shujaat,* Photocopy British Museum, Add. 1653; Hindi trs. in Rizvi, *Adi Turk Kalin Bharat,* Aligarh, 1956.

Fatawa-i-Alamgiri, Urdu trs. by (1) Maulana Syed Amir Ali, 10 vols. Delhi, 1988 and (2) Maulana Mufti Kafi-ul Rahman, 42 parts, Deoband.

Farishtah, Muhammad Qasim Hindu Shah, *Gulshan-i-Ibrahimi,* also known as *Tarikh-i-Farishtah,* Persian Text, Lucknow, 1865.

Firoz Shah Tughlaq, *Futuhat-i-Firoz Shahi,* Aligarh, 1954.

Gulbadan Begum, *Humayun Nama,* trs. as *The History of*

Humayun, by Mrs A.S. Beveridge, London 1902, Indian Reprint, Delhi, 1972.

Hamdullah Mustaufi, *Tarikh-i-Guzidah*, ed. E.G. Browne, London 1910.

Hamiduddin Bahadur, *Ahkam-i-Alamgiri*, trs. by Jadunath Sarkar under the title *Anecdotes of Aurangzeb*, Calcutta, 1912, Third ed. 1949.

Hajiuddabir, *Zafar-ul-Wali bi Muzaffar Wali, An Arabic History of Gujarat*, ed. by Sir Denison Ross, 3 vols., London, 1910, 1921.

Hasan Nizami, *Taj-ul-Maasir*, trs. by S.H. Askari in *Patna University Journal* (Arts), vol.18, No.3, 1963; also in E.D. II.

Hidaya Kitab al Siyar wail Jihad Mujtabai Press, Delhi, 2 vols., 1331, 1332 H.; *Hidayah* by Shaikh Burhanuddin Ali, Urdu trs. entitled *Ashraf-ul-Hidayah* by Maulana Jamil Ahmad Sukrodvi, Deoband, 1980-88. Also see Hamilton under modern works.

Ibn Battuta, *The Rehla of Ibn Battuta*, English trs. by Dr. Mahdi Husain, 1953; French trs. as *Ibn Batoutahs Voyages* by C. Defremery and B.R. Sanguinetti, Paris, 1857.

Ibn-ul-Asir, Shaikh Abul Hasan, *Kamil-ut-Tawarikh* (written 12th cent. C.E.), trs. in E.D.II.

Isamic, Khwaja Abdulla Malik, *Futuh-us-Salatin*, Persian text ed. by Agha Mahdi Husain, Agra, 1938. For English trs. see Mahdi Husain under modern works.

Jahangir, Nuruddin Muhammad, *Tuzuk-i-Jahangir* or *Memoirs of Emperor Jahangir*, trs. by Alexander Rogers and edited by Henry Beveridge, Delhi Reprint, 1968. See also Price for *Tarikh-i-Salim Shahi*.

Jaisi, Malik Muhammad, *Padmavat*, ed. by R.C. Shukla, Allahabad, 1935.

Jamil Ahmad Sukrodvi, see *Hidayah*

Juwaini, *Tarikh-i-Jahan Gusha*, Gibb Memorial Series, 1912.

Kamboh, Muhammad Saleh, *Amil Saleh*, Bib. Ind., 3 vols., Calcutta, 1923, 1927, 1939.

Khafi Khan, Muhammad Hashim, *Muntakhab-ul-Lubab*, ed. by Kabir-ud-din Ahmad, Bib.Ind., Calcutta, 1869, 1925.

Khondmir, Ghayasuddin Muhammad, *Khulasat-ul-Akhbar*, trs. in E.D., IV.

Minhaj Siraj Jurjani, *Tabqat-i-Nasiri*, Bib. Ind., Calcutta, 1864; English trs. by Major H.R. Raverty, London, 1881.

Mir Gholam Hussein Khan, *Siyar-ul-Mutakherin,* Eng. trs. by Haji Mustafa, revised by John Briggs, Indian reprint, Allahabad, 1924.

Mir Masum, *Tarikh-i-Masumi* also called *Tarikh-i-Sind,* ed. by Daudpota, Poona, 1938.

Mufti Kafi-ul-Rahman, see *Fatawa-i-Alamgiri.*

Muhammad Bihamad, see Bihamad

Muhammad Ufi, *Jami-ul-Hikayat,* trs. in E.D., II.

Mustaad Khan, Saqi, *Maasir-i-Alamgiri,* trs. and annotated by Jadunath Sarkar, Calcutta, 1947.

Niamatullah, *Makhzan-i-Afghana,* trs. by Nirodbhushan Roy as *History of the Afghans,* Santiniketan, 1958; also B. Dorn's trs., 2 parts, London, 1829-36.

Nizamuddin Ahmad, *Tabqat-i-Akbari,* Bib. Ind., 3 vols., Calcutta, 1927-35; also trs. by B. De.

Otto Spies, see Alqalaqashind.

Padmanabh, *Kanhadade Prabandh,* translated and annotated by V.S. Bhatnagar, New Delhi, 1991.

Price, Major David, *Tarikh-i-Salim Shahi,* trs. under the title of *Memoirs of the Emperor Jahanguer, written by himself,* London, 1829; Indian edition, Calcutta, 1906. Also see Price under Modern Works.

Qazvini, see Amin.

Ranking, see Badaoni.

Reynolds, see Utbi

Rizqullah Mushtaqi, *Waqiat-i-Mushtaqi,* Photo copy of the British Museum Ms. Ad. 11633.

Sarwani, Abbas, *Tarikh-i-Sher Shahi,* trs. in E.D., IV.

Shah Nawaz Khan, Samsam-ud-daula, and his son Abdul Hayy, *Maasir-ul-Umara,* trs. by H. Beveridge and Baini Prasad, 3 vols., Calcutta, 1911-14.

Shihabuddin al Umri, *Masalik-ul-Absar fi Mumalik-ul-Amsar* (written in middle of 14th cent. C.E.), trs. in E.D., III; Hindi trs. in Rizvi, *Tughlaq Kalin Bharat.*

Tarikhi-Alfi by Maulana Ahmad and others, trs. in E.D., V.

Timur, Amir, *Malfuzat-i-Timuri,* trs. in E.D., III.

Utbi, Abu Nasr Muhammad, *Kitab-i-Yamini,* trs. by James

Reynolds, London, 1858; also in E.D., II.
Ufi, Muhammad, *Jami-ul-Hikayat*, trs. in E.D., II.
Vidyapati, *Kirtilata*, Allahabad, 1923.
Wassaf, Abdullah, *Tajziat-ul-Amsar wa Tajriyat-ul-Asar*, also called *Tarikh-i-Wassaf* (written 1327 C.E.), Bombay, 1877.
Yahiya Sarhindi, *Tarikh-i-Mubarak Shahi*, Bib. Ind. Text edited by M. Hidayat Husain, Calcutta, 1931; English trs. by K.K. Basu, Baroda, 1932.
Yazdi, Sharafuddin, *Zafar Nama*, 2 vols., Bib. Ind., Calcutta, 1885-88.

Foreign Travellers' Accounts

Barbosa, Duarte, *The Book of Duarte Barbosa*, 2 vols., London, 1918-21.
Bernier, Francois, *Travels in the Mogul Empire* (1656-1668), revised by V.A. Smith, Oxford, 1934.
Della Valle, *The Travels of Pietro Della Valle in India*, trs. by Edward Grey, 2 vols., London, 1892.
Du Jarric, *Akbar and the Jesuits*, see Payne.
Finch, William, see Foster
Foster, William, *Early Travels in India* (1583-1619), contains narratives of Fitch (pp.1-47), Mildenhall (pp.48-59), Hawkins (pp.60-121), Finch (pp.122-87), Withington (pp.188-233), Coryat (pp.234-87) and Terry (pp.288-322), London, 1927.
Ibn Battuta, see under Original Sources.
Major, R.H., *India in the Fifteenth Century*, contains extracts from narratives of Nicolo Conti, Santo Stefano, etc., London, 1857.
Manrique, *Travels of Frey Sebastian Manrique*, trs. by Eckford Luard, 2 vols., London, 1927.
Manucci, Niccolao, *Storia do Mogor*, trs. by W. Irvine, 4 vols., London, 1906.
Marco Polo, see Yule
Mundy, Peter, *Travels of Peter Mundy in Asia*, ed. by R.C. Temple, London, 1914.
Payne, C.H., *Akbar and the Jesuits*, contains in trs. Du Jarric's account of the Jesuit Missions to the Court of Akbar, London, 1926.

Pelsaert, Francisco, *Jahangir's India*, trs. by W.H. Moreland and P. Geyl, Cambridge, 1925.

Tavernier, *Travels in India*, trs. and ed. by V. Ball, London, 1925.

Terry, Edward, A *Voyage to East India*, London, 1655.

Thevenot, *Indian Travels of Thevenot and Careri*, ed. by Surendra Nath Sen, New Delhi, 1949.

Varthema, *The Itinerary of Ludovico di Varthema of Bologna*, ed. by Sir Richard Temple, London, 1928.

Yule, Sir Henry, and H. Cordier, *The Book of Ser Marco Polo*, 2 vols., New York, 1903.

Modern Works

Aghnides, Nicholas P., *Muhammadan Theories of Finance*, New York, 1916.

Ahmad, Muhammad Aziz, *Political History and Institutions of the Early Turkish Empire of Delhi* (1206-1290 A.D.), Lahore, 1949.

Ameer Ali, Sayyid, *The Spirit of Islam*, London, n.d.

Arnold, T.W., *The Preaching of Islam*, Westminister, 1896.

Arnold, T.W., *The Caliphate*, London, 1924.

Arnold, T.W., and A. Guillaume, eds., *The Legacy of Islam*, Oxford, 1931.

Ashraf, Kunwar Muhammad, *Life and Conditions of the People of Hindustan*, Calcutta, 1935.

Askari, S.M., *A Study of the Rare Ms. of Sirat-i-Firoz Shahi* in *Journal of Indian History*, vol.LII, April, 1974.

Bharatiya Vidya Bhavan, see Majumdar, R.C.

Bhatnagar, V.S., see Padmanabh under Original Sources.

Biswas, Satya Krishna, *Banshasmriti* (Bengali), Calcutta, 1926.

Bosworth, C.E., *The Ghaznavids: Their Empire in Afghanistan and Eastern Iran*, 994-1040, Edinburgh, 1963.

Brown, Percy, *Indian Architecture (Islamic Period)*, Third ed., Bombay, n.d.

The Cambridge History of Islam, in two volumes, ed. by P.M. Holt, Ann K.S. Lambton and Bernard Lewis, Cambridge, 1970.

The Cambridge History of India, Cambridge University Press
vol.III, ed. by Wolseley Haig, Delhi reprint, 1958.
vol.IV, ed. by Richard Burn, Cambridge, 1937.

Caroe, Sir Olaf, *The Pathans*, London., 1958.

Davis, David Brion, *Slavery and Human Progress*, Oxford, 1984.

Davis, "Slaves in Islam", Review article on Bernard Lewis's *Race and Slavery in the Middle East*, New York Review, 11 October, 1990.

Digby, Simon, *War Horse and Elephant in the Delhi Sultanate*, Oxford, 1971.

Devendra Swarup (ed.), *Politics of Conversion*, New Delhi, 1986.

Dorn, Benhard, *History of the Afghans*, being trs. of *Makhzan-i-Afghana*, London, 1829.

Easton, Stewart C., *The Heritage of the Past*, Newyork, 1957.

Eaton, Richard Maxwell, *Sufis of Bijapur* (1300-1700), Princeton, 1978.

Elliot, H.M. and J. Dowson, *History of India as told by its own Historians*, 8 vols, London, 1867-77; vol.II, Aligarh reprint, 1952.

Elphinstone, Mountstuart, *The History of India*, 2 vols., London, 1843.

Elst, Koenraad, *Negationism in India: Concealing the record of Islam*, New Delhi, 1992.

Elst, Koenraad, *Indigenous Indians: Agastya to Ambedkar*, New Delhi, 1993.

Encyclopaedia Britannica

Encyclopaedia of Islam, 1913-38.

Encyclopaedia of Social Sciences, 1949 *reprint*.

Gardner, Alexander, *Memoirs*, ed. by Major Hugh Pearce, Patiala reprint, 1970.

Gazetteers, Imperial and Provincial Series.

Gazetteers of Alwar, London, 1878.

Gibbon, Edward, *Decline and Fall of the Roman Empire*, 2 vols., Everymans Library ed., n.d.

Goel, Sita Ram, *Islam vis-a-vis Hindu Temples*, New Delhi, 1993.

Guillaume, A., *Islam*, 1954.

Guillaume, A., *The Life of Muhammad*, OUP, Karachi, 1987.

Habib, Mohammad, *Sultan Mahmud of Ghaznin*, Delhi reprint, 1951.

Habib, Mohammad, *Compaigns of Alauddin Khilji*, being trs. of Amir Khusrau's *Khazain-ul-Futuh*, Bombay, 1933.

Habib, Mohammad, *Collected Works,* entitled *Politics and Society During Early Medieval Period,* edited by K.A. Nizami, vol.I, 1974; vol.II, 1981.

Habibullah, A.B.M., *The Foundation of Muslim Rule in India,* Revised ed., Allahabad, 1961, first published, Lahore, 1945.

Hamilton, Charles, *Hedaya* trs., of *Hidayah,* 4 vols., London, 1791, Reprint of vols. 1 and 2, New Delhi, 1985.

Hazard, H.W., *Atlas of Islamic History,* Princeton, 1954.

Herklots, see Jafar Sharif.

Hitti, P.K., *The Arabs: A Short History,* London, 1948.

Hodivala, S.H., *Studies in Indo-Muslim History,* Bombay, 1939.

Hughes, T.P., *Dictionary of Islam,* W.H. Allen & Co., London, 1885.

Indian Antiquary.

Indian History Congress, Proceedings.

Indian Heritage, vol.I, Bombay, 1955.

Ira Marvin Lapidus, *Muslim Cities in the Later Middle Ages,* Cambridge, Mass., 1967.

Ishwari Prasad, *A History of the Qaraunah Turks in India,* vol.I, Allahabad, 1936.

Ishwari Prasad, *History of Medieval India,* Fourth impression, Allahabad, 1940.

Jafar Sharif, *Islam in India or the Qanun-i-Islam,* trs. by G.A. Herklots, ed. by William Crooke, London, 1875, 1921.

Journal of the (Royal) Asiatic Society of Bengal.

Kidwai, Salim, "Sultans, Eunuchs and Domestics in Medieval India", in *Chains of Servitude,* New Delhi, 1985.

Kolf, Dirk H.A., *Naukar, Rajput and Sepoy: the ethnohistory of the military labour market in Hindustan* (1450-1850), Cambridge 1990.

Lach, Donald F., *Asia in the Making of Europe,* vol.I, Bks I and II, Chicago, 1965.

Lal, K.S., *History of the Khaljis,* New Delhi, 1980, first published 1950.

Lal, K.S., *Twilight of the Sultanate,* New Delhi, 1980, first published, 1963.

Lal, K.S., *Studies in Medieval Indian History,* Delhi, 1966.

Lal, K.S., *Growth of Muslim Population in Medieval India,* New Delhi, 1973.

Lal, K.S., *The Mughal Harem,* New Delhi, 1988.
Lal, K.S., *Early Muslims in India,* New Delhi, 1984.
Lal, K.S., *Indian Muslims: Who Are They,* New Delhi, 1990, 1993.
Lal, K.S., *The Legacy of Muslim Rule in India,* New Delhi, 1992.
Lamb, Harold, *Tamerlane the Earth Shaker,* London, 1929.
Lapidus, see Ira Marvin.
Levy, Ruben, *The Social Structure of Islam,* Cambridge, 1957.
Lewis, Bernard, *Race and Slavery in the Middle East, A Historical Enquiry,* Oxford, 1990.
Lewis, Bernard, *Islam,* from the Prophet Muhammad to the capture of Constantinople, 2 vols., Macmillan, 1974.
Mahdi Husain, *Tughlaq Dynasty,* Calcutta, 1963.
Mahdi Husain, *Shah Namah-i-Hind* or trs. of Isami's *Futuh-us-Salatin,* 3 vols., Aligarh, 1976-77.
Majumdar, R.C. (ed.), *Struggle for the Empire,* Bombay, 1957.
Majumdar, R.C. (ed.), *The Delhi Sultanate,* Bombay, 1960.
Margoliouth, D.S., *Mohammed and the Rise of Islam,* London, 1905, Indian reprint, with an introduction by Ram Swarup, New Delhi, 1985.
Mazumdar, B.P., *The Socio-Economic History of Northern India* (1030-1194 A.D.), Calcutta, 1960.
Meer Hassan Ali (Mrs.) *Observations on the Mussulmauns of India,* London 1832; Delhi reprint 1975.
Modern Cyclopaedia, 8 vols.
Moreland, W.H., *India at the Death of Akbar,* London, 1920.
Moreland, W.H., *From Akbar to Aurangzeb,* London, 1923.
Moreland, W.H., *The Agrarian System of Moslem India,* London, 1929.
Muhammad Aziz Ahmad, *Political History and Institutions of the Early Turkish Empire of Delhi* (1206-1290 A.D.), New Delhi, 1949, 1972.
Muir, Sir William, *The Life of Mahomet,* Indian reprint with an introduction by Ram Swarup, New Delhi, 1992.
Mujeeb, M., *The Indian Muslims,* London, 1967.
Mukerjee, Radhakumud, *Economic History of India* (1600-1800), Allahabad, 1967.
Nazim, M., *The Life and Times of Sultan Mahmud of Ghazna,* Cambridge, 1931.

Nigam, S.B.P., *Nobility under the Sultans of Delhi,* New Delhi, 1967.

Nizami, K.A., *Some Aspects of Religion and Politics in India during the Thirteenth Century,* Aligarh, 1961.

Om Prakash, *Religion and Society in Ancient India,* Bharatiya Delhi, 1985.

Orme, Robert, *A History of the Military Transactions of the British Nation in Indostan,* 3 vols., Fourth ed., London, 1803.

Page, J.A., *A Guide to the Qutb,* Archaeological Survey of India, Memoir 38.

Price, Major David, *Memoirs of the Principal Events of Muhammadan History,* 3 vols., London, 1921. Also see Price under Original Sources.

Qureshi, Ishtiaq Hussian, *Administration of the Sultanate of Delhi,* Fifth ed., New Delhi, 1971, first published, Lahore, 1942.

Ram Swarup, *The Word as Revelation: Names of Gods,* New Delhi, 1980.

Ram Swarup, *Understanding Islam through Hadis,* Indian reprint, New Delhi, 1983.

Rizvi, Saiyyad Athar Abbas, *Adi Turk Kalin Bharat,* Aligarh, 1965.

Rizvi, Saiyyad Athar Abbas, *Tughlaq Kalin Bharat,* 2 parts, 1956, 1957.

Rizvi, Saiyyad Athar Abbas, *Uttar Timur Kalin Bharat,* Part II, Aligarh, 1959.

Saksena, Banarsi Prasad, *History of Shahjahan of Dehli,* Second Impression, Allahabad, 1961.

Sarkar, Jadunath, *History of Aurangzeb,* 5 vols., Calcutta, 1912-25.

Sarkar, Jadunath, *Fall of the Mughal Empire,* 4 vols., Third ed., Calcutta, 1964.

Sarkar, Jadunath (ed.), *Later Mughals* by Irvine, 2 vols., Calcutta,, 1921-22.

Sarkar, Jadunath, *A Short History of Aurangzeb, Calcutta,* 1930.

Sewell, Robert., *A Forgotten Empire* (Vijayanagar), New Delhi reprint, 1966.

Sleeman, Sir W. *Rambles and Recollections of an Indian Official,* ed. V.A. Smith, Oxford, 1915.

Smith, V.A., *Akbar the Great Mogul,* Delhi reprint, 1962.

Stephen Carr., *Archaeology and Monumental Remains of Delhi*, Calcutta, 1876.

Sykes, P.M., *A History of Persia*, 2 vols., London, 1915.

Talib, S. Gurbachan Singh, *Muslim League Attack on Sikhs and Hindus in the Punjab 1947*, New Delhi reprint, 1991.

Thomas, Edward, *Chronicles of the Pathan Kings of Delhi*, London, 1871.

Thornton, Edward, *Gazetteer of the Territories under the Government of the East India Co. and of the Native States on the Continent of India, Compiled by the Authority of the Court of Directors and chiefly from the documents in their possession*, 4 vols., London, 1854.

Titus, Murray, *Islam in India and Pakistan*, Calcutta, 1959.

Tod, James, *Annals and Antiquities of Rajasthan*, 2 vols., London, 1957.

Tripathi, R.P., *Some Aspects of Muslim Administration*, Allahabad, 1936.

Wink, Andre, *Al-Hind, The Making of the Indo-Islamic World*, vol.I, *Early Medieval India*, OUP, Delhi, 1990.

INDEX

Abbasid Caliphs, provide great impetus to slavery, 133
Abdulla Khan Uzbeg, captures Hindus in Kalpi-Kanauj area, 73
Abyssinians, much demand for, 79, 133, 135
Africa, Islamic slave-making in, 60, 61; becomes synonymous with slavery, 61
Ahmad Vali, Bahmani Sultan, captures Hindu women and children, 72
Aibak, Qutbuddin, 27, 33, 35, 36, 37, 41, 43, 44, 56, 84, 86, 122, 125, 130, 135, 157
Aibak, Saifuddin, slave noble, 37
Akbar, 72, 80, 113, 128, 129, 166
Akbarabadi-Mahall, Hindu concubine of Shahjahan, 166-67
Alauddin Bahman Shah, gets Hindu girls as booty, 71
Alptigin, 25, 35
Amir Khusrau, Alim and Sufi, 50; delighted over how Muslims can seize, buy or sell Hindus at will, 50; resents Hanafi law accepting Hindus as *zimmis*, 66; shows contempt for Hindus, 81
Amir Timur, 55, 56, 86, 119
aphorisms and maxims, on how Muslims obtain multiple wives, 154
Arabia, pre-Islamic slavery in, 10, 12
Arabs, enslavement of Hindus by, 17-19; take pride in keeping slaves after Islamization, 6
Arhai din ka Jhonpra, Hindu temple at Ajmer converted into mosque, 84
Armed peasants, resist enslavement by Muslims conquerors, 62-65
Armenians, enslaved in millions, 61, 132
Asaval, slave-taking at, 49
Asni, slaves-taking at, 20
Athens, slaves in, 2
Aurangzeb, 114, 132, 166, 169, 170
Avadh, slave-taking in, 47
Azarbaijan, Muslims nobles and their slaves arrive from, 145

Babylon, slavery in, 1
Badaon, slave-taking at, 70, 136
Baghdad, slave markets at, 7, 30
Balban, Ghiyasuddin, 9, 30, 35, 36, 37, 43, 45, 47, 53, 74, 77, 78, 85, 90, 91, 122
Balbani slave-nobles, 37
Balkh, slave markets at, 7
Banu Quraiza, massacre and enslavement of, 42
Banaras, slave-taking at, 44
Baran, slave-taking at, 20
Barbary States, slave-taking from, 7
Basrah, slave markets at, 30
Battle of Talikot, Hindus captured and enslaved after, 72
beardless young boys, Muslim fondness and demand for, 105, 125
Bengal, slave-taking spreads to, 71; famous for eunuch-making factories, 117
Berbers, sold in thousands by Muslim slave merchants, 133
Bhojpur, slave-taking at, 47, 48
Bidar, trade in 'Black people' at, 136
Bihar, slave-taking in, 43
Black slaves, 7, 13, 61, 176; in India, 80-82
Black Sea Coast, booming slave-

markets on, 61
Bokhara (Bukhara), the king of, a big slave-catcher, 8; renowned centre of slave trade, 7, 25, 131, 135
booming slave markets, 61
Brahman and Buddhist teachers, slaughtered by Muslim invaders, 43, 67
Brahmanabad, slave-taking at, 18, 21, 119
Brahmanas, captured and enslaved, 49, 54; treated with great harshness, 68
British, the, continue the Muslim slave trade, 138
Buddhist University centres in Bihar, destroyed by Muslim invaders, 67
Bukhara Haji, pious slave merchant, 28
Bulgarians, sold in millions as slaves, 61, 132
Burqa, the continuing symbol of slavery, 177

Cairo, slave markets at, 7
Caliph Walid I, sells Hindu princesses captured in Sindh, 18, 120
Cambay, slave-taking at, 49
Ceylon, slave markets in, 137
Chandwar, slave-taking at, 70
Chief Qazi of Nishapur, great slave trader, 27
child slave, price of, 123
Children, separated from parents and sold as slaves, 54
Chittor, massacre during the invasion of, 49
Christian captives, sufferings of, 134
Christian monasteries, employment of slaves in, 6
Christian nations, major partners in Muslims slave trade, 6
Christian slaves, drawn by Muslims from many countries, 13
Christianity, sanctions slavery, 5
Church Fathers, supporters of slavery, 6
Circassians, sold in millions as slaves, 61, 132
Concubinage, 167-72; very common among Muslim royalty, 159
Coptic monks, castrate young boys for sale to Muslim slave merchants, 132
Cordova, slave markets at, 7

Damascus, slave markets at, 7
Damsels of Paradise, as portrayed in the Quran, 152-53
daughters of Hindu princes and Ranas, rough treatment of, 22
Debal, slave-taking at, 17, 21, 155
Deccan, the, slave markets in, 71
Delhi, slave markets at, 7, 9, 28, 30, 50, 51, 52, 53, 117, 123, 126, 127, 131, 136
Delhi, looks like Dar-ul-Islam, 45
Delhi Sultanate, policy of, 58
Devagiri, slave-taking at, 49, 91
Deval Rani, captured Hindu princess, 160; forced into several harems, 161
Dewshrime or capture and conversion of young Christian, Jewish and Gypsy boys, the practice of, 57-58

Egypt, slavery in, 1, 7, 9, 13; booming slave markets in, 61
Enslavement, Hindu resistance to, 61-67
Etawah, slave-taking at, 70
Ethiopians, sold in thousands as slaves, 133

Eunuchs, practice of making, 112-18, 132; factories for making, 133; collected as profitable commodities and presented as gifts or revenue, 117
European slave traders, 176

Fatawa-i-Alamgiri, on slavery, 140, 141, 149
Fatehpuri-Mahall, Hindu concubine of Shahjahan, 167
Female slave, partnership in a, 147
Female slaves, taken in Sindh, 18
Figures of slaves made, 43-45
Forcible marriages, 158-61
Foreign girls, import of, 130
Foreign Muslims, influx of, 45; as slave-nobles, 74, 75
Foreign slaves, import of, 89, 130-35
forest-village dwellers, multiply due to fear of enslavement, 66

galley slaves, 134
Gardner, Alexander, on Muslim slave trade in the nineteenth century, 7, 8
Georgians, sold in millions as slaves, 61, 132
Ghazni, slave markets at, 7, 27, 28, 106, 131
Ghilman or handsome young slaves, love of, 105-12
Goa, slave markets at, 129, 135, 137
Golkunda, slave markets at, 117, 135
Gondwana, slave-taking in, 48
Greece, slavery in, 1, 2, 7
growth of Muslim population, enslavement as a factor in, 42
Gujaraf, slave-taking in, 49, 71
Gulf countries, Indian and Sri Lankan girls sold in, 177
Gwalior, slave-taking at, 45, 48, 71

Habshis, see Abyssianians
Hadis, 139, 153, 154
Hajjaj, 18, 19, 21, 120
Hanbal, Imam Ahmad bin, 140
handsome and elegant maidens, captured in great numbers in Gujrat, 49
Hanifa, Imam Abu, 139, 141
Harem, largest State Department under Muslim rule, 112
Harems of the Muslim elite, 164
Haryana, slave-taking in, 47
Hedayah, the, 55, 126, 140, 141, 145, 147
Hijras, origin of, 172; proliferation of, 173-74
Hindu and Sikh girls, abducted in 1947, 130
Hindu buildings, materials from, 83
Hindu concubines, women without influence in Muslim households, 160
Hindu Kush (Hindu-killer) mountain, captive Hindus dies en masse in crossing of, 138
Hindu learning, attack on, 67-68
Hindu masons, forced to work as slaves, 85
Hindu prisoners, distribution and sale of, 17
Hindu slaves, Ghaznavid capture of, 19-24; employed on building construction, 83-89; in the army, 89-93; as makers of weapons, 98-99; in palace and court, 99-104
Hindu soldiers, always slain after Muslim victory, 18
Hindustan, the new heaven of Islam, 45
Holy shrine of Pir-i-Nimcha, centre of slave trade, 8

Hugli, slave-market at, 137

Ibn Battutah, describes how Hindu princesses were presented as gifts, 52, 127
Ibn Khaldun, defends slavery, 41, 80, 124
Iltutmish, Shamsuddin, 9, 28, 29, 32, 33, 36, 37, 41, 43, 44, 45, 53, 74, 77, 84, 86, 122, 131, 135, 157
Indian girls, high price paid for, 127
Indian Muslims, forget how they were converted, 70; despised as base by foreign Muslims, 75
Indian people, survival strategy of, 63
Indian slaves, money value of, 121; low price of, 126-28
infidels, Christianity and Islam allow no natural or human rights to, 5
Internal trade, in slaves, 136-38
Iran, slavery in, 9
Iranians, occupy high positions under Muslim rule, 78
Iraq, slavery in, 9; Muslim nobles and their slaves arrive from, 45
Isfahan, slave markets at, 117
Islam, 6, 7, 9, 10, 150; Caliphs of, 15; converts to, 59; permits polygamy, 153; rules of, 153; slavery an integral part of, 13, 41; slavery widespread in, 25; status of slaves in, 11-13; stickler about rules, 175
Islamic jurisprudence, 46, 140; law, 55; usage, 91
Islamic lands, importation of black slaves into, 81
Islamic markets, supply of white slaves to, 132
Islamic slave trade, the Prophet sets the precedent for, 11
Islamic slavery, extension of, 13-14
Islamization of India, obstacles in the way of, 68
Italy, booming slave markets in, 61

Jahangir, 55, 73, 102, 114, 116, 128; demands daughters of Hindu kings, 156, 159
Jaipal, Hindu Shahiya king of Kabul sold as a slave, 22, 24, 120, 124
Jalesar, slave-taking at, 70
Jalor, slave-taking at, 50
Janissary regiments, 57
Jauhar, way for Hindu women to escape enslavement, 163-64
Jaunpur, slave markets at, 71
Jesus Christ, sees nothing objectionable in slavery, 5
Jihad, provides zest for slavery, 7

Kabul, slave markets at, 128
kafir women, could be married by Muslims even if married before capture, 161
Kalinjar, slave-taking at, 42
Kalpi-Kanauj area, slave-taking in, 73
Kamala Devi, Hindu queen captured and forced into harem, 49, 160
Kampil, slave-taking at, 47, 70
Kanauj, slave-taking at, 20, 121
Kanhardeva of Jalor, frees Hindu captives, 54, 55
Karkhanas, employment of slaves in, 96
Karkhi, Imam, 141
Kashmir Valley, slave-taking in, 121
Katehar, slave-taking in, 47, 48, 70, 91
Khalji, Alauddin, 48, 49, 51, 84, 90, 91, 92, 93, 94, 101, 107, 109, 123, 125, 126, 160; collects large number of slaves, 50; pigion-boys of, 101; collects a thousand

concubines, 72
Khalji, Ikhtiyaruddin Bakhtiyar, 32, 33, 34, 41, 43, 63, 67
Khalji, Jalaluddin, 48, 109
Khalji, Qutbuddin Mubarak, 107, 125, 161, 172
Khaljis, enslavement under, 48-51
Khan of Khiva, major slave merchant, 8
Khandesh, slave-taking in, 49, 71
Khokhars, enslavement of, 43, 125
Khor, slave-taking at, 70
Khurasan, slave markets in, 9, 45, 120, 125
Khusrau Khan, handsome Hindu enslaved and used as sex object, 75, 107, 108, 109, 161
Kol (Aligarh), slave-taking at, 41
Korrah, the whip for disciplining slaves, 88
Kufa, slave markets in, 7

Lal Kunwar, Hindu concubine of Jahandar Shah, 165
Lodi, Bahlul, 63, 71, 77, 160
Lodi Gardens, tombs in, built by Hindu slave labour, 87
Lodi, Sikandar, 39, 68, 71, 77, 87, 108, 160

madrasas, built by slave labour, 84
Mahaban, slave-taking at, 20, 121
Mahmud of Ghazni, slave-taking by, 19, 20, 22, 23, 24, 26, 77, 120, 121, 122, 124; his passion for possessing slaves, 106
Malik bin Anas, Imam, 140
Malik Kafur, high-priced Hindu slave, 49, 75, 94, 107, 113, 125
Malwa, slave-taking in, 48, 50, 71
Mandor, slave-taking at, 136
Manumission of slaves, 34, 142-47; a pre-Islamic Arab custom, 139; four kinds of, 142; partial, 144
Marathas, armed peasants who resist Islamization, 62
Mashaikh (sufis), urge complete Islamization of India, 45
Masjid Quwwatul Islam, built by Hindu slave labour and from materials of Hindu temples, 83
Masjid-i-Jami in Samarkand, built by Hindus enslaved by Timur, 119
master, cannot be slain for murder of his slave, 148
Masulipatam, slave markets at, 135
Mathura, slave-taking at, 20, 121
Mauretania, provides black slaves in modern times, 176
mausoleums, built by Hindu slave labour, 84
Mecca and Medina, great centres of slave trade, 7
Mediterranean Islands, booming slave markets in, 61
Megasthenes, saw no slavery in India, 5
Mewat, slave-taking in, 47, 54
Mongol prisoners, enslavement of, 50
mosques, built by slave labour, 84
Mughal buildings, built by Hindu slave labour, 88
Mughal Generals and nobility, make profit by slave trade, 73
Mughals of India, exchange slaves with Ottomon and Safvid empires, 10
Muhammad bin Idris, Imam Abu Abdulla, 139
Muhammad bin Qasim, 9, 17, 18, 19, 21, 58, 119, 120, 155, 160, 162, 163
Muhammad Ghauri, 26, 27, 28, 37, 43, 56, 77, 125
Muhammad, Imam, 141

Muhammad, the Prophet, 6, 10, 11, 12, 23, 133, 139, 150, 154, 175; did not restrict number of slave girls and concubines, 151; special place for women in the life of, 152
Muhammadan legists, 58
Muizzi slave-nobles, 37
Multan, Muslim slave merchant at, 8
Muslim etiquette, apes manners forced on slaves, 39
Muslim harems, filled with concubines and eunuchs, 167
Muslim population, slave-taking to plant or raise, 69; concubines increase, 152
Muslim psychology, regarding sex, 150-58; about women, 152-53
Muslim slave system, legacy of, 173
Muslim slave traders, partners of Christian nations in slave trade, 6
Muslim slave-catchers, most successful in Africa, 177
Muslim sultans, very fond of handsome young slaves, 105

Naharwala, slave-taking at, 49
Nasiruddin, Sultan, 47; awards prizes for slave-catching, 54; presents slaves as gifts, 47, 122-23
Nazirs and Khwaja Saras, names for eunuchs in the harem, 112, 113
Negroes, sold as slaves in thousands, 133
Nimsar, slave-taking at, 71
Ninduna, slave-taking at, 20
Nishapur, slave markets at, 25, 135

Other Backward Classes (OBC), fall-out from Muslims rule, 64, 66
Ottoman Empire, 9, 10, 13, 176

Paiks, Hindus employed in Muslim armies only as, 91, 92, 93, 94; not entitled to share in booty, 95
Palace and Court, large-scale slave labour used in, 99
Paradise, Prophet Muhammad's idea of, 152
Patiali, slave-taking at, 47
Persia, Muslim nobles and their slaves arrive from, 45
perverted passions, public expression of, 105
Pipli, slave market at, 137
Popes, supporters of slavery, 6
Portuguese, great slave traders, 137

Qandhar, slave markets at, 128
Qasr-i-Lal, built by slave labour, 85
qasrs (palaces), built by Hindu slave labour, 84
Qazi Khan, *fatawas* of, 141
Qazis, manupulate sale and manumission of slaves, 149
Qubacha, Nasiruddin, 29, 30, 33, 35, 36
Quran, 6, 10, 151, 153, 154, 159, 175
Qutb Minar, built by Hindu slave labour, 84, 86, 87
Qutbi slave-nobles, 37

racial slavery, originated in medieval Muslim societies, 79
Raja of Kampil, enslavement of the eleven sons of, 56
Rajas, leaders of Hindu resistance to Muslim enslavement, 62, 63
Rajasthan, provided only a small number of slaves, 50
Rajputs, 62; chivalry of, 50
Rani Ladi, queen of Raja Dahir, captured and enslaved, 120, 160
Ranthambhor, slave-taking at, 47, 48, 49
Rapri, slave-taking at, 70

Rawar, slave-taking at, 18, 21
Raydan, Imad-ud-Din, Indian-born Muslim noble despised by Turkish nobles, 74, 75, 113
Rewa, slave-taking at, 71
Rome, slavery in, 1, 3, 7
royal slaves, very large number of, 107
Rum (Turkey), Muslim nobles and their slaves arrive from, 45
Rupmati, Hindu concubine of Muslim noble, 166
Rural slaves, no trade in, 129

Saket, slave-taking at, 70
Samanid rulers, great collectors of slaves, 25
Samarkand, great centre of slave trade, 117, 133, 135
Scheduled Castes and Tribes (SC/ST), multiplied under Muslim rule, 64, 66
Sevana, slave-taking at, 50
Sex objects, enslavement of young women as, 150
Sex slavery, interest of Muslims in, 157
Shahjahan, 73, 156, 162, 164; intolerable conditions in the time of, 58
Sham (Syria), Muslim nobles and their slaves arrive from, 45
Shamsi slave-nobles, 37, 47; a list of, 135
Sikhs, armed peasants who resist Islamization, 62
Sindh, Arab invasion of and slave-taking in, 17, 19, 120
Siwalik, slave-taking in, 47, 54
slaughter of the Hindus, 44
slave girls, 102, 122, 168, 169, 171, 172; behaviour of, 164-67; defects in 145; distribution of, 161-63; parts of their bodies freed individually, 170; prices of, 123, 125, 156; could be easily swapped, 170; sorting and grading of, 119; all of them could be used as concubines, 145
Slave Kings, 31-35
Slave markets, 7, 23, 156
slave merchants and brokers, 124; steal children for sale as slaves, 133
slave nobles, 35-40; strife among, 76-80
slave trade, 6, 7; centres of, 136; viewed as sinful by Hindus, 136
Slave-catching, channels of, 70
Slave-taking, a matter of policy, 46-48; most successful missionary activity, 69-73
Slavery, 1, 2, 3, 4, 133; becomes a divinely ordained institution, 5; prominent feature of Muslim society, polity and economy, 139
Slaves, as per Islamic law, 30; barter of, 147; as makers of weapons, 98; become too numerous, 53; sale and purchase of, 120-23, 147, 149; sale price of, 123-26; in Muslim armies, 89-93; amputation of, 148; internal trade of, 136-38
Slavs, enslaved in large numbers, 61, 132, 133
Somnath, slave-taking at, 49
Sorath, slave-taking in, 54
Spain, booming slave markets in, 61
Sparta, slavery in, 2
Spartacus, leader of slave revolt in Rome, 3
St. Paul, supports slavery, 5
St. Thome, slave market at, 137
stone-cutters, 12,000 Hindu slaves employed as, 86
Subuktigin, 25, 26, 41, 135
Sudan, provides black slaves in

modern times, 176
Sufferings of the enslaved, 53-57
Surat, slave-taking at, 49; slave market at, 135
Sylhet, famous as a eunuch-factory, 116

Taj Mahal, built by Hindu slave labour, 88
Tajuddin Firoz, captures 60,000 Hindus, 71
Tamluk, slave market at, 137
tanks, built by Hindu slave labour, 84
temples, turned into mosques by Hindu slave labour, 87
Thanesar, slave-taking at, 20, 121
Third Battle of Panipat, slave-taking after, 155
Tirmiz, slave market at, 135
Tombs of Sufi Shaikhs, built by Hindu slave labour, 87
trade-marts for slaves, between India and Khurasan, 128
Tughan Khan, slave noble, 37
Tughlaq, Firoz Shah, 53, 56, 58, 68, 86, 90, 95, 96, 107, 109, 111, 127; born of a forcibly married Hindu lady, 156, 158; *Karkhanas* of, 97; special slaves of, 57-59
Tughlaq, Muhammad bin, notorious for enslaving people, 51, 52, 56, 86, 97, 101, 111, 126, 156, 162; personal slaves of, 109
Tughlaqs, enslavement under, 51-53
Tughril Khan, slave noble, 37
Turanians, obtain high posts under Muslim rule, 78
Turkestan, slave markets in, 8, 45
Turkish nobles, inborn arrogance of, 37, 74, 75
Turkish slaves, 14, 15, 16, 26, 27, 29, 35, 36, 76, 77, 85, 147

Udaipuri-Mahall, Georgian concubine of Aurangzeb, 166
Ujjain, slave-taking at, 45
Ukrainians, sold in millions as slaves, 61, 132
Ulama, 45, 46, 140
Umar, the second Caliph, 6, 155

Vanmanthali, slave-taking at, 49
Vijayanagar kingdom, slave-taking in invasions of, 72

Waihind, slave-taking at, 20
War, prescribed on religious grounds, 6
wealthy palaces of Arabia, slaves still serving in, 177
White slaves, 7, 61, 133
women and children, special targets for enslavement, 18, 42, 47, 150

Yaldoz, Tajuddin, 28, 29, 35, 36, 157
Yusuf, Imam Abu, 141

Zamindars, lead resistance to Islamization, 62, 63, 64
Zeba, mother of Sikander Lodi, a captured Hindu woman, 160